The Ambitions of
JANE FRANKLIN

The Ambitions of
JANE FRANKLIN

ALISON ALEXANDER

ALLEN&UNWIN
SYDNEY • MELBOURNE • AUCKLAND • LONDON

To James

First published in 2013

Allen & Unwin
83 Alexander Street
Crows Nest NSW 2065
Australia
Phone: (61 2) 8425 0100
Email: info@allenandunwin.com
Web: www.allenandunwin.com

Cataloguing-in-Publication details are available
from the National Library of Australia
www.trove.nla.gov.au

ISBN 978 1 74237 569 4

Front cover images: portrait of Jane Franklin, courtesy the Simpkinson family; Joseph Lycett, 'View
of the Governor's retreat, New Norfolk, Van Diemen's Land', courtesy Allport Library and Museum
of Fine Arts, Tasmanian Archive and Heritage Office. Back cover image: Auguste Etienne Francois
Mayer, 1805-1890, 'Hobart-Town, Ile Van Diemen' [1841?], National Library of Australia, nla.
pic-an8901165.
Maps by Trudy Cowley
Index by Alison Alexander
Set in 12/16.5 pt Garamond by Midland Typesetters, Australia
Printed and bound in Australia by Griffin Press
10 9 8 7 6 5 4 3 2 1

Australian Government

This project has been assisted by the Australian
Government through the Australia Council for
the Arts, its arts funding and advisory body.

MIX
Paper from
responsible sources
FSC® C009448

The paper in this book is FSC® certified.
FSC® promotes environmentally responsible,
socially beneficial and economically viable
management of the world's forests.

CONTENTS

INTRODUCTION

After a brisk but stormy sea journey of four months, in January 1837 Jane Franklin arrived in Hobart with her husband Sir John, the new governor of Van Diemen's Land. He was received with official pomp—ships firing salutes, crowds cheering on the wharf, troops presenting arms. Jane, being only his wife, landed privately, but she was determined to take her part in exploring their new domain. As soon as they could, they set off on a tour of inspection.

At a time when most ladies sat at home with their embroidery, the commandant of the convict-powered coal mine near Port Arthur was astounded by Lady Franklin. The vice-regal party arrived after sunset, but she insisted on going down the mine—it was dark underground anyway, she pointed out. 'Ladies and all dive first thing into the Mines … minutely examining everything', wrote the commandant, stunned.[1]

'Entered farthest hole in cliff', she wrote in her diary. 'Get in here slightly stooping.' They continued down a passage, inspecting the iron rollers, deep shaft, solitary cells, buckets, rope … Another passage, 'more stooping'; on and on, 'very wet and muddy and being bent double, got worn out'. Stout Sir John was also suffering, the dim candlelight making the perspiration streaming from his head look like smoke, as if his head were on fire, but Jane Franklin persisted. They finally emerged through another passage—'came out with blackened hands & draggled petticoats'—and continued their inspection, this time visiting the prisoners' barracks, the kitchen and even the bakehouse. Only then, about nine in the evening, did they sit down to a 'good supper of Wallabi'.[2]

Jane Franklin's life was shaped by her two overriding ambitions—for herself and her husband. From an early age she wanted to live life to the full, doing and seeing everything she could. She never turned down an opportunity, whether it was to climb a mountain, make a balloon ascent, spear a shark, dally with a charming man, or, as above, investigate a coal mine—even if it meant being wet, muddy, bent double and worn out. Probably the most travelled woman of her time, she made long, adventurous trips to every continent except Antarctica. The range of her activities in her seven years in Australia was unique, from starting a scientific society to building a Greek temple in the bush and founding an agricultural settlement. To achieve her ambitions, she skilfully negotiated the restrictions which society placed on women at this period, managing to win her own way while remaining praised as a pattern of charming femininity. Her accomplishments seem to make her an admirable feminist prototype, daring and determined—a wonderful woman to write about, as she vanquishes her opposition, defies men (and women) who dare question her and overcomes all obstacles.

But it was not for these achievements that Jane Franklin became famous throughout the western world. Her feminist credentials fall short here, for this fame came as she achieved her second ambition: supporting her husband through thick and thin, almost single-handedly turning him into an acclaimed success instead of a failure and possible cannibal. In pursuit of this aim she organised and sent out five expeditions, influenced politicians and the press, and flattered royalty and wealthy men into assisting her. Even in distant America, she gained moneyed supporters and presidential sympathy. Her efforts saw her husband accepted as the epitome of the gallant English gentleman winning against the odds, discovering the Northwest Passage. Explorers were the ultimate heroes of the mid-nineteenth century: the Franklins became a world-famous couple. That such a stellar reputation was built on thin foundations made her achievement all the more remarkable: she was a genius at public relations. And capable: though her ambitions were quite divergent, she fulfilled both admirably.

Jane Franklin and her ally, John's niece Sophy Cracroft, were determined to manage her reputation not only during her lifetime but afterwards, leaving a huge archive of her writings for posterity. Now in the Scott Polar Research Institute in Cambridge, these records describe what she saw and did over six decades—millions of words, a treasure trove for modern historians.

Others have used this archive to write about Jane Franklin: why another biography? Jane or Sophy culled the immense hoard so that only positive material remained. Someone even went to the trouble of copying out letters with negative sections omitted—anything showing Jane Franklin in a bad light, dominating her husband or manipulating other people (a few originals remain for comparison). Previous biographers relied on this archive, so enormous that it should provide ample source material. Building on Jane Franklin's earlier reputation, believing everything she wrote, they generally depicted her as a wonderful woman undertaking interesting activities, but at the same time charming, gentle and retiring, as a lady should be. They took it for granted that such a lady was also truthful.

But there are many more records scattered around the globe (Australia, New Zealand, England, Canada) which missed the cull. The Internet and the computer make these accessible and manageable in a way inconceivable even twenty years ago, and I feel fortunate to be the first historian to be able to use them to create a more complete picture.

A flash of realisation—that Jane Franklin did not always tell the truth—transformed my reading of these records. What lay beneath them? The gaps left by the culling: what did they hide? I found a different person from the vapid creature of mid-twentieth-century biography. Instead, what emerged was a determined, intelligent, driven, self-absorbed yet sensitive woman, who described in vivid detail the subterfuges and intrigues she used to get her own way—as entirely justified, always on the side of righteousness, truth and the good of mankind (not womankind, in whom she had little interest). In fulfilling her two ambitions, especially turning her gentle husband into a hero, her achievements were immense. Vital lessons learnt in her tough years of political involvement in Van Diemen's Land, enabling John to cope with a situation that was otherwise beyond him, allowed her in turn to triumph in Britain.

However, I stopped short of trying to get inside Jane Franklin's head. She was such an extraordinary woman that I felt it would be highly risky (and I had hideous nightmares of meeting her in the after-life). I have presented the activities and thoughts of the woman who emerges from all these records, for the reader to decide: what was she really like?

1

A GIRL WHO DID
NOT FIT IN

When Jane Griffin was six, her father commissioned a portrait of his four children. The son and heir stands bathed in light, tall and handsome, the focus of the painting. His three sisters sit in his shadow, indistinguishable in their matching white dresses, except by height. Fanny, the eldest, gazes adoringly at their brother; little Mary peeps out sweetly from under Fanny's shoulder; and Jane, the middle one, sits slightly apart from the others, staring glumly at the floor.

No one looking at Jane in her cradle would have prophesied world fame—the third child, and a girl at that, daughter of obscure silk-weavers in the narrow streets of Spitalfields, a far from fashionable district of London. Both her grandfathers were silk-weavers, descendants of Protestant Huguenot refugees who fled Catholic France at the end of the seventeenth century. Jane felt her Calvinist heritage gave her steadfastness and determination, as well as intellectual vitality.[1]

Jane's father's family, the Griffins, came from Normandy and were undistinguished. Her father John, born in 1757, worked with his own father as a silk-weaver at the family home, a tall, narrow house with a shop on the ground floor, two storeys of living quarters, and weaving looms in the best light at the top. In 1781 Jane's grandfather was admitted as a liveryman of the Worshipful Company of Goldsmiths, one of London's twelve great trade guilds, which now admitted other crafts. Admittance meant a craftsman was successful and respectable, and Jane's father John was admitted in his turn in 1791.[2]

As an adult, Jane rarely mentioned the Griffins. She preferred her mother's family, the Guillemards, who were much grander. In France they had been landowners; as silk-weavers in London they became wealthy. In 1786 Jane Guillemard married John Griffin, and bore him children at two-yearly intervals: in 1788 Fanny, a sharp-witted, strong-willed girl; John, the only son, in 1790; Jane, named after her mother, on 3 December 1791; and sweet-tempered Mary in 1793. Jane Griffin senior died in 1795, in childbirth according to descendants. John Griffin did not marry again, but employed a member of their Huguenot circle, Mrs Peltrau, as housekeeper. She brought up the children, and her daughter saw to their early education. Sadly, young John died at fourteen of a lung disease, possibly tuberculosis.[3] For Jane, the loss of her mother and brother could have been shattering, but in later writings she does not refer to either death. She was never one to dwell on the past.

Apart from these bereavements, her childhood sounds happy enough. John Griffin was a fond and easygoing father, and a letter he wrote to Jane when she was twenty reads as from one equal to another, as he passes on gossip and jokes about Fanny's high sense of decorum.[4] After a century in England, Huguenots like the Griffins were well assimilated into English life, attending the Anglican church and using English names. However, Jane grew up surrounded by Huguenots. They formed the family's social circle, and when Jane was ten, she and Mary, always close, were sent to a boarding school run by Huguenots, Mrs Peltrau's sisters.

The school was small, with only six to eight girls. Two became Jane's lifelong friends, one recalling Jane telling her the plot of the popular novel The Mysteries of Udolpho as they walked in the garden or went to their dancing lesson. The school ensured fluency in French, but otherwise was not stimulating. Girls learnt by heart from text-books, with questions discouraged. One of Jane's textbooks survives. Published in the year she used it and written 'on a new plan' (so the Peltrau ladies tried to keep up to date) it contains hundreds of histori-cal events arranged by the day of the year they happened, isolated facts with no context. Jane made some annotations—for example, she or the teacher knew that Napoleon won the battle of Lodi in 1796 not 1797—which suggests some level of intellectual activity, but learning these facts by heart would be terribly boring. In old age Jane described her education as 'meagre', and recited one particularly fatuous fact she had to learn. To the question 'What is metaphysics?' the book gave the meaningless reply: 'A science more sublime than physics'.[5] However, such schooling was standard for girls. Jane Austen suffered similarly.

Jane Griffin's school report when she was twelve shows that she excelled (as far as that went) in arts subjects like Reading, French and History, was less good at Sums, and unenthusiastic about Work (needlework), with comments like 'very well but little' or even 'none'. Her conduct was excellent except for one lapse, laughing impudently at the French master. At sixteen a throat infection meant she was brought home in case she shared her brother's delicate constitution, so she was 'freed from the shackles of school'[6]—free to fulfil her ambition to seek adventure, to do and see everything she could.

This gentle if dull upbringing, doubtless disciplined but without any strict authoritarian figure, meant Jane's natural liveliness was never crushed, while young John's death left no son to be favoured, no brother whose superior education showed up hers. In a family where she was the clever one, she flourished. As often happens, each child was assigned a label: Mary was the pretty one, Jane clever, and Fanny difficult, inheriting the Guillemard trait of irritability.

Despite finding school inadequate, Jane never rebelled outwardly, though she managed to avoid things she disliked, such as needlework. If her later adventurous life is a guide, she might have been a tomboy. She was possibly her father's favourite, as she seems to have been in adult life, and if she was Papa's little princess it would explain her later self-confidence and sense of entitlement. But tomboyish inclinations and a dislike of girlish activities meant growing up could have been hard, especially with no mother to love and guide her. Jane's mentors were her father and her uncle, neither much help in the difficult process of becoming a young lady.

After Jane left school, two advantages lifted her life above the humdrum. One was her uncle's encouragement. Her mother's brother, John Guillemard, was the other clever member of the family. The Guillemard wealth meant he could leave silk-weaving, and he gained a Master of Arts at Oxford University and was appointed to the commission establishing the boundary between Canada and the United States. This could have led to an impressive career, but his eccentricity meant he gained no more such appointments. He lived as a gentleman, became a Fellow of the Royal Society and took an interest in his bright niece. When she was seventeen, he and his wife, a childless couple, took her to Oxford. They attended balls in the conventional way, but also inspected every college and attended academic functions.[7]

Perhaps Jane was unhappy that as a girl she could not attend university, for two years later her uncle took her on a six-month visit to relations at Tredrea Cottage in Cornwall, where he instructed her as, perhaps, she would have been instructed at Oxford. The rest of the family did not take this seriously. 'Fancy then you are at Tredrea College, where you are fully occupied during the term, to take your degree if you have leisure & like it, learn a little latin, & qualify it if not disagreeable by a subordinate qualification, the knowledge of Whist', joked her father, and her sister Fanny sent Jane an essay on Pedantry.[8] (No wonder Jane preferred Mary.)

Her immediate family might laugh, but Uncle Guillemard did not. As dusk descended they would draw their chairs round the fire and he would examine her in, say, grammar, or what it meant to be a Christian. Jane often felt ignorant, and when an algebra problem defeated her, she was so annoyed with her own stupidity that she burst into tears. Uncle Guillemard was all sympathy. 'Don't think it's stupidity, my dear', he said; she only needed to pay a little more attention.

Life at Tredrea was not all study. Out for a ride with her uncle, Jane wrote,

> I canter'd fast, & my petticoats disarrang'd by the violent motion, refused to cover my legs, & shocking to relate, rose above my knees; my scanty, flimsy habit too light to be kept down by its own weight, experienced a similar fate, & only served just to shade my garter from observation ... my cruel Uncle ... was maliciously amused with my misfortune, & came on tittering behind me & making caustic observations on the fine figure I should cut in Hyde Park [where London society rode in prim respectability].[9]

Back in London, Jane continued her intellectual development, drawing up a plan for her 'employment of time & improvement of the mind'. Mornings were for study, afternoons for compiling her papers, evenings for needlework, music (rare mentions) and conversation, with 'easy natural reflections' on her reading; then, in her room, she would summarise her day's work. Beneath the plan, many years later Jane wrote, 'Alas! alas'—but though she might not have carried out the plan rigidly, she did take learning seriously, becoming engaged, as historian Penny Russell comments, in 'a sort of dilettante intellectualism'. Jane's lengthy reading lists include memoirs, sermons and books about travel, history, geography and education, as well as poetry and novels by Jane Austen and Walter Scott.[10] Like many autodidacts building on an inadequate education, she loved facts—all facts, without discrimination as to their importance, and little idea of any underlying theory. Just like her school textbook.

Jane's other stimulus was travel, which her father loved. He retired early from silk-weaving, and each summer the family went on a long holiday. Before they left, Jane read all she could about the district they were to visit; she left nothing undone to reap fruit from any opportunity, commented her obituarist and niece Sophia Cracroft. Her lengthy journals described where she went, what she saw, what she did, whom she met, the district's principal products and buildings ... No detail was too minor. As she travelled she took notes in pencil on a piece of paper which she slid up her glove when she was not writing, and in the evenings she turned the notes into fluent prose. She wrote these journals until she was in her late seventies, producing books full of detail about many parts of the world, a mine of information for modern researchers.[11] At first the journals dealt with her travels only, but soon they described home life too. She never so much as hinted why she wrote so much; recording everything seemed to be a compelling need.

Her powers of observation were acute, sometimes uncharitable. She regretted 'that Miss Browne should have that unfortunate taint of vulgarity about her', and described her friend Anne Hind as 'shewy-looking, stiff in the limbs, & excessively talkative'. (She rarely mentioned anything as unladylike as limbs, except for one startling entry, when in Egypt she described a man 'wriggling his bottom'.)[12] This is a self-confident writer who feels her judgements are as good as anyone's.

Socially Jane was less comfortable. She blushed easily and was shy and nervous, and a birthmark on one temple would not have helped a teenager's self-confidence, though she could cover it with her hair. At a ball she did not have the courage to look a partner in the face, and she could not cope with compliments from a young man. Perhaps she was unwilling, or did not know how, to play the role society allotted to girls, an empty-headed butterfly admiring the superior male—irritating for someone more intelligent than most of her partners. As she grew older, parties often featured in her diary as 'stupid'. It was not that she was unattractive; although she was described as more 'piquante' than beautiful, she was small and slender, with dark hair and blue eyes, and her portrait, painted in 1816 when she was 24, depicts a pretty young woman—Jane thought it true to life but Fanny, among others, did not. The three Misses Griffin were described, tepidly, as 'sensible and agreeable, & *not unpretty*'.[13]

Jane's description of a visit with Mary to Anne Hind, in whose home 'stylish smartness' reigned, shows that she felt superior to the usual young-lady interests of clothes, music, needlework and chatter, though 'we entered into it as much as we could'. Mary found this easier, playing duets with Anne while Jane read Johnson's *Journey to the Hebrides*. Jane enjoyed a timid male visitor's horror at being 'unwillingly caught in a party of ladies', especially when, at dinner, Mrs Hind's muslin tippet slipped from her shoulder and left the strap of her corset visible. Jane was so amused she found it hard not to laugh, and she was glad when any foolish thing was said, giving her an excuse. Fortunately many were, she wrote in her condescending way.

At a final meal, wrote Jane, Mr Hind admired 'our dressed heads & smart pink low gowns', saying, ' "you look like strawberry cream, fit to be eaten", a remark which did not a little nettle our friend Anne who had a pink gown in her wardrobe too & a prettier one than ours which her father only a few days before had most unmercifully abused'.[14] In later years Jane showed almost no interest in dress, but in her youth she enjoyed looking attractive.

There was a purpose to this social life. As Jane Austen's novels show, young ladies were expected to find husbands, to establish themselves with homes and financial support, and fulfil their expected role as wives and mothers. Other roles were seen as second-rate: paid work was only done from financial necessity, and remaining single was an admission of failure. 'You will be an old maid! and that's so dreadful!' exclaims Harriet Smith in Jane Austen's *Emma*.

The Griffin girls would have expected to marry men from a similar background to theirs, well-to-do gentry. By the time John Griffin's daughters were entering society, he was accepted as a gentleman; when in 1824 the Athenaeum Club was founded for literary and scientific gentlemen, he was invited to become a member.[15] However, his background in trade left the Griffins socially vulnerable.

By now the family had a better address. The silk industry in Spitalfields was declining, the district was going downhill, and like other wealthy weavers the Griffins moved, in 1815 leasing a terrace house,

21 Bedford Place, off Russell Square. It was a comfortable upper-middle-class home, one large room wide with five storeys: kitchen in the basement, dining room and drawing room on the ground floor, two floors of family bedrooms, and servants' bedrooms at the top. The 1841 census showed John Griffin employing five servants, and ten years later there were six: butler, footman, cook, lady's maid and two housemaids. Mrs Peltrau left, and Fanny, the eldest daughter, probably ran the house; Jane mentioned only once that she herself did the housekeeping, as an unusual event.[16]

John Griffin maintained a keen interest in the Worshipful Company of Goldsmiths—to the point of garrulity, according to Jane. In 1814 he was elected to its governing body and moved up its hierarchy, in 1819 becoming Prime Warden (chairman), a most prestigious position, for which he needed a coat of arms and a motto. The College of Heralds provided one, with the central figure a mythical griffin, and the motto *Nosce te ipsum* (Know thyself). However, Jane disliked any mention of this trade-related activity, and only attended the Company's annual dinner for ladies reluctantly, to please her father.[17]

It was not among the mercantile Goldsmiths but in general cultured society that the Griffin girls looked for husbands. The only one to marry young was Mary. In 1814, aged 21, she married Frank Simpkinson, a London barrister who was not a favourite with his sister-in-law Jane. Of one of her suitors she wrote, 'Mr Simpkinson in his usual manner began to abuse him as a person whom he could not bear the sight of, & me as an arrant flirt'. Perhaps they saw each other as competitors for Mary's affection.

In 1819 Jane recorded the birth of one of Mary's children. Mary dined at Bedford Place, but, feeling uncomfortable, went home after dinner instead of to a party. Her labour began that night. Jane was called, and heard the baby's first cry at 5.30 a.m. 'I could not believe it was the new-born babe & thought it must be a cat or kitten on the staircase—I saw a new-born babe for the first time on Mrs Tathams's lap & thought no object in nature could be less attractive.' She saw the child, kissed Mary, then walked home in the early morning. 'I left my white satin shoes & pink striped gown behind, & was habited in this morning's walk in Mary's plaid petticoat with one of her white dressing gowns over it—I trusted to meeting no acquaintance on my road.'[18] So when heavily pregnant, Mary dined away from home and even considered going to a party, and Jane was more interested in her appearance than her new nephew.

Jane received only a little guidance from her father about her future. He told her he disapproved of coquetry (to little effect), and when she was thirty warned her against a clergyman with little money. She replied that she was trying to repress her suitor, 'tho' not on the grounds of Papa's objections as to money –. Papa's countenance brightened at this information', and even more at her mention of several ex-suitors. He had only been aware of one and, while proud that his daughter was sought after, was also grieved that she had not accepted any. He asked her why: she gave, she said, a short and inadequate explanation, then begged him to say no more.[19]

John Griffin did not often take such an interest in his daughters' romances. He was far more absorbed in travel. As soon as peace with France was signed in 1814, the family visited the continent. They stayed away for over two years, Jane and Fanny for the whole period, others coming and going. Now in her early twenties, Jane adored it. She was such an ardent traveller that in an uncomfortable carriage she could rejoice that, since it was French, at least it meant that they were in France—though when 'supper was in the vilest French style' she found it hard not to look 'a little sulky à l'anglaise'.[20]

As usual, Jane described everything they did and saw. She read voraciously, sometimes clandestinely in her room for fear of being teased, and often wrote her journal while the others were at dinner—she was never very interested in food. Then in Geneva she met Adolphe Butini, a clever, vivacious young man. She danced with him at a ball, wearing a white satin dress decorated with lace, ribbon and net, and a crimson velvet corset tied behind with white ribbons. There were more dances and outings, and Jane thoroughly enjoyed herself, if somewhat guiltily: 'what a life!—to spend the evening in displaying one's dress, & the morning in preparing for it'. Geneva, she said, changed her from a shy person shrinking from society, doting on books but ashamed of being laughed at about them, to—she did not say, but clearly someone more outgoing.[21]

In 1816 the Griffins returned to England. Now Jane understood better how to be a young lady. She was more confident, though still worried by nervousness; Fanny accused her of self-indulgence, though Mary sympathised as she always did ('Mary deserves all the intenseness of my affection for her'). Nervous or not, once Adolphe broke the drought Jane mentions many men in her diary, and she and Fanny enjoyed numerous flirtations. 'I said', 'he said', 'Fanny said', furious crossings out—such entries run on for pages.[22]

Between 1814 and 1828 these affairs followed a similar pattern: initial attraction, talking, dancing and so on; the suitor becoming enthusiastic and sometimes proposing marriage (at least half a dozen did); with much anguish and agony ('agitating, poignant, heart-rending') Jane curbing any ardency and moving to a successor; the spurned man usually marrying someone else, which she often felt deeply. Two men most attracted her. She alternately dismissed and yearned after Adolphe Butini: 'I know that Adolphe loves me better than any one else has ever loved me, better than anyone can ever love me again … [But] I still think & ever must believe the individual whose name I dare not write, to be superior to most men.' This was Peter Roget, another Huguenot, later to compile the thesaurus. He never proposed. He missed a rare opportunity, for Jane Griffin would have been a wonderful wife for a thesaurus compiler, with her acute mind and dogged perseverance. It is easy to picture her, bustling up to him: 'Look dear, I've found another usage of …'[23]

Why did Jane Griffin refuse these suitors? Many were eligible, including a colonel and a baronet. '*Whenever* I marry, *whoever* I marry, I will open my whole heart to him who will then possess supreme & exclusive dominion over it', she wrote, and, 'Shall I really make as good a wife as I intend to be? or is it one of my romantic fancies to think that the supremest bliss of a woman is to be found in her sanctified affection towards her husband?' Did she not meet her ideal? Did she want a husband who, like her, enjoyed travel, reading and possibly adventure, and none measured up? Or was she afraid of sex? She loved flirtation, but there is no hint of physical arousal as she records with nonchalance fervent kisses pressed on her hand. Once Mary said a wedding made her uncomfortable, for she could not help 'feeling for the situation of the bride'.[24] Facing the wedding night? Apprehension about sex and their mother's death in childbirth might explain Jane and Fanny marrying so late.

Another possible factor is that Jane was looking for more in a husband. Her nephew Frank Simpkinson said that 'her idea was fame—fame almost at any price',[25] and while there were other factors in Frank's sourness, perhaps Jane was looking for a man through whom she could use her talents.

Jane Griffin must have known that she had gifts above the ordinary. Though not brilliant or deeply intellectual, she had a quick intelligence and a clear mind. She had drive and determination, and was capable of extremely hard work. In the twenty-first century she could have run her own business—and had the business been in public relations, she might have founded a worldwide empire. There were no such opportunities in her time. Literature was one way, publishing poetry, novels or travel books, but Jane declared that 'I shall certainly <u>not</u> write a book', and never did.[26] She was not likely to become an actress or a singer, she was not interested in charity, and there was no other way a woman could achieve fame except through a husband. Perhaps Jane did not see in any of her suitors that spark she could fan into fame. (If she was looking for it, she missed an opportunity with family friend Benjamin Disraeli, future novelist and prime minister. True, Jane was a decade older, but so was his eventual wife.)

Despite refusing her suitors, Jane aimed to marry eventually. She sometimes felt 'in a state of torturing uncertainty … equally ignorant of my future fate, yet surely … this suspence is drawing <u>nearer</u> to a close'. At times she feared she never would marry. Birthdays became increasingly gloomy. When she turned 28, 'I had a sick head-ach & sat all day over the fire, reading … & brooding over my own dismal affairs'. In 1821 Fanny ignored her sister's thirtieth birthday because she thought Jane would prefer not to have it noticed, and Jane wrote sadly in her diary that she had recently lost two former suitors to others '– and what now remains to me?'[27]

'Plenty' was the answer, plenty more love affairs. For example, in 1823 Jane was alone in the drawing room with a man who begged for a lock of her hair, '& having a pair of scissors in his hand, he succeeded in effecting his purpose'. In exchange he gave her a prayer book, and then:

> We had a long & ample explanation of our feelings—I said the strongest things I could possibly think of to induce him to give up all thoughts of me—I told him I was 5 or 6 years older than himself, that even if he could marry now which was impossible I shd be indisposed for it … Nothing I could say however had so much effect as my tears, which fell fast & which he viewed with distress & compunction … He shed no tears, he yeilded without a murmur to my wish that this shd be our last, our farewell meeting, but he embraced me with a fervour, & detained me when I would have torn myself from him with a tenaciousness of passionate affection which I should hardly beforehand believed I could have permitted—But it was our parting moment, I had denied & resisted all his prayers & importunities, we were parting probably for ever.[28]

And so on, and so on. Though she believed she had to marry, she does not sound enthusiastic to do so—but she did relish the drama of rejection.

So her life continued: summer trips abroad, the rest of the year based in London with its entertainments and flirtations as well as more intellectual activities, such as art exhibitions, German lessons and music lectures. Never musical, Jane struggled, and told a friend she had none of the accomplishments expected of young ladies, such as playing music, sketching or doing embroidery. Instead she had her reading, writing and journal-keeping, and heard reports that people were frightened of her and Fanny, as bluestockings.[29]

There were occasional excitements. Jane was shocked when a Miss Wright who stayed with the Guillemards between posts as governess was revealed as Uncle Guillemard's illegitimate daughter—not so much because of her uncle's moral laxity, as for fear that she would no longer be first in his affections. Her own most dashing activity was a balloon ascent. She and Fanny arrived in time to see the balloon filled with gas (Jane provides much detail about this, even that the man in charge wore striped linen trousers) then climbed into the red and orange car beneath. The balloon was tethered to the ground by 100-metre ropes, and the two women rose to almost this height then were lowered, three or four times. They could have gone higher, but Fanny was frightened. A crowd stared, but Jane had exchanged 'my well-known Vienna plush bonnet' for an old black one, and held a handkerchief to her face lest she be recognised.[30]

Fanny was involved in charitable work, but Jane was not. However, she had some interest in social conditions. Once in Devonshire she visited a prison ship, where she saw about 750 political prisoners huddled together in a hold; but she took less notice of the men's suffering than of their admiration of their female visitors. (Natural enough, at seventeen.) Later she became interested in the work of Quaker reformer Elizabeth Fry, and in 1823 she, Mary and four friends visited Newgate prison to watch Mrs Fry lecture female prisoners whom she had reformed from swearing, fighting harridans. They were mostly strapping, ugly women, wrote Jane, but she had to admit they behaved well as Fry read a chapter of the Bible and discussed it, stressing the rewards of good behaviour. Jane was disappointed with this quiet and gentle approach, surprised that it could have produced such a change.[31] It was not her way.

By this stage she had an income of her own. Her father provided his daughters with a lump sum, and Jane bought shares in the East

India Company and voted in elections for the company's directors, her only public activity. She was canny about money, once selling clothes she had bought in France to her sisters and friend for their original price, though they were second-hand.[32]

Physically fit, with plenty of travel, entertainment and suitors, Jane was outwardly content in these years, yet beneath the diaries' endless pages of romantic hand-wringing and trivia is a woman who is frustrated with this superficial life, and struggling to find a purpose for herself. Then, in her thirties, Jane Franklin's life changed. She met Eleanor Porden and, through her, the explorer John Franklin.

2

THE FRANKLIN
CONNECTION

Who was John Franklin? A century ago everyone knew, but today the glow around such heroes of exploration has faded, and the question needs an answer. John Franklin was born in 1786 in the Lincolnshire village of Spilsby, into a large, god-fearing, close-knit rural family, quite different from the Griffins with their urban sophistication. Formerly country squires, the Franklins had come down in the world, only keeping their status as gentry by the skin of their teeth. John's grandmother had to open a shop to survive and John was born in a room above it, not a promising start; but his father prospered and became a landowner. However, the eleven Franklin children grew up without the money or family influence so useful in getting on in the world. Fortunately John had another valuable asset: popularity. Almost everyone liked this transparently honest, decent, kind man. It helped him in obtaining the patrons so vital for promotion—but getting on was still hard work.

As a boy, John fell in love with the sea and insisted on joining the navy, which was more open to promotion by merit than other careers such as the church (his father's desired destiny for him). Like

Jane Griffin's, John's formal education was limited, and at fourteen he enlisted as a volunteer, the lowest rank of officer. He found himself fighting in the Battle of Copenhagen, where he was horrified by the sight of dead bodies lying in the harbour.[1]

The family had one naval relative, Captain Matthew Flinders, who married John's aunt. In 1801 he took the boy on his three-year voyage to Australia. Young John enjoyed exploration and natural history (botanist Robert Brown was on board), circumnavigated Australia, was shipwrecked and rescued, and took part in a dramatic action in which British merchantmen chased off a much more powerful French squadron. He loved it all.

After returning to England in 1804, John fought in the battle of Trafalgar, in charge of his ship's signals. Men were killed all around him—including his best friend, who was shot and fell dead on the deck while they were talking—but John escaped injury, although the noise of gunfire left him slightly deaf. With the French defeated, naval activity became mostly mundane, though during the Anglo–American war of 1812 John took part in the battle of Lake Borgne near New Orleans. There he received his only wound, a slight one. He was promoted to lieutenant but no further, probably due to his lack of a patron (Flinders had died) rather than any professional failing, since he was a competent, conscientious officer. He influenced his crew by kindness not severity, and was never afraid to show his strong religious piety, usually ridiculed at this period.[2]

In 1815 the long war with Napoleon ended. Britain's huge navy was drastically downsized, with most officers retired on half pay. Franklin wanted to stay in the navy, preferably with promotion, and pleaded with Robert Brown for help. Brown told him that exploring expeditions were talked of, and he would do what he could. Perhaps this included introducing Franklin to Joseph Banks, the famous naturalist. Banks advised Franklin to learn surveying, which he did, and then recommended him to the Admiralty as an explorer.[3]

The Admiralty's interest in exploration came about because John Barrow, its senior public servant, envisaged it as an inspiring and useful activity for the remnant navy. In 1818 he organised expeditions to the holy grails of Arctic exploration: the North Pole, which he believed was a rocky outcrop surrounded by an open Polar Sea, and the Northwest Passage, linking the Atlantic and Pacific oceans round the north of America.

Fortunately for Franklin, Barrow liked him, and appointed him second-in-command of the North Pole expedition. There was enormous public interest, and Franklin revelled in meeting important people. 'It really seems quite ridiculous to find myself placed among these parties when I consider how little I know of the Subjects which usually form the topic of their conversations', he wrote to his sister. Among the crowds was Jane Griffin, whose party was shown over one of the ships. She noted Lieutenant Franklin's role—but then Adolphe Butini visited, 'a much more interesting event than any thing I have hitherto mentioned'.[4] So much for Arctic exploration.

The Northwest Passage expedition under John Ross only reached the west coast of Baffin Bay, and the North Pole expedition also made little progress, solid ice blocking its route north from Spitsbergen. However, it was in the interests of everyone concerned to depict these ventures as successful, praising bravery and daring exploits if achievements were meagre. John Franklin returned to London a minor celebrity.

Among his new acquaintances was Eleanor Porden. Her father was an eminent architect, and Eleanor was an intelligent young woman, who attended her first lecture at the Royal Institution aged nine, and at sixteen published *The Veils*, a 'clever scientific poem allegorizing the Rosicrucian system' that won her membership of the Paris Institute. Though quite different—she the urban sophisticate, he the rural innocent—John and Eleanor fell in love; 'seldom can two such absolutely diverse personalities have decided to brave the sea of matrimony together', as a descendant wrote. There was no engagement yet, for Eleanor was nursing her much-loved elderly parents, and John was organising his next expedition.[5]

Eleanor became acquainted with Jane Griffin, who described her as 'a plain, stout short young woman, having rather a vulgar, tho' a very good-natured countenance'. They became friendly, though not intimate, each writing of the other with reserve. Perhaps Jane was envious of this younger woman who had achieved literary fame and was so cheerfully self-confident and witty. Eleanor was teased, wrote Jane, about

> her universal talents—she makes all her own clothes, preserves & pickles, dances quadrilles <u>con</u> <u>amore</u>, belongs to a poetical bookclub, pays morning visits, sees all the sights, never denies herself to any body at any hour, & lies in bed or is not dressed till 9 o'clock in the morning.

One evening at a lecture, a man behind Eleanor remarked loudly that instead of going to scientific talks, young women would be better at home making puddings. 'We did that before we came out', Eleanor told him good-humouredly (and truthfully).

The Griffin and Porden families invited each other to a few dinners and parties, not many; the Pordens hosted more notable people, and discussion was more erudite. Eleanor was playful as well as intellectual, and Jane enjoyed a hoax she played on Fanny. After a lecture at the Royal Institution, Fanny accidentally spilled a few drops of an evil-smelling liquid, and Eleanor sent her a fake bill from the Institution's clerk for cleaning the room. Jane and Mary, the clerk, Peter Roget and Uncle Guillemard all joined in the hoax with enthusiasm. Fanny actually had her purse out to pay the bill when they acknowledged it. Jane thought it succeeded admirably.[6]

Meanwhile, John Franklin was away exploring. With the North Pole proved inaccessible, Barrow concentrated on the Northwest Passage. The map between Baffin Bay and Bering Strait was blank except for the mouths of the Mackenzie and Coppermine Rivers. In 1819 Barrow sent Edward Parry to sail west from Baffin Bay, and John Franklin to descend the Coppermine River and travel east along the coast. Parry sailed as far west as Melville Island. A magnificent achievement: he returned a hero.

John Franklin also made his name, though his expedition was a disaster. Inexperienced in organising overland travel, the Admiralty relied on promises of help from Canadian fur companies; but these were at loggerheads, the season was poor, and locals were not interested in explorers. So help was minimal, but the party was too big to live off the land, as it included a number of French-Canadian voyageurs employed to do the manual work that officers never did.

Without the British navy's lash to enforce automatic obedience, Franklin proved no natural leader. He encouraged the sport of sliding on sledges down snowy riverbanks, but once 'when I was thrown from my seat and almost buried in snow, a fat Indian woman drove her sledge over me, and sprained my knee severely'. It is hard to picture anyone running a sledge over a strong leader like the Duke of Wellington; Franklin was clearly not a figure of awe, as he enjoyed frolics with the local population. Unimaginative, a man of his times, he could not understand people different from himself—he was appalled, for example, when men who carried provisions through 553 miles (890 kilometres) of deep snow broached a cask of rum on New Year's Eve. He did recognise, if condescendingly, some of the locals' good points such as cheerfulness, admiring an Indian chief who 'often surprised us by his correct judgment of the character of individuals'.[7]

The British party consisted of Franklin; John Richardson, surgeon and naturalist; two midshipmen, George Back and Robert Hood; and seaman and attendant John Hepburn. Leaving England in 1819, the party crossed Canada to Point Lake, where voyageurs built Fort Enterprise. There was some dissension among the Britons. Franklin and Richardson became lifelong friends, with Franklin relying on Richardson's advice, but none of the others liked the capable but bumptious Back, and Richardson and Franklin were horrified when Back and Hood had affairs with local women, Hood fathering a child. They found one woman, Greenstockings, particularly attractive, and today she is seen in a similar light to Mathinna in Van Diemen's

Land, the personification of the tragedy of indigenous people abused by Europeans.

In June 1820 the party rowed down the Coppermine and turned east: five Britons, eleven voyageurs, two hunters and two Inuit interpreters. They achieved 640 miles (1000 kilometres) to Point Turnagain, but Franklin explored too long and had to return across the Barren Lands, where he had been warned that food was short. The party struggled on, living on lichen, skins, bones and leather. When they killed an ox, 'the contents of its stomach were devoured upon the spot, and the raw intestines, which were next attacked, were pronounced by the most delicate amongst us to be excellent'.

Starving and disorganised, they just managed to cross the Coppermine. Franklin sent Back ahead to search for food; Hood, very weak, remained with Richardson, Hepburn and some voyageurs; the rest straggled on towards Fort Enterprise, some dying on the way. There was no food at the fort, but they could only stay there, scrounging for skins or bones. Richardson and Hepburn joined them, claiming that a voyageur, Michel Teroahauté, had eaten two other voyageurs and killed Hood. Claiming self-defence, Richardson killed him.

Everyone in the fort had died or was dying when Indians sent by Back saved them. Franklin then started turning disaster into success. In their 'long, fatiguing, and disastrous travels' of 5550 miles (8900 kilometres), the British had 'discovered' 640 miles of coast, and that was what mattered. Eleven people died, but Franklin and the Admiralty managed to pass this off as an unfortunate by-product of success, and criticism in Britain was muted.

Back home in 1822, Franklin wrote his narrative of the expedition. He called this task 'a sad plague', but Eleanor Porden almost certainly helped him. Barrow edited it, and the book depicted the British positively—Hood, for example, not as a seducer of indigenous maidens but as a gallant hero who died holding a copy of *Scripture Help*. They were a brave band of brothers overcoming overwhelming odds and uncooperative Canadians. No problem was their fault. The story is gripping, with its exploration, starvation, cannibalism and death. The book became a bestseller, with Franklin lionised as a celebrated Arctic explorer, the Man Who Ate His Boots.[8] Explorers were the men of the moment, popular heroes comparable with film stars and sporting giants today. They faced incredible dangers and privations, conquering not just distance but endless other problems, to bring back that Victorian goal: knowledge, filling in the blank spaces on the map. They were also rare, with only a handful who really achieved. Franklin, Parry, Back and a few others became household names, revered for their courage and gallantry, ideal British heroes.

Back in England, Eleanor Porden's parents had died, and she was left alone but for her grumpy elder sister. When John returned the two agreed to marry, but their engagement had its ups and downs. Eleanor felt John was too absorbed in his own family to appreciate her friends, and he took offence when she compared flat Lincolnshire to the Arctic wastes. 'Cannot you take a joke?' she asked him. 'I was determined to play with you a little. You know I dearly love to turn any one's meaning inside out!' More seriously, he told her he hated seeing the name of anyone connected with him in print, as hers had been when her poems were published. She was shattered. 'My tastes and habits had been fully known to you from the first moment of our acquaintance'; why had he changed his mind? She would never oppose any such interest of his, and he himself was writing a book about his voyage. 'If you have liked what I really am, if a sincere attachment to yourself, and an earnest wish to render towards you the attention and the duty of an affectionate wife, be sufficient to make you happy, I am willing to be yours', she wrote. 'But you must not expect me to change my nature.' John gave in.[9]

Then there was religion. Both were Anglicans, but John had Puritan tendencies. 'I should be inclined to say that my religion like my character, was of a gayer nature than yours', Eleanor wrote. 'The simpler our Religion is, the better.' But John disapproved of the Pordens' literary salon, the Attic Chest, meeting on Sunday, and rashly sent Eleanor some ardent evangelical writings, which she received coldly.[10]

They were greatly attracted to each other, however, John a hero and a rock of strength to lonely Eleanor, she enchanting with her optimism and gaiety: 'it is my constant endeavour that no circumstances shall depress me'. She sent him an amusing valentine 'from Miss Green Stockings to her faithless Admirer', and he tried to live up to her, writing a poem about a balloon ascent. Others saw their happiness, and when Jane Griffin called on Eleanor in April 1823, 'we joked her upon Captn Franklin's great 4to [book] which we found on her table— she told us if we had come 5 minutes sooner we shd have seen him, but we suspected we said that if we had come then, we should not have been admitted at all'.[11]

Eleanor and John were married that August. Eleanor visited John's family and did her best, and John was pleased that she was as enthusiastic about Arctic discovery as he was; but their tastes differed. Eleanor loved London's social and intellectual life, and her wit and charm attracted many friends to their house. 'I am quite harried by visiting and comp[an]y and long for a little quiet', wrote John to a friend. 'This is the consequence of marriage!' Eleanor was more positive, writing to John's sister that twelve months was 'Time enough for us to get tired of each other, according to some people's opinion but I see no signs of such an event at present'.[12]

Eleanor was soon pregnant and had a worrying cough, but John was too busy to coddle her. Early in 1824 he was appointed in charge of a second expedition to the north American coast, organised from England this time—his job. Family concerns frequently called him to Lincolnshire, especially the devastating deaths of six family members in two years. In London, he often socialised without Eleanor ('It is 11 but your brother is not yet come home from a dinner party', she wrote to his sister, tolerantly seeing this as part of John's 'necessary visiting'). He usually stayed at home on Sundays, recorded Jane Griffin, but was allowed to come to the Griffins' dinner (on a Sunday!), and later to their party where 'the ladies gathered round their favorite hero Captn Franklin after the dance'. The Griffins met him at a party at the Disraelis': 'As soon as Captn Franklin saw Fanny & me, he gave us each an arm,

& seemed to have us under his protection the greater part of the evening which surely must have made us objects of envy.' The sisters went to Woolwich to see him test his boats, even daring to try out the portable boat, the 'walnut shell'. Jane and John clearly liked each other, but speculation that they were having an affair is surely over-enthusiastic: he sounds an unlikely participant, while she wrote like this about many men, and was just starting a flirtation with her Spanish teacher.[13]

Jane was friendly with Eleanor, visiting her and taking her out driving for her health. Jane found one visit rather heavy until Eleanor began to speak of her husband, when 'her heart was full & her tongue eloquent'. The Griffins went to a dinner at the Franklins', where Jane met Edward Parry, John Barrow and the rest of John's Arctic friends. Eleanor was making an effort for John, but she was unhappy with his frequent absences, writing: 'I suppose you are the best judge, but it seems that none of your family can do anything without you, and your self-love is flattered by it, you vain animal!' She was besieged by men asking to be taken on the expedition: 'I wish you would come home and do your own business, for I feel it very ridiculous to have all these gentlemen coming to me to try the effect of petticoat influence.' John went to a ball without her, and she told his sister that he had been in such demand by the ladies that 'I wonder they left a bit of him for me. Such a flirt he is!'[14]

Their daughter Eleanor was born in June 1824, and was so like her father that, said one of his friends, 'it was like looking at Captn Franklin thro' the wrong end of a telescope'. They both adored her. 'Baby is very well and grows as fast as ever, fat, fair and funny', Eleanor wrote to John. 'I had been laughing and playing with her half the morning, for she has got such a trick of crowing and chattering at me, that there is no getting away from her'; and later, 'Goosey is making believe to talk, and even gets out some sounds very like "Mama." ' In August they had a happy family holiday in Tunbridge Wells, where they convinced themselves that Eleanor's health was improving. The baby, wrote her fond father, was 'getting so fat & heavy as to be beyond Mamas power of tossing—and almost enough to tire Papa's stouter arm'.[15] But back in London, John was often absent again.

Disastrously, in January 1825 Eleanor was diagnosed with tuberculosis, a fatal disease. John's expedition was due to leave in February, and they both decided he must go. Though he still had the occasional evening out ('Captn Franklin kept me in continual talk', wrote Jane Griffin) he cared for Eleanor devotedly, admiring the courage with which she faced death. Jane visited Eleanor in early February and found her 'very unfit to see any body'. A few days later, when the Griffins called to leave farewell presents for Captain Franklin, they were told she was dangerously ill. John left on 16 February, and Eleanor swapped a husband's care for that of her grim sister and John's sister Hannah, who started to read the Bible to her, chapter by chapter. She had only reached the twenty-fourth when on 22 February Eleanor died, aged 29.[16]

Sympathetically, Jane Griffin visited Eleanor's sister who wept, but 'did not scruple to allude to her faults', regretting that Eleanor had been harsh and hasty, maintaining her opinions too stoutly against her husband's. 'I said I thought her manners had been softened either by her illness or her marriage, probably by both.' Elsewhere Jane also supported her friends. At a party the Disraelis passed on gossip about the Franklins' parting, and 'my voice trembled with agitation not unmixed with anger while I replied to all this unfeeling nonsense'. There were certainly rumours, then and later, that the Franklins' marriage was unhappy, but their letters sound devoted and family tradition described a happy couple. Rumours could have started because of John's neglect of Eleanor, because he was unresponsive at her literary evenings, because she stood up to him or, most obviously, because he left her on her deathbed, though, as he pointed out defensively, she insisted on it.[17]

The next Arctic expedition was successful. From the mouth of the Mackenzie River, Richardson sailed east to the Coppermine, and Franklin west. He only reached half as far as he aimed, but 374 miles (601 kilometres) was a respectable achievement, and there were no disasters. Franklin was encouraged by thoughts of his daughter, 'Miss Fatty' as he called her. 'I have fancied myself a witness to her prattle, her imitations, and her fondness of pictures—and the delightful appellation of Dad Dad has more than once escaped my mouth in the manner she was wont to salute me.'[18] Nothing of this endearing warmth came through in his book about the expedition, which without Eleanor's help was stodgy and did not sell well.

In London, Jane Griffin made 'great progress in intimacy' with her Spanish teacher, and the family went on a trip to Scandinavia. When Captain Franklin called, only the day after he returned home, they were still away. He soon found them in, told them he had named a cape after them, and gave them reindeer tongues from Canada. They asked him to dinner but the evening was difficult for, to Jane's embarrassment, her brother-in-law Frank Simpkinson, who knew nothing about it, would argue with the expert Franklin about the Northwest Passage. Nervously, Jane visited little Eleanor. After this, no details remain. Either Jane or her executor, Sophy Cracroft, destroyed journals and letters from early 1828, perhaps removing evidence of any negotiation over marriage, religion, wifely independence or any other matter. The clean sweep does suggest some challenges. But in July, John Franklin informed Mr Griffin that he and Miss Jane were assured 'not only of our entertaining the warmest affection for each other but likewise that there exists between us the closest congeniality of mind, thought, and feeling'.[19] He asked for her hand in marriage, and Jane's father consented.

Later that year Jane wrote to 'My dear Captain Franklin' that,

> whenever I think I am imposed upon my spirit rises, and I struggle harder to resist than perhaps is quite consistent with that meek and resigned spirit which men endeavour to teach us is not only becoming but obligatory, and which we poor women endowed with acute sensibilities, though with less energy and much less power than men, often find to be our surest and safest way to happiness.

So she was depicting herself as struggling to behave in the submissive way society expected of women. She continued:

Do not be alarmed at these moralising reflections ... You are of a much more easy disposition than myself, in spite of that energy and firmness of mind which, when the occasion calls for it, you can display as well or better than most men, and without which you never could have won my regard. [My task is to] combat those things which excite my more sensitive temper; while it must and shall be yours, as my beloved and most honoured husband, to control even this disposition whenever you think it improperly excited ... You will put this letter by and turn it to account at some future time when I am in a rebellious mood; and upon this consideration I trust you ought to feel infinitely obliged to me for furnishing you with so valuable a document. How soon shall I repent of it myself?[20]

Why did Jane Griffin accept John Franklin when she had spurned so many other men? At 42 he was middle-aged, short, stout, balding, with little money. But he was famous, a 'lion' in London society, recently presented with an honorary degree at Oxford University and the Gold Medal of the Geographical Society of Paris. He was also nice, liked by all. Eleanor's niece remembered sitting on his knee playing with his epaulettes, and described him as mild and kind, 'his manner very quiet, though not without a certain dignity, as of one accustomed to command others'. He was decent, dependable and affectionate, brave and noble. John Richardson said he 'had a cheerful buoyancy of mind, which, sustained by religious principle of a depth known only to his most intimate friends, was not depressed in the most gloomy times'. His piety is demonstrated by a sheet among his papers headed 'Concise rules for self-examination. Have I this day walked with God?' Of twelve rules, eleven concern God—had the reader submitted to his will, sought him through prayer, tried to glorify him in social inter-course—while the twelfth encourages using every opportunity to help others.[21]

Did Jane fall in love with John? Their letters sound more like those between good friends than passionate lovers—yet is it fair to judge from letters? From the one quoted above, Jane admired his energy and firmness of mind, and wanted someone to calm her, guide her through life—but Jane used words not so much to express truth as to get what she wanted (in this letter, she was encouraging him to show this energy and firmness). She felt perfectly competent at guiding herself through life. Did she speculate that time was running short and it was now or never—especially since he was such a nice man? Did his invincible cheerfulness attract this nervous woman, or his adventurous life beckon her adventurous side? Having seen how Eleanor stood up for herself, did Jane see in John a husband who had been 'broken in', who would not dominate her? Was she swept away by his renown (he was by far the most famous of her suitors) and saw in him a man through whom she could obtain greatness? Given that she spent much of the rest of her life advancing his career by any possible means, this sounds likely, but all these explanations are possible, perhaps mixed together. As for John—he was a warm-hearted man, probably missing family life. He wanted a wife, and a mother for his daughter. Eleanor's niece commented that his wives both had 'superior intellect and uncommon force of character'; he was clearly attracted to clever, strong women. Jane admired and liked him, as she made plain, asking him to dinner and taking him presents. She wrote that it must have been her 'strange compound of contradictory qualities [which] made me so very irresistible in your eyes, and brought your gallantries at last ... to a close'; he took his time, nine months, to propose.[22]

In July 1828 the Griffins were about to leave for Russia. John Franklin wished to come with them, but Jane's sense of propriety forbade it; they might be placed in awkward situations in the long, rough journey. He was to join them in St Petersburg. On the way, in Hamburg, Jane bought her Spanish teacher a snuffbox (she found it hard to let go of past loves) and the party was taken on a tour of the sights. These included public houses surrounded by crowds of 'degraded beings ... painted & tricked out like the dancers outside of a show & looking like animated waxen dolls.—I never saw such a sight before, & don't suppose that any other place could exhibit such'.

An English driver would never have taken ladies to see such a terrible exhibition, but the German one drove slowly and deliberately past![23] So in all her previous travels, 36-year-old Jane Griffin had never knowingly seen prostitutes.

At St Petersburg the engaged couple were feted, the famous explorer meeting other explorers, scientists and even the Empress Mother. At one reception the couple were received by a general in full uniform, wearing his medals. 'Captn F. had nothing to say, told me he did not hear very well, & was vexed he had not on his uniform', wrote Jane. 'I s[ai]d he had better apologise & at his request, did it for him.' Then all was well.[24] This vignette shows a pattern that lasted their entire married life: John the established hero, but diffident, needing her advice and practical help; Jane his protector against the world, determined to make him successful.

3

AN OCCASIONAL
MARRIAGE

On 4 November 1828 Jane Griffin and John Franklin were married. She was 36, he was 42. None of her writing survives from this period, but from her new husband's letters everything sounds happy—though his letters almost always did. The wedding went well, every face beaming with joy, the path from the church strewn with flowers. He and Jane passed a week together 'in perfect retirement', and then went to Paris. John Franklin the famous explorer was celebrated, feted at meetings of the Geographical Society, where he refused the seat of honour as 'rather too prominent for a nervous man'. Jane accompanied him when she could, but was irritated that women were not asked to dinners.[1]

Back in London, John was a malleable husband—'you have only to make known your wishes and they are obeyed'. Perhaps he obeyed Jane in another step: requesting a knighthood for his achievements as an explorer. He was duly knighted.[2] He had to brave the head of the British navy to ask this favour, and it seems unlikely that a modest man who refused a prominent seat in December would do this in April of his own accord: more likely his wife encouraged, perhaps even pushed, him. From whatever cause, he and Jane became Sir John and Lady Franklin, a huge step up the social ladder.

From now on, Jane's title was 'Lady Franklin'—not 'Lady Jane Franklin', for her husband was only a knight and she was not the daughter of a peer. Only her closest intimates called her 'Jane', and no one ever called her 'Lady Jane'. This is not mere trivia. 'Lady Jane' has a friendly, easygoing sound, which was not for Jane Franklin. The formal, keep-your-distance 'Lady Franklin' was always used. This was the Establishment's aim, of course: to keep the riffraff at bay.

Financially, the Franklins were comfortable—not rich, but with enough money from Jane's father and John's first wife to live as they pleased. Legally Jane's wealth belonged to her husband, but John allowed her full control. He was never much interested in money. More than this, he wanted employment. No exploring expedition was likely, so he haunted the Admiralty asking for a ship. The Australian Agricultural Company offered him the position of manager in New South Wales; Jane had a burning desire to go there, wrote John, but he declined in case it harmed his prospects in the navy. His friend and fellow explorer Parry went instead.[3]

Married life might have been challenging for Jane, after 36 years of being single. They lived in John and Eleanor's former home, where as well as the ghost of Eleanor senior there was the presence of Eleanor junior. The little girl, now five, had been living with her aunt, John's sister Isabella Cracroft. As soon as the engagement was announced, Jane tried to be a good stepmother. She referred to 'dear little Eleanor', bought Eleanor dolls (and, missing no opportunity for instruction, asked her to tell her what they were made of), and asked Isabella to make sure Eleanor loved her new Mama. It was easy enough with Eleanor at a distance, but much harder when she was living in the house. John adored his daughter, describing her as cheerful and affectionate, but Jane's version was that Eleanor was vivacious, self-satisfied and intellectually sharp. 'This is not to my mind the beau ideal of the female countenance or mind, but we must work upon the materials we find and strive to mould them to our purpose', she wrote to John.[4] She never had much affinity with children.

Late in 1829 Jane became ill, often a sign that she was unhappy, and Eleanor returned to the Cracrofts. Jane went to a health resort and saw a succession of doctors. John mentioned rheumatism, but there was clearly something else that attacked Jane on and off for decades, often but not always when she was unhappy. Modern doctors suggest migraines and nervous dyspepsia, debilitating illnesses in the short term which have little effect on long-term health.[5]

Sometimes illness meant Jane missed out on treats. Once John decided she was too ill to accompany him in a visit. After he left she wrote to him, wishing she had yielded with a better grace and not given way to her feelings, but she wanted to go, and the sacrifice cost her dearly. Of all her letters only this, written a year after their marriage, breathes passion—but then she tells him that at a party her host said she produced an extraordinary sensation, and every gentleman present asked him who the very pretty young lady was. In other words, John was a brute but other people appreciated her. John apologised, but enjoyed his holiday. When Jane was better they returned to London (and Eleanor), and gave dinners and parties. In summer Jane took the waters at Brighton, and they attended royal levees and receptions. Jane described this period as given up to shameful vanity, trifling and idleness, though it was the normal way of life for the upper class, and, as so often, she used words for a purpose, in this case to inspire her husband to better things.[6]

In September 1830 Franklin was appointed to a ship, *Rainbow*. Jane wanted to accompany him, but he thought she should wait till spring's better weather. She submitted. One November morning, John brought Eleanor into Jane's bed to take his place there—Jane's opinion of the substitute can be imagined—and left for the Mediterranean. (This acknowledgement that John and Jane shared a bed is the only information about their sex life in all their hundreds of thousands of words.) Based on the Greek west coast, Franklin was the senior officer of a British–French–Russian fleet overseeing the fragile independence of the new Greek state, free after centuries of Turkish rule. Backed by naval authority and supportive officers he performed well, his superiors praising his work.[7]

Jane's nephew Frank Simpkinson, a young officer with Franklin, said everyone loved him for his kindness and courtesy—'I never saw him in the least out of temper, or heard him speak harshly to any of his officers'. The ship was nicknamed 'Franklin's Paradise' under Franklin's benign sway; he left administration to his first lieutenant. The navy considered flogging vital for discipline but Franklin hated it, trembling from head to foot whenever it was carried out, wrote Frank. Nevertheless, he accepted its necessity. Though deeply religious, he did not 'worry' the crew with prayer meetings (as Frank put it), but on Sunday afternoons gave the midshipmen a sermon in his cabin. He rebuked Frank for failing to remember the text of the Sunday service, and for rushing up and kissing his aunt when she was welcomed aboard; Franklin felt such displays should be reserved for the privacy of the cabin.

Franklin had human weaknesses. He was absentminded, once appearing on deck with only half his face shaved and the rest still lathered, to the midshipmen's joy. He was nervous on horseback and, when a party of officers rode on shore, warned the midshipmen not to come near him in case they frightened his mount—so they galloped furiously round him, pretending they could not control their horses.[8] Echoes of the woman driving her sledge over him: this kindly figure sounds a challenge for his wife to turn into a hero of achievement.

After John left, Jane Franklin returned to London, to Bedford Place, where she enjoyed dinners, parties, opera and theatre. However, she was often ill, and there was a dreadful occasion when the heated bag of hops the doctor prescribed (in desperation?) was too hot and nearly burnt her in her bed.[9] She and Eleanor attended a party where the King was present, and she was pleased to pass on a report that the King called Sir John 'a great friend of his'. She was interested in public events—she was conservative, though not as much as her sisters, who thought a cheaper postal system dangerously radical—but her diary mostly describes family activities. Fanny, aged 42, married Ashurst Majendie, a geologist of Huguenot descent who lived in style at Hedingham Castle in Essex. John Franklin approved, thinking Fanny would have to give up her 'whims and peculiarities', picturing her sallying forth with her husband and her geological hammer 'in search of all that is new in Science'. Mary's son ran away from school, and Mary and Jane spoke their minds to the headmaster about the atrocious system of fagging. At Bedford Place the butler caught a thief pocketing the spoons in the dining room, locked him in and sent for the police. Jane stood on the stairs with a poker while the female servants, 'as pale as death', kept watch at the windows until the police arrived.[10]

And there was Eleanor. For a woman who had had little to do with children, care of the six-year-old was a worrying burden. She had been ill as a baby, and Jane wrote to Eleanor's aunt that she was very anxious about her, caring for her like a hothouse plant. Subtext: I am a doting stepmother; but the letter has an over-anxious, even desperate undertone: what is this duty thrust on me? To show John how well she was bringing up their daughter, Jane described how she found Eleanor crying because Jane's maid had set her a verse of the Bible to learn. Assuming Eleanor was being naughty, Jane

> *immediately set her two verses, insisting they should be perfectly said the next day, and advising her, tho' I did not insist about it, to set about it resolutely at once more particularly as I was writing to Papa, and should be so glad to give a good report of her,—the truth, I assured her I was always obliged to tell him.— She instantly said she would learn them now.*

Jane also refused to send Papa a letter Eleanor wrote him because she thought the maid helped her. 'Left to herself and to me, she is almost all I could wish, and my influence over her is almost unbounded', she wrote.[11]

Jane obviously felt that, like Eleanor, John needed moulding. In one letter he rashly expressed a wish for a quiet life. This rang alarm bells. Jane urged him to gain promotion, to get to know important people (she was horrified when he refused a chance to meet the King of Greece, and made him ask for another opportunity), to contribute to science, improve his navigation, please the admiral, strive for employment in exploration 'and come back as usual with an increase of credit and of fame'. She almost wished for war to break out so that he could get more work. John had such drive, such energy, the King spoke well of him, and when 'all the latent energies of your nature' were aroused, his achievement would be limitless. Nothing meant more to her than her husband's success; 'I feel no satisfaction in any sense of superiority, such as you sometimes attribute to me, but the greatest joy and purest delight in all that you possess over me.'[12] By now the reader must be wondering how great a regard Jane had for exact truth. Perhaps she would have argued that society gave women little power, forcing them to be devious to have any influence. This was the argument of Mary Wollstonecraft's 1792 book, *A Vindication of the Rights of Women*—though Jane Franklin would never have championed such a radical feminist. She dreaded being seen as an unwomanly freak.

As a girl, Jane managed to live more or less as she wished while also meeting society's expectations. As an adult she managed this also. She knew she had a forceful, critical mind, huge energy and a desire to be active; she also knew that to be accepted in society she had to conform to its ideal of what a woman should be—submissive, retiring, obedient to the dominant male. Fortunately she looked appropriate, petite, slim and attractive, and she was often described as gentle, amiable and charming, so she could play that part; and she managed to subsume her strong character in the role of wife, where she could be as active as she wished for her husband's sake, claiming that all she did aimed at supporting him. It took some verbal manoeuvring, but Jane excelled at this.

Meanwhile, she tried to join John. Even if war did break out, it would not matter to her, and she would not be in the way, she wrote to him desperately. England and stepmotherhood bored her, and joining her husband—that important wifely duty—was a chance to escape. There was also the tantalising suggestion of feminine freedom, for she was intrigued to hear that a Mrs Lyons went round the Mediterranean by herself. However, at present she was shackled by society's rules. A gentleman might travel to the Mediterranean alone, but a lady must have a female companion, and this was hard to organise. It was also difficult to find transport. Arrangement after arrangement fell through, but 'I ... don't think things <u>impossible</u> for me which are only a little <u>difficult</u>', and finally in August 1831 she left for the Mediterranean with her father and an American couple, the Reverend Dr and Mrs Kirkland. She also took two servants and her iron bedstead, which travelled everywhere with her. The doctor said the Mediterranean would be bad for Eleanor's health, so she went back to the Cracrofts. Perhaps Jane dropped a hint to the doctor—but who could blame her for not wanting to travel with a six-year-old. A second reason for not taking Eleanor, as she wrote to her husband, was that 'I fear the child might sometimes be an obstacle to my being with you ... I cannot resolve upon anything that is to separate me from you'.[13] Time was to prove this claim somewhat inaccurate.

Jane Franklin spent the next three years in the Mediterranean, mostly travelling. There were difficulties. It was often hard to find companions, servants and transport. Erratic transport meant erratic mail, and she and her husband often did not hear from each other for months. In letters home she complained about bugs, mosquitoes, fleas, smells, weather (cold, hot, steamy) and a succession of uncongenial companions and inadequate servants, but this was probably so that her family would not think she was having too much pleasure. The upper classes expected to enjoy their usual round of dinners, parties and balls, but travel was meant to be for a worthy cause, such as duty, education, self-improvement or writing a book. Travelling for enjoyment was frowned on as frivolous. John told his sister that Jane did not travel out of vulgar curiosity, 'but in order to inform herself and broaden her mind so that she can be more interesting to others'. He extolled her benevolent heart, simplicity and frankness of mind, and her shyness and reserve—which was often taken for pride, of which she had none, he wrote.[14]

Whatever Jane's motive for travelling, her diaries show her revelling in it—mostly, for there were genuine difficulties. But she never minded discomfort or novel food or routines, and loved new places, new experiences, new people. At forty she was fit, energetic and courageous. Gradually she became more liberated, and in these three years she blossomed. Though nominally obedient to John, who imagined he was in charge of her—'I have given my consent', he wrote of her plans—in fact she did as she pleased, while he was proud of his dearest Jane's adventures.[15]

Jane joined her husband rarely, for a total of six months in four years. A really devoted wife would surely not have chosen to be away for so long. Was she disillusioned, was the man she married not the hero she had assumed? She was certainly irritated at the pusillanimous way he kept warning her of danger, urging her not to be rash ('above all things don't worry yourself about me', she wrote, exasperated).[16] Was marriage distasteful? Were they having problems?—in her letter above, he accused her of feeling superior to him. Was she hesitant about sex or pregnancy? These were the last years in which she could conceive, and perhaps she wanted to avoid it, particularly as her mother died in childbirth; and she was not the maternal type. Apparently lacking physical passion, perhaps she (or John) disliked sex. Or was it that she adored travel? John's job did mean some compulsory separation, but they could have been together much more than they were.

In late 1831 Jane's party travelled around Spain and northern Africa, riding forty miles inland from Algiers to Tetuan—the first European women to make the trip, Jane reported. Seventy-two-year-old Mr Griffin and Jane's maid were both thrown from their mules, but no one suffered serious injury, wrote Jane—she was never very sympathetic about other people's travelling misfortunes—and despite Tetuan's bugs, mosquitoes and stench, she enjoyed living higgledy-piggledy in a small windowless Moorish house. She wrote to Mary that she had done things which would have killed her in England, but pure air, warmth, the absence of 'wearing and importunate household affairs' and 'the amazingly tonic power of great excitement' improved her health enormously—though when Mary envied her happy lot, Jane replied reprovingly that she was so sensitive to the miseries of the world that she could never be a very happy person.[17]

At Gibraltar poor bruised Mr Griffin returned home, and Jane and the Kirklands joined Sir John at Corfu for some months. In March 1832 the three travelled to Alexandria on an American warship. There Jane met the first of the trio of men she thought wonderful: the ship's noble, highminded, gentlemanly, generous captain. She wrote so enthusiastically about the American navy that Sir John had to point out that the British navy was just as capable, but there was no denying that the captain was ingenious. The Pasha in Alexandria never met foreign women, but on his duty visit to the American ship the captain introduced Mrs Kirkland and Lady Franklin, and the Pasha had to greet them. Jane was thrilled.[18]

In Alexandria she met her second hero, the English consul, Mr Thurburn—kind, hospitable, gentlemanly and accomplished. She also met a Mrs Light, who was accompanied by her handsome 'preux chevalier'—'gallant knight'—Captain Bowen. Both were wearing Turkish dress, and Mrs Light smoked pipes with the gentlemen, shot wild birds, navigated the yacht she lived in, and could 'do anything she had a mind to'. She and her husband were indifferent to each other, wrote Jane. Though English residents discussed her with apprehension, they accepted her. Here was liberation! Jane loved Egypt, writing to her long-suffering family that though she had a miserable time on a boat trip on the Nile because of bugs, cockroaches, ants, fleas, spiders and rats, the hot dry climate suited her. Dysentery was no problem as long as 'it does not go too far', and apart from plague it was a very healthy country.[19]

But cracks were appearing in her relationship with the Kirklands, as often happens with travelling companions. They accused Jane of moving too slowly, while she complained that they rushed through places without seeing them properly. Still, they continued their trip through Palestine and Syria, the ladies wearing tarbooshes and scarves to hide their faces, in deference to local custom. Jane

loved the Holy Land. She wrote to Mary ecstatically: after riding for
hours under a hot sun, the travellers found themselves in a filthy shed
crowded with horses and Bedouin in the wretched village of Jericho,
Jane's inflamed leg making her entirely lame. But a poultice relieved it,
starvation cured her stomach upset, and next morning they rode off
towards Jerusalem with their Egyptian servant and an escort of twelve
Bedouin, 'wild looking creatures' wearing striped blankets with handkerchiefs on their heads, muskets at their backs, lances in their hands,
and scimitars in their sashes. As they crossed the desert the Bedouin
excited each other with wild screams, letting off their muskets, 'thrust-
ing their lances at full gallop, wheeling, pursuing, receding, sweeping
across our path, yet always with the nicest care just avoiding being in
our way'. Wonderful![20]

At Constantinople the Kirklands returned to England, and Jane
was left alone. She loved it. She travelled around the Bosphorus and
climbed the ancient Mount Olympus, today's Uludag. With her guide
and her male servant (she was past needing a female companion) she
rode up to a plateau where gypsies were pasturing their cattle. Their
family patriarch ordered skins and carpets for Jane to sit on and bread
and cheese for her to eat, and the women and children came to look,
fascinated by her clothes, lifting her skirts to see if she wore trousers,
'which I took pains to shew I did'. She camped that night, and early in
the morning gypsies brought flowers to her tent. Jane adored the climb
up the mountain, stopping to gather hardened snow which, mixed
with local firewater, 'made no unpalatable beverage'. Their guide was
shocked at them drinking alcohol, but the gypsy patriarch accepted it
as 'English sherbet'.[21]

Back in Constantinople plague was a worry, so Jane moved on to
Smyrna and Athens. She gained a reputation for adventurousness,
a Turk writing in his memoirs that of all foreign ladies who trotted
over the classic soil of ancient Ionia, the most enthusiastic was Lady
Franklin. English ladies shocked the locals by riding astride—if Jane
did this, it was another unconventional, though practical, activity. She
relished travelling alone: 'I feel every day what a blessing it is to go

about independently in my own way without etiquette or observance.' In Athens she was annoyed when respectful English officers cramped her movements. 'I cannot go out without sending for the services of some officer to accompany me, and my room is a perpetual levee from breakfast time till dark.' John must understand why she resisted joining him and suffering more such frivolity—but when she did go, 'I will make the best of it and be as charming as you think it is always in my power to be, you cunning flatterer!' At least in Athens she could hobnob with the English admiral, making sure he praised Sir John.[22]

A French ship took her to the Greek west coast. She was horrified at the officers' boisterousness and atheism, the way they drank rum at breakfast and took God's name in vain, but admired their good nature and vivacity. At one stop on shore, she told them that the ancient Pierian spring was nearby, and repeated the quotation: 'A little learning is a dangerous thing; Drink deep, or taste not the Pierian spring'. They were entranced. An officer held the wooden bucket to her mouth and she 'swallowed a thirsty draught', but they told her to stop, as they needed it more than she did. The 'coarse way we lived' (or all that male admiration) suited her health astonishingly, she wrote, but after the French left she became weak and feverish, and worried about when John would become an admiral. Finally in December she joined him at Patras, but after only a fortnight she was off on a tour of the Ionian islands.[23]

Jane was pleased with herself for managing so well: 'all things concur to confirm me in my long experience of the same theory that difficulties are almost sure to vanish as you approach them'. She assured Mary that she would not be spoilt by praise of her travels. There was nothing extraordinary about them (oh no!), and she shrank from fame, for she did not want to be thought 'a strong bodied, as well as strong minded person, bold, masculine, independent, almost everything in short that I most dislike ... I hope I shall never be talked of as one of your bold, clever, energetic, women, fit for anything. I am no doubt possessed of great energy and ardor, but I would rather hide than show it.' It was important to conform outwardly with society's expectations. In any case, she continued, physical weakness, intense shyness and fear of ridicule restrained her energy; she was 'a mass of contradictions'. She told her husband she was a 'very ordinary sort of person … a strange compound of contradictory qualities'.[24]

She continually urged him to promote his career. Why had he not paid his respects to high officials; this might be useful, provide an opening, and otherwise the admiral might think he was not interested. 'You must excuse me my love if I presume to advise & often to differ from you,' she concluded. John replied patiently. He had to do his duty; he did not want to purchase a position by obsequious pretence; she imagined him fearful, but he had an important charge and his great pride was to fulfil it; he did not want to check her, but he knew what was happening and she did not: he felt 'a painful struggle between affection for you and duty'. She continued to push, even suggesting that he gain fame and promotion working for a foreign country. Certainly not, he replied. Such men were considered adventurers, and this step would end his chances of promotion at home. He would not do anything 'for the mere desire of travelling and still less for the mere empty shadow of increasing my fame'.[25] How did Jane react to that: 'mere' desire of travelling, fame an 'empty shadow'?

Early in 1833 Jane's friends Mrs Hanson and Louisa Herring arrived from England at her request; but now she had tasted independence, and was waspish about them—'Mrs H. dresses not fit to be seen, & has a tres mauvais ton [very bad tone], & Louisa is as deaf as a post'. After some months' travelling the others returned home, and Jane was alone again. 'Oh, my dear Independence, I return to thee, and love thee better than ever!' She intended going back to Alexandria, for the Thurburns had invited her to the exciting destination of Thebes. Sir John 'most gladly acceded to her wishes', he innocently told his friend John Richardson. He himself was about to return to England, but 'travelling agrees surprisingly' with Jane, and she would remain to avoid the English winter. He was looking forward to the time when 'my dearest Jane & I and our dearest little girl are seated in some snug Box in the Country'.[26] No hope!

Anxious to see John before he left, Jane went to Athens, but he was not there. So she climbed Mount Hymettus. After riding most of the way on donkeys, she and her guide set off at 5 p.m. on the hour's walk to the top. They scrambled over almost inaccessible places and kept finding higher summits to climb, only turning back at sunset. Trying for a more direct route they became lost, and could see 'nothing but a great pit of darkness'. The hillside was so steep they slid down, grabbing anything possible to slow their descent. 'I was much impeded by the strong bushes of prickles & briars which generally caught my petticoats behind, & I left a very considerable portion behind me—my shoes were actually in tatters,' she reported with some pride.[27]

She made more attempts to see her husband, and was furious when the admiral told her that he had given him a roving commission. Surely he could have roved to visit his wife, and taken her to Alexandria? He interpreted his commission as roving on duty only, but she never could appreciate that for John duty came first and everything else second. It was at least partly for appearances: 'I wish that in the eye of the world you may <u>appear</u> to have corresponded to my effort to meet you.'[28]

They finally met at Malta, he returned to England, and she spent a boring few months trying to organise transport to Alexandria. She was irritated at advice against visiting Cyprus merely because the Greeks and Turks were quarrelling, the English consul's family died of disease and the French consul of poisoning. These were poor reasons, wrote Jane. The Turks and Greeks would do her no harm, no one would poison her, and half the English consul's family were probably still alive. However, she enjoyed buying land near Athens; unlike John she liked Greeks, and felt she was supporting the new Greek nation.[29]

Finally in December 1833 she arrived at Alexandria, and was welcomed by the Thurburns. She also met 'the Swedish countess', another liberated woman: talkative, independent, travelling by herself. Despite her shocking reputation and John's warning, Jane liked her: she 'is not more cracked, than people who choose to have their own way, when that way is not exactly that of the world around them, generally are'. However, Jane decided against travelling with her. The

Countess was notorious, just what Jane did not want. In Greece she had been (or told John she was) appalled to find herself described as a lady of great distinction and a celebrated traveller—even this was too notorious for her.[30]

The Thurburns' party set off for Cairo in January 1834, Jane on her own boat with two servants. 'Oh, what horrors!' Smelly rats clawing her face stopped her sleeping; lice were everywhere, even on her stays; the boatmen were uncooperative (not surprisingly, after she insisted they go on instead of eating dinner) and she was always hours behind the others, missing excursions and meals. She felt neglected—'evidently the most insignificant person of the party, perhaps was felt to be somewhat of a bore'. When she finally caught up she burst into hysterical tears, made worse when a callous man said it was nothing but lack of food. Jane found even the Thurburns unsympathetic.

In Cairo she met the Reverend Johann Lieder, a Prussian who had been working in Egypt since 1826 with the Anglican Church Missionary Society. He was about to go to Upper Egypt, and Jane persuaded him to take her. In telling her family, she showed her skill at using half-truths. It was improper for a woman to travel alone with a man, but at the same time a woman had to have someone in charge of her (Sir John was glad the Thurburns had this role). Jane told her family that she was in the charge of a most respectable and suitable man, a learned, pious, benevolent Anglican missionary, and also a doctor, homeopathic but handy in emergencies. One imagines a venerable white-haired professor. She did not mention that Johann Lieder was tall, handsome and at 36, seven years younger than she, that he wore dashing oriental dress—a red tarboosh, pistols in his pocket, a sword buckled round his waist—and was susceptible to feminine charms.[31]

They left Cairo in mid-February, each in a separate boat, uniting for meals and sightseeing. Jane was in her element. As they progressed up the Nile, she described ever-more romantic moments. Mr Lieder, as she always called him (or occasionally Leider or Leader), gave her Arabic lessons and was determined that she would be able to read the first chapter of the Koran. Luckily it was short. In one of his letters of introduction she was called 'la sua signora'—'your woman' or even 'your wife'—and she did not let him forget it. He 'seemed to live only to serve me' (such a pleasant change from someone who always put duty first), and when they went ashore and she was given a room with a dirty floor, he 'laid down his little Persian carpet for me to lie on & lay down on it with me to take tea'. He did not stay long as she was, or said she was, unwell.[32]

They crossed the Nile on a raft, and Mr Lieder picked some sweet-smelling flowers for Jane and said ' "would that he could even with bloody fingers pull off all the thorns in my path thro' life"—I told him it was better I should meet with some & put the flowers in my bonnet.' He tried to cure her with homeopathic powders, forbidding her to drink tea while taking them; unfortunately he boarded her boat just as she was going to drink some, but nimble-witted Jane explained that she had not begun the powders yet, and this was a last treat. They conversed until late in the night, often discussing spiritual matters. Mr Lieder was not satisfied with her faith, wrote Jane, and she asked him 'not to persuade by the force of my affections, but of that of my reason only'. She played an April Fool's joke on him, and he played the guitar to her, one night until two in the morning.

This was shocking behaviour by English standards: a married lady travelling with a man, missionary or not, let alone the carpet, raft and guitar. She was aware that her actions would be frowned on, and was relieved to miss the Thurburns' boat. Other English gentlefolk received her coldly, but two colonels called on Lady Franklin, and she and Mr Lieder visited a Coptic bishop and discussed the prospects of the Christian church. Reading her diary is like reading a thriller: whatever will she do next?

They continued up the Nile, looking at temples, statues and tombs. Jane performed many feats with Mr Lieder's assistance, climbing down into a hot, smelly mummy-pit (other travellers did not believe there were mummified crocodiles, but Jane knew there were, for she bought several from her guide) and up a monument at Luxor, 'to great agitation of Mr L. whose strength & kindness enabled me to do it'. When a storm threatened, Mr Lieder rushed through mud and water to Jane's boat, '& falling on his knees & clasping me round waist asked if I was alarmed. It was impossible to proceed further, tho' his own boat was half an hour ahead—& it was now dark, I prevailed on him to leave me & walk to it'. Once she went on ahead, contrary to their agreement; she apologised, and he 'received me with his usual tenderness & kindness & seemed more grieved than hurt or offended at my having left him behind'. Finally they achieved their aim, Wadi Halfa at the second cataract, 1500 kilometres from Alexandria. They crossed the river on stepping stones to a black rock above a rapid, and sat on the brink of the Nile, their 'ne plus ultra', as Jane wrote—'nothing greater'. What could be more romantic?

However much they might try and put off 'the day of separation', Johann Lieder was there to do missionary work. Perhaps fortunately, this was translating the New Testament and Koran into Nubian rather than giving moral instruction. They parted. Jane's diary entries become brief.[33]

Soon they were reunited, and Jane's next diary does not survive. Did it contain entries even more daring than being clasped round the waist? They went down the Nile together, and Jane's first surviving letters for three months were written from Cairo in May, telling her family how anxious she was for news of them. Mr Lieder had kindly lent her his house in Cairo, and he had decided 'not to abandon the charge of me' until he could hand her over to her friends the Leeves in Greece. She felt so afraid when she was alone, but no serious harm could happen to her if Mr Lieder were near. 'I trust you agree that in the circumstances I am placed, I could not do better', she wrote to Sir John—Mr Lieder was 'so kind a friend'. And could John tell Eleanor that 'she is my own dearest child'? His own letters were such a comfort to her. So Jane was brazening this out, portraying Lieder as a benevolent friend and herself as a devoted wife and mother. She succeeded so well that Sir John told the Leeves he was much obliged to Lieder.[34]

What are we to make of all this? My reading is that Jane was disillusioned with marriage, finding that the hero she had chosen for her husband was stolid, stout, lethargic and unromantic. He put duty ahead of her, baulked at advancing his career as she wished, was irritatingly cherishing, tried to check her activities by imagining dangers, and instead of being daring, painstakingly tried to please her—'I hope this is the kind of letter you wished from me'.[35] She was ripe for infatuation with someone nearer her ideal. The American captain and Mr Thurburn were unresponsive, but Johann Lieder was not—and he was Sir John's opposite, dashing, admiring, giving up his duty for her. Even so, a sexual liaison seems unlikely. Jane tended to be prudish, her writing about Lieder is strikingly passionless, and pregnancy would be disastrous. More likely, she was enjoying again the romantic flirtations of her salad days. Still, the mechanics do not really matter. Even if Jane remained technically faithful to John, for five months the dominant man in her life was not her husband.

However, at some stage cold reality surfaced. This delicious relationship had no future, as she well knew. Johann Lieder had to return to his work, she had to return to England. Mrs Light and notorious adventuresses like Hester Stanhope and Jane Ellenborough might live as they liked in the eastern Mediterranean, but they had to stay there. Jane Franklin had no wish for such a life in the long term. Divorce was extremely difficult and expensive, and brought notoriety and social ostracism; surely the possibility did not so much as cross her mind. Her only possible future lay as the wife of Sir John Franklin. So she farewelled Johann Lieder and returned to John, to 'work upon the materials we find and strive to mould them to our purpose', as she had written about Eleanor. (Lieder worked in Cairo for nearly forty years, training Coptic priests and translating religious texts. He married an Englishwoman, like him interested in archaeology.[36])

Jane Franklin's skills at public relations were such that, despite this extended idyll, she was never censured. This was a huge achievement, for if known the story would have brought extreme social disapproval. John Franklin never hinted at any suspicion. He was a trusting man who took things at face value. When his first wife told him her health was better, he believed her. When his second wife told him that

Mr Lieder was merely a kind friend, he believed her too. In any case, as he told her humorously, he was not of a jealous disposition, 'or I must have put a stop to your travelling without me on account of your numerous charms'. However, there was some friction, not over Johann Lieder, but about Jane staying away so long. She obviously went on the attack in a letter now lost; in reply, John recalled that they had agreed that she would stay in Egypt for the winter. 'I never for one moment let it be supposed by anyone that you were staying out contrary to my wishes—nor did such a thought enter my mind.' But he wished she would come home now. She replied in August, explaining that there had been delays (well, there would be), and mentioning Lieder only in passing. As soon as she could she was coming home, and she was 'ever my dearest love, your most affectionate wife'.[37] She finally arrived in England in October 1834, well over a year since she had last seen her husband.

4

TO VAN DIEMEN'S LAND

Back in London after an absence of three years, Captain Franklin had to find work, a difficult business. He called on influential men and had an audience with the King: 'your shy timid husband' found the courage because 'I knew you would have wished me to do so', he told Jane. More enjoyable was a visit to his sister Isabella Cracroft and her happy, affectionate family, including his daughter Eleanor. He enjoyed the children's pleasure when he could not answer their riddles, and loved spending time with dear Eleanor. Jane would be glad to know that he was thinner, and 'I have not had the slightest disposition to drowsiness in the Evening nor of the lethargy you thought me to possess'.[1]

This enthusiastic husband met Jane when she landed and thought she looked well, but after a few days she collapsed with a fever, and continued ill on and off through 1835. She yearned after Johann Lieder, and at a meeting of the Church Missionary Society had the nerve to ask for news of him. When a letter arrived from the Leeves without a message from him, she was hurt. However, she pulled herself together and took up her career as Sir John Franklin's wife. 'Everybody who knows me at all ... [knows] that I am devoted soul and spirit to Sir

John', she wrote later, and so she was—though whether it was to his person, his interests, or his interests as she saw them, is not clear. She wanted her husband to succeed, she told him, even if it meant being away from her. She would find this exceedingly painful, of course, but his credit and reputation were dearer to her than the selfish enjoyment of his society, 'nor indeed can I properly enjoy your soc^y if you are living in inactivity when you might be in active employ'.[2] There was no chance of that snug little seat in the country he coveted.

Jane did what she could for his career by giving presents to the children of Francis Beaufort, the navy's hydrographer, to 'appear kind in the eyes of their father', as she wrote frankly. Otherwise she resumed her social activities. At one dinner she asked an obstreperous radical if he approved of ladies being excluded from the House of Commons, 'for it was very clear I said, that as soon as we had vote by ballot & universal suffrage (to both of which measures I suspected he had a leaning) this subject would inevitably be brought forward'. Jane herself disapproved of these measures, strongly.[3]

They visited Eleanor, and John's family in Lincolnshire. Jane showed decent interest, but her diary does have a hint of Lady Franklin doing her duty to the less fortunate. More enjoyable, as ever, was travel. They went to Ireland, touring with Colonel and Mrs Sabine and a Professor Lloyd. The professor told friends he was 'vastly amused' when, travelling through a difficult pass, Lady Franklin said again and again, 'John, you had better go back, you are certainly giddy'. At last she had to admit that she herself could proceed no further, and Sir John asked Sabine to help carry her back. 'The Colonel thought it nervous work and hesitated, until encouraged in a grave matter-of-fact way by the excellent husband. "Don't be afraid, Sabine; she never kicks when she's faint!"'[4] The professor could see through Jane's stratagems—but John, though he might smile, was always loyal.

It was an unsettled time. The Franklins had no home—in London they stayed with Jane's father—and the future was uncertain. John was helped by his closest friends, John Richardson, Francis Beaufort and Edward Parry. All were deeply involved in Arctic exploration, and they helped each other's careers. All were, or appeared, religious, upright, humane, decent men; all lost at least one wife, and saw each other through these hard times; all were interested in science as well as exploration. Richardson was a Scottish naval surgeon, while the other three joined the navy early, and Beaufort, like Franklin, had to make his own way with little patronage. They were all devoted family men (though Beaufort was a little too devoted; after his first wife died, his diary reveals he had an incestuous relationship with his sister—'Did it to Harriet', 'Fresh horrors with Harriet, O Lord forgive us', 'Wicked Sunday'. No one else knew this at the time, and it shows what could be hidden under an outward appearance of absolute respectability. Beaufort remarried, and Harriet went to live with a sister). Patron of them all was John Barrow, secretary at the Admiralty, who had power over appointments to exploring expeditions. He appreciated these men, being similar himself—from an even more humble background, hard-working, modest, a mild family man.[5]

Franklin wanted an exploring appointment. After his second expedition ended in 1827, British achievement in the Arctic was limited. Parry failed to reach the North Pole. In an expedition down Prince Regent Inlet another explorer, John Ross, was frozen in for four winters and barely managed to escape. George Back was sent on a rescue mission, and mapped the Great Fish River to its mouth on the north American coast. In 1836 a new expedition was sent to complete Franklin's survey of the coast; it must have disappointed him when Back was appointed. He failed, drifting helplessly in the ice for ten months, such an appalling experience that he never went to the Arctic again.

The other Arctic explorers disliked John Ross, who attacked them in a book about his expedition. Beaufort told Jane Franklin a good story. Showing her a map in Ross's book, he asked her to count the Clarence Islands. Nine. Beaufort said there were only three at first, but when Ross proposed to the King, the former Duke of Clarence, that they be called the Clarence Islands, he (Ross) added more to provide one for each of the Fitzclarences, the King's illegitimate children. Jane relished such insider gossip.[6]

Whether John Franklin actually wanted to govern a colony is not known; certainly his closest friend, John Richardson, believed his wife pushed him into it. His first offer of such employment came in March 1836: lieutenant-governor of Antigua, a small island in the West Indies, on the understanding that acceptance would not affect his naval career. He told the secretary of state for the colonies (the ultimate power in colonial affairs) that he must consult his wife. Finally he declined, because he would be secondary to the local governor, the climate was unhealthy and the income insufficient. Jane behaved nobly, he told his sister. She 'forcibly and ably' stated her opinion, and left the decision to him.[7] (She was against it, and he declined.)

The next offer was lieutenant-governor of Van Diemen's Land, a more prestigious post with no local superior, double the salary and an excellent climate. Everyone advised him to go. Of Britain's forty or so colonies, Van Diemen's Land was one of the more important. Though Tasmania is now a minor part of Australia, in 1836 it had a third of the total population and was much larger than the tiny new settlements of Port Phillip or Western or South Australia. Jane Franklin saw it in a romantic light—'Australia, where to breathe the very air is happiness, where sickness is turned into health, & existence ... is in itself enjoyment', she had written. Her family, however, mourned her departure to the end of the world.[8]

Who would they take with them? Jane could no longer avoid having Eleanor with her. In her twelve years Eleanor had mainly lived with the Cracrofts, most recently in Guernsey. This seemed suitable. Isabella Cracroft was a poor widow whom Sir John supported financially, and her daughter Catherine was Eleanor's age. However, Eleanor later said life in a succession of small, unattractive houses on a limited budget was restricting. She seldom saw her adored father, and a letter he sent on her tenth birthday reads dauntingly, exhorting her to love God, study hard and be grateful for God's mercies. Papa was sure when they lived together she would love her new Mama. It sounds unlikely, for Jane wrote in terms that threatened friction: Eleanor 'thinks there is no reason whatever why at 14 she should not go to all sorts of balls & parties

& picnics just as many young ladies in Guernsey do, an idea which I tell her she must get as quickly out of her little head as possible'. Nevertheless, John was sure that under his dearest Jane's 'judicious correction and instruction' Eleanor's mind and principles would be properly formed.[9]

It was usual for governors to assist relations and friends who needed positions, husbands or broadening experience. John took two nieces: his orphaned ward Mary Franklin, aged 22, pretty and popular; and Isabella Cracroft's daughter Sophia (usually called Sophy), aged 21, lively and sharp-witted. She had no money and might have to become a governess; better that she and Mary find husbands in Van Diemen's Land. Then there was staff, often pushed on Franklin: Beaufort's protégé Alexander Maconochie as private secretary, with his wife Mary and family; nineteen-year-old Henry Elliot, son of the Earl of Minto of the Admiralty, as aide-de-camp; John Barrow's unsatisfactory son Peter; and John Hepburn, Franklin's mainstay on the disastrous Canadian expedition. Jane worried. What job could Hepburn do, she asked John Richardson. She had a housekeeper, but needed a lady's maid, a butler and a governess for Eleanor; a pious lady, but not too puritanical or 'enthusiastic'. Jane thought of teaching Eleanor herself, to attach 'my husband's child to me by the ties of gratitude & tenderness', but decided Eleanor's wilfulness and vanity required a firm governess. They chose Miss Williamson, who, wrote John, had a ladylike manner even if not 'first rate requirements' as a teacher.[10]

Jane was worried about John's influenza and chronic cough, as she wrote to his sister Hannah when he was staying with her. Could Hannah refuse him spirits and more than half a pint of wine a day? He could never resist temptation, and he was touchy about his health and would tell Hannah that this was nothing but Jane's fancy, but doctors backed her up. And could Hannah please not persuade him to stay longer? If he did not return by the fifteenth, public men would think him unreliable, 'for he has failed much already'. Exasperatingly, he wrote that he would arrive on the nineteenth.[11] Men!

On 24 August 1836 the Franklins boarded their ship, *Fairlie*, under Captain Ager. Their party consisted of 23 people, including their four servants and the Maconochies' three—'Mama has got a French maid who cannot speak English, so we have to talk French to her', wrote Eleanor.[12] Also on board were Van Diemen's Land's new archdeacon, several more clergymen and too many other passengers, who had heard that the new governor was on board and hoped for introductions and patronage.

William Henty, a passenger, liked the Franklins. Sir John was affable, he wrote, and 'his Lady appears also gentle & kind in Manner … Sir John & his Lady try to put every one at their ease & require no State'. Activities were organised: church services (Maconochie interrogated his children and Eleanor about each sermon); a Sunday school (Jane Franklin tried teaching a class of girls, but this 'drudgery' soon faded away); and evening lectures, in which Maconochie shocked people by comparing the two genders, which 'put the ladies a little to the blush and brought down on him a scolding from his wife'. Or they danced on deck, Sophy Cracroft providing music on the Franklins' piano. 'Sir John & his Lady are great Encouragers', wrote Henty.[13]

Jane enjoyed seeing the sights: other ships, porpoises, the Southern Cross, a shark being disembowelled. She threw a harpoon, tasted flying fish, took lessons in perspective from an artist, and described how long a chameleon took to die when she drowned it. Most of all she enjoyed reading and writing in her cabin. She loved long sea voyages, with their leisure, quiet and freedom from anxiety and responsibility. Her health was generally good, though when she realised that the leeches in her large medicine chest were dying, she had them applied to avoid waste—it was fortunate, really, that she happened to be suffering from 'my head'.[14]

With so many godly persons on board, Captain Ager must have wondered what he had struck. Once another ship almost ran into them, and Ager let slip an oath. The archdeacon composed a prayer of thankfulness for *Fairlie*'s escape, and asked forgiveness for those guilty of blasphemy—'his voice trembled as he spoke'. Jane Franklin too saw some laxity—Eleanor and the young Maconochies talking, stretched out on cushions on the deck in an idle way. 'I promised myself if it continued to be necessary to take Eleanor in hand again myself.'[15] This does not sound hopeful for the stepmother–daughter relationship.

Nor does another interaction. In Cape Town, a French officer kissed Eleanor's hand, then asked Jane's permission. She laughed, saying that doubtless Eleanor was flattered; so he kissed her hand again, and, wrote Jane, 'hoped she would pardon him. "Oh oui!" she replied with great eagerness,—& the most lively expression of delight dancing in her eyes. The event I afterwards found was thought worthy of minute mention in her journal—"He twice kissed my hand." '[16] Perhaps Eleanor showed her the entry, but perhaps also Jane Franklin read her stepdaughter's private diary.

They stopped at Cape Town for a fortnight. Jane was busy sightseeing—the observatory, the Cape of Good Hope, churches, a menagerie—but listed nine sights even she could not fit in. She made a six-day excursion into the interior and, despite opposition from John, climbed Table Mountain, five hours on foot. Her diary shows she could be demanding of other people, taking it for granted that they would put themselves out for her, provide a meal when she turned up unexpectedly, and not mind when she did not arrive as arranged, though she would not have been the only lady to think along these lines. She penned her usual frank descriptions:

> The Admiral has 2 little boys, one of whom is trained to throw off a number when he comes in at the dessert & at the highest pitch of his voice to scream out a toast to the health of the King & the return of the war & Buonaparte. The child's odious shrieks paralyse the tongues & stun the ears of every one at table whether accustomed to this daily folly or not.[17]

Jane never did like children much.

The voyage from Cape Town to Hobart was unpleasant, with weather so rough passengers often had to sit on the floor to eat dinner. Jane was busy writing up a 16 000-word description of Cape Colony, using her own notes and 25 reference books.[18] Finally the four-month trip came to an end. On 5 January 1837 they sailed up the River Derwent to Hobart.

Van Diemen's Land had been settled by the British in 1803 as a convict colony. The first twenty years were rambunctious. A settled community grew only slowly, as too many of the little colony of convicts, guards and settlers revelled in theft, drunkenness, adultery and corruption. 'Kindly, but dissolute', wrote historian John West of this period.[19]

Change came in the 1820s. More convicts and immigrants arrived. Settlement moved into the centre of the island, taking up the Aborigines' hunting grounds. They retaliated, attacking settlers to drive them away. Settlers too retaliated, and many Aborigines and some Europeans died. From 1824 a competent lieutenant-governor, George Arthur, organised the colony. An efficient police force reined in theft and bushranging. Convicts mostly worked for settlers. The sad remnants of the Aboriginal population were rounded up and moved to Flinders Island. Industries developed, mainly exporting wool, wheat and whale oil. The colony prospered. Under Arthur, convict Van Diemen's Land became a stable community, and by 1837 the colony of 43 000 people had a veneer of normality and respectability.

Socially it was layered, like all British communities. At the top was a small group of officers and gentlemen, officials sent out to rule, led by the governor. Next came free settlers. A mixed bunch, they ranged from respectable god-fearing citizens to unprincipled adventurers. It was often a struggle to establish themselves in a hard environment, but many succeeded and had to be accepted by the official class—who could not forget that (for example) the now-wealthy Archer family were descended from a miller. Lower down the social scale were the working classes, almost all ex-convicts, who generally melded into the community, working as labourers as they had in Britain. At the bottom were convicts, who mostly lived relatively peaceably in the community. Only a small sub-stratum of convicts and ex-convicts lived by crime.

Van Diemen's Land

Bass Strait

Flinders Island

Wybalenna •

• George Town

● Launceston

• Campbell Town

Lake St Clair

Swansea •

Hell's Gates

+*Frenchmans Cap*

• Oatlands

Macquarie Harbour

Franklin River

Bothwell •

Grass Tree Hill

Bridgewater
New Norfolk
Lenah Valley
Mt Wellington +
Richmond
Lindisfarne

Huon River
Hobart Town

Saltwater River

Fernlands •
Betsey Island Port Arthur
Oyster Cove
Tasman Peninsula

Bruny Island
Cape Pillar

Port Davey

South West Cape
Recherche Bay

West Coast expedition, 1842

---- walked or carried

—— rode

Physically the colony consisted of Hobart in the south, a combination of raucous port and decorous capital; the smaller town of Launceston in the north; and farming properties around these towns, through the fertile midlands and on the east coast. With convicts as such mostly invisible, the colony looked like any other British settlement. Hobart, the Franklins' home, had a population of 14 000 and resembled any small town in England, with churches, schools, shops, hotels and gracious Georgian homes for the wealthy.

In charge of the colony was the lieutenant-governor (in practice, always called the governor). From 1803, Van Diemen's Land's governors and their womenfolk had been a mixed bag. John Bowen had no talent for administration and lived with a convict's daughter. Efficient David Collins lived with a succession of convict womenfolk. John Murray, autocratic, drunken and corrupt, fought a duel over his wife's adultery. Mary Geils was the first respectable wife but her husband Andrew, 'venal and rapacious', did not last long. Margaret Davey was also a respectable wife with a difficult husband: inefficient Thomas Davey was an eccentric drunkard, but Margaret hosted six balls and was present at one of the few official functions, laying the foundation stone of a church. William Sorell was so efficient and popular that his one major flaw was at first ignored: the lady he introduced as Mrs Sorell was not his wife. This limited her official role, and led to Sorell's dismissal. So by 1824 none of the governors' womenfolk had made a mark, in official duties at any rate.[20]

The person with whom Jane Franklin would be compared was Eliza Arthur, wife of Governor George Arthur and mistress of Government House from 1824 to 1836. Busy enough bearing and caring for her thirteen children and running Government House, she also did her duty as governor's wife, hosting weekly dinners for about twenty people—visitors, officials and colonists—and annual balls on the King's birthday: three or four hundred guests, ornate decorations, a band playing and a plentiful supper.

Eliza also assisted worthy causes—the first concert, the Mechanics' Institute and the Van Diemen's Land Society, which held lectures on natural sciences. She attended the laying of several foundation stones, was patroness of three charitable associations, and assisted female migrants, brought to the colony to redress the gender imbalance. Eliza's travel was limited by pregnancies and childcare, but she accompanied her husband on some of his tours round the island, and in 1836 took two of the children for a holiday to Sydney. She was not involved in politics, though she did copy documents for her husband.[21]

Eliza Arthur's hospitality, support for local activities and blameless domestic life meant that, though George Arthur was unpopular and she herself dutiful rather than warm-hearted, the press never criticised her. She set the pattern of what was expected of a governor's wife: hosting official entertainments, gracing functions and community activities, supporting her husband but letting him take centre stage. Succeeding governors' wives have been expected to follow this pattern.

In 2012 the Tasmanian governor's wife, Frances Underwood, commented that it is difficult to walk into Government House and take up the role of governor's wife. Tradition is strong, rituals are laid down, many of the staff have been there for long periods, and the newcomer feels obliged to fit in. Making any change is difficult. Everything runs well, why alter it?[22]

It could well have been a similar situation 170 years earlier when Jane Franklin arrived to take up the reins. People approved of Eliza Arthur, and twelve years is long enough to set down tradition, especially if it is the sort of tradition people want. Change can be resented, unless it fits in with what people think appropriate.

If Jane Franklin was going to be compared with unassuming, dutiful Eliza Arthur, Sir John was even more obviously going to be compared with her husband. Efficient, determined, a natural administrator, Arthur transformed the colony, but was an autocratic ruler, running it his way, trying to crush opposition.

This opposition arose for several reasons. Personally Arthur was reserved and formal. He increased his power by appointing relatives to important positions—standard practice, but Arthur did it on a major scale. Worse, he used his position to speculate in land and make a fortune, which infuriated people. So did his attitude towards free settlers: as they enjoyed free labour and land, they could not expect British rights such as trial by jury and an elected parliament. Opposition grew, expressed in petitions to Parliament in Britain and in hostile newspapers in Van Diemen's Land, often with outrageous attacks. Many people appreciated Arthur's orderly, moral rule, but the controversy so embittered colonial life that most were anxious for his term to finish. However, the all-important British Colonial Office saw efficient, economical Arthur as a model governor. He served an unprecedentedly long term of twelve years, and was then knighted and promoted.

The colonists welcomed Franklin's appointment as governor. His knighthood added lustre to the colony, as did his fame as an explorer and hero. With his 'open manly countenance' and 'great personal courage and determination' he was 'anything but an intriguing artful politician; he is a straight forward man in all his actions.' What a relief after Arthur! Lengthy biographies ('a matter in which every colonist is naturally interested') stressed Franklin's zeal in the service of his country. Newspapers prophesied a golden age. Sir John would right wrongs, introduce liberal measures, and destroy the corruption and tyranny of Arthur's time. Colonists were moved to verse:

MEMOIR OF CAPT. FRANKLIN.
In battle fearless, and in danger brave,
Bearing his country's red-cross flag aloft,
Triumphant over foes and elements,
No peril stopp'd him!

And more wittily:

Franklin, R. N. as Governor of Van Dieman's Land.
Captain Franklin has spent his best days with intent,
To find out an end to the earth;
He finds it at last, when his search is past,
In a snug Vandemonian berth.

To which a wag replied:

> *When he saw the d–d place,*
> *He made such a grimace,*
> *His eyes how they twinkled and quivered;*
> *And he roar'd out quite fast,*
> *"To the Devils at last,*
> *Past doubt 'tis to them I'm delivered."*[23]

In 1836 this was just a joke.

5

THE GOVERNOR'S LADY

As soon as *Fairlie* anchored off Hobart in January 1837, Jane
Franklin reported their safe arrival to her father. Though it was
summer it was almost as cold as January in England, she wrote, but
'the island seems to be in a most flourishing condition—everybody
growing rich, the convicts behaving well'. The following day Sir John
was to make his public landing, 'while we ladies walk quietly through
the garden to the Government House'.[1] Was this a statement of fact:
John was the governor, the ladies merely appendages, their background role understandable? Or was Jane disgruntled at being ignored?
However, if the colonists thought they could relegate Jane Franklin to
walking quietly, they were mistaken.

Next day thousands thronged the wharf to greet Sir John. Vessels
fired salutes, and when he set foot on land 'the air was rent with cheers'.
Interest was enormous: 'Of course every thing that the Governor said,
did, or even looked, has been the theme of every tongue.'[2] People soon
realised how thoroughly nice he was, so unpretentious he liked to
rise early and walk round the docks chatting to fishermen, and much
was made of the story that Canadians revered Franklin as the man

who never killed a fly. 'Though teased by them beyond expression' he would patiently blow them away, saying 'the world was wide enough for both'.[3]

Hobart was illuminated in honour of the new governor, with splendid decorations, firecrackers and thousands of people crowding the streets. The most gratifying event, noted a newspaper, was that a stranger accompanied by two ladies strolled along Hobart's streets, pleased by their happy tranquillity. Someone recognised him as Sir John, and called out this exciting news. People rushed to see him, with cheers and shouts. Sir John bowed to them, enjoying himself thoroughly. When some wayward cracker came in contact with his party, 'he seemed as much amused with the fun as the grown up boys did who let them off'. Eleanor was one of the ladies; her stepmother was not, but she could not miss out on the excitement: 'Mama went out after we came in although I had left her ill'.[4]

On 11 January, five days after the family landed, Sir John held a levee, where he received about 650 gentlemen. In the evening, Lady Franklin held a 'drawing-room' (reception) for the ladies of the colony, accompanied by their husbands. This was the culmination of five busy days. As governor's wife, Jane was in charge of domestic arrangements. She had to settle the party into their new home, see what was there and organise servants. Then she had to organise the drawing-room for an unknown but vast number of people. Rooms had to be prepared, tablecloths found and ironed, flowers arranged, variegated lamps unearthed, refreshments organised. Huge quantities of tea, coffee, lemonade, punch and food must be prepared, and cups, saucers, glasses, plates and cutlery found, cleaned and laid out. The Franklins' large punch bowl must be located among the baggage. The ladies' evening clothes had to be unpacked and ironed, their hair elegantly done ... However did Jane Franklin do it in the time? Fortunately she was a first-rate organiser.

At 8 p.m. everything was ready. Carriages drew up and guests entered Government House, which was brilliantly lit with the multicoloured lamps. Lady Franklin, Sir John by her side, received her guests, about 550 ladies and their menfolk, at least 800 people. They enjoyed refreshments, with the magnificent punch bowl much admired. Every room was full, and the guests were so delighted they were reluctant to go home at the advertised hour, eleven o'clock. It was a great success, and even the touchy colonial newspapers could find no fault.[5] Jane Franklin triumphed in her first challenge as governor's wife.

In the next few weeks Sir John received many expressions of loyalty and respect. At social events his wife was often at his side. Most newspapers merely mentioned her presence, but an anti-Arthur journalist did note

> *the extraordinary difference between the much respected Lady Franklin and Mrs. Arthur. We like not to refer to the female portion of any political member of society, but, yet, we cannot help remarking the general feeling on the subject. Mrs. Arthur was all austerity (we were going to say, proud) in her comportment to her visitors and the townspeople in general. Lady Franklin, in a few words, is the very reverse of Mrs. Arthur.[6]*

Commandant Booth came up from the penal station at Port Arthur to meet the new governor, and attended a family dinner at Government House. 'Sir John & Lady Franklin unostentatious & agreeable persons … a very agreeable evening', he wrote in his diary.[7]

Three weeks after they landed, the Franklins set out on a tour of the island. Wherever they went, they were cheered by crowds, presented with addresses of welcome, entertained—endless cheers, salutes, addresses, dinners and balls. At one ball, the chairman proposed the health of Lady Franklin. He was sure Her Ladyship was as much interested in the prosperity of the colony as His Excellency, and they hailed her arrival with the same enthusiasm, convinced that to her influence they would owe that restoration of harmony which was so desirable. (*Hear, hear!*)

Sir John replied on his wife's behalf. Lady Franklin took a warm interest in the prosperity of the colony and every individual present (*loud cheers*). It would be her study to promote social harmony and kindly feelings 'everywhere within the sphere of her influence'. (*Hear, hear!*) Captain Maconochie rose—out of order, but perhaps the plentiful refreshments dulled his concern about such a trifling point. There was nobody to whom such a compliment could be more deservedly paid than Lady Franklin, he proclaimed, and the proposer had been wrong in proposing the toast to Lady Franklin and her friends, since everyone present was her friend. So he proposed a toast to 'Our Noble Selves', which was drunk amidst much laughter.[8]

What a pity Jane Franklin's description of the scene does not survive. Did she accept that men replied on her behalf, or did she writhe in irritation, having to sit smiling while men condescended to her or made fools of themselves? Was she irked at the assumption that her sphere of influence would be mainly social? Did she enjoy the way 'our highly distinguished Governor' was so loudly and warmly honoured while she was mentioned occasionally as an appendage, or accept that this was to be expected? Newspaper reports show her behaving impeccably, often described as affable—though praise of her 'refined affability' hints that this was restrained rather than enthusiastic.[9]

In Launceston, Sir John held a levee and Lady Franklin received the ladies at another quickly organised drawing-room. The triumphant progress continued, and 'the affability of His Excellency and Lady Franklin was unwearied and most engaging'. At one ball the toasts were accompanied by relevant songs, Sir John Franklin with 'Rule Britannia' and Lady Franklin with 'Bonnie Lassie', a pleasant compliment for a 45-year-old.[10]

Not everyone thought Lady Franklin bonny. Jane Williams, a young widow living with her parents at Bothwell, a remote inland town, wrote of 'great preparations being made among the folks here to give Sir John & Lady Franklin & suite a dinner & ball ... Mama says she will not go without I accompany her, & Papa insists that I go.' On the day, 'we were all formally introduced to Sir John & Lady F., who was dressed like the pictures of 2 centuries back, &, as well as her two nieces, is very plain ... Sir John very affable & agreeable.'[11] The young woman from the backblocks felt confident enough to scorn the looks and fashions of Lady Franklin, straight from London.

Back in Hobart, the Franklins settled into their new routine. Sir John's role was relatively straightforward, governing the colony. Jane had to work out her 'sphere of influence'. There were no instructions for governors' wives, but one activity was obvious: entertainment. Eliza Arthur had her weekly dinners and annual balls, and Jane Franklin had to follow suit. In July and August 1837 she held a series of five weekly conversaziones—intellectual gatherings becoming popular in England, the type of entertainment she enjoyed, which might lift local standards and encourage science and culture.[12]

A major question was who was to be invited to Government House. In Britain social distinctions were clear—only the gentry, ladies and gentlemen, would be asked. In Van Diemen's Land social distinctions were more fluid, and pure-bred gentry scarcer. People of less exalted origins who made money and gained influence had to be invited, but where did one draw the line? Especially after the Franklins had announced on their arrival, rather rashly, that they wanted to do away with distinctions, rejecting only two classes in their invitations (ex-convicts and tradesmen, perhaps?).[13]

For the first drawing-rooms there were open invitations, so guests chose themselves. But certain persons close to Lady Franklin (unnamed) disliked having to mix with the common herd, and persuaded her to be more exclusive. So she divided colonists thought worthy of gracing Government House into four grades, who were invited to between one and four conversaziones. This was bound to offend everyone except those in the top grade, and a storm of criticism broke out. The Franklins said that they wanted to do away with distinctions—yet they divided society into four grades, entirely rejecting some people. An esteemed settler ignored in favour of some petty government clerk! Everyone was talking about it: jokes appeared about entertainments called by heathenish names, and 'grade cards' were laughed at in the

Supreme Court. Several newspapers defended the Franklins, claiming they could ask whom they liked to their own parties, but the reply was that these were not private but public entertainments. No conversazione was described in the press, however—probably because, as several editors pointed out, they were not invited.[14]

There was criticism that these parties were boring, 'exceedingly dull, and insipid'. Louisa Anne Meredith, wife of a prominent free settler, sympathised with the Franklins' effort to encourage interest in art and science, but thought few colonists appreciated them—especially young ladies:

> Lady Franklin's attempts to introduce evening parties in the "conversazione" style were highly unpopular with the pretty Tasmanians, who declared that they "had no idea of being asked to an evening party, and then stuck up in rooms full of pictures and books, and shells and stones, and other rubbish, with nothing to do but to hear people talk lectures, or else sit as mute as mice listening to what was called good music. Why could not Lady Franklin have the military band in, and the carpets out, and give dances, instead of such stupid preaching about philosophy and science, and a parcel of stuff that nobody could understand?"[15]

Surveyor James Calder, reminiscing thirty years later, admired both these gatherings and Lady Franklin:

> What was a reunion, or an 'at home', in Lady Franklin's time? It was an intellectual treat. No burlesque of a queen's drawing room. Nothing beyond the usual forms and conventionalities of genteel life. It partook more of a conversazione, Lady Franklin, after taking the initiative, taking care that the subject introduced was not beyond the capacity of the company. Her study was to make every person at home and happy, and admirably did she succeed, for an evening at Government House was considered the most enjoyable of all parties.[16]

It is easy to see why conversaziones were not universally popular. Many young people at any time would sympathise with the Tasmanian belles, and the hint of condescension in Calder's account—Lady Franklin taking care the topic would not be too hard for her listeners— could be irritating. Calder added that while Lady Franklin's at-homes gave her pleasure, 'a large assemblage of incongruous people made her ill'; probably one reason she moved away from drawing-rooms, since this sounds like a description of the first one.

Though newspapers criticised the graded conversaziones, they did not descend to personal attacks. The Franklins, newcomers, were merely misguided. What Jane thought is not known, since none of her writing between March and October survives. Probably this woman who acknowledged that she was extremely sensitive to criticism was upset, perhaps devastated. However, she did not give up the grade idea easily. In 1838 the Franklins were in Launceston again, and Lady Franklin discussed an entertainment with local leaders. One told her it was much desired she would make no social distinctions in her parties. She told him about the four grades for her conversaziones, and he replied, tactfully, that a drawing-room like her first might be more desirable. She gave in, and held a soiree.[17] (Drawing-rooms, soirees and at-homes were all much the same, large gatherings with refreshments, music and sometimes dancing.)

There had been criticism when the King's Birthday of 1837 passed without recognition, and the Franklins gave in here too, Jane telling Mary that they felt it was polite to hold a ball, as the Arthurs had. The first one, in 1838, came at a bad time, for Jane, Mary and Sophy had all been ill with some disease which made their hair fall out. Sophy and Mary had their heads shaved, and Jane wore a cap. She detested it, as she hated any form of heat: 'I had rather display my grey hairs than be eternally condemned to a heating envelope.'[18]

She issued about 950 invitations for the ball, and there were enormous preparations: borrowing extra silver plate, hiring gilt chandeliers, and organising supper, coloured lamps which formed a crown and all the other details such a huge event required. And at the lowest possible price—tradesmen charged Government House higher rates, so this was challenging. Because of a bushranger scare and bad weather only about 350 people attended, but George Boyes, the colonial auditor, approved of the event as infinitely superior to any of the Arthurs' balls. Jane Franklin too was pleased. 'It went off however extremely well … the supper was said to be the prettiest that had ever been seen at Government House', she told her sister Mary. The *Colonial Times* was impressed: the assemblage was brilliant, the punch superlative, and the dancing 'extremely active, if not elegant'.[19]

Inelegant dancing at the antipodes was a far cry from sophisticated London, and Jane Franklin herself did not enjoy the function. 'I went through the fatigues of the Birthday evening uncommonly well', she continued to Mary. She received the guests with Sir John, then:

> *I did not enter the rooms till near eleven, when the dancing being at it's height in the great dining room, I waited for the pause between the quadrilles, (all the other rooms being deserted for this) and then was conducted by Sir John round this and an adjoining drawing room …*
>
> *After bowing and curtseying to all these people and standing about till tired and worn, I returned to the now empty Drawing room threw myself on the sofa and had a cry, which doing me a wonderful deal of good I brightened up, and feeling better and stronger as the evening advanced, sat up till between two and three in the morning, by virtue of my sofa to which I had occasional resort.*
>
> *I wore my oldest court dress never worn but once before, but somewhat discoloured as to the crape, tho' fresh enough still in it's deep border of green leaves, and silver grapes. It's deficiencies in this upper part, were entirely concealed by an ample shawl, in which I was still (enveloped as I had hitherto been in flannel) very glad to wrap myself.[20]*

It sounds unusual, the hostess of a ball appearing so late, vanishing for a cry (and reappearing with red eyes?), wearing an old and discoloured dress; but no one criticised her.

After this, the Franklins gave a ball each year for the Queen's Birthday on 24 May, with 400 people the average attendance. Jane gave in to urging from Sir John and others that 'nothing but the want of character should exclude', so invitations were widespread. It is difficult to describe the balls accurately as by now newspapers were aligned either for or against the Franklins, with the same ball described as 'a splendid entertainment' and 'the most pitiful thing ever'. However, there was gradually less to criticise. At first objections were made that no shopkeepers were invited, refreshments were meagre, balls were dull—and twice bad weather did limit attendance; but over the years invitations became more general, decorations more splendid, refreshments more lavish, and the urbanity and kindness of the distinguished hosts more gratifying. Once Lady Franklin displayed objects of vertu and literature, but usually entertainment was the only aim. Once she had to leave the ball before supper owing to indisposition, and in 1841 she was absent, Sophy Cracroft receiving the guests in her place. Several people expressed regret, 'for the winning address and pleasing manners of her Ladyship, no one present could imitate'. There was only a little criticism of her absence, however; provided an enjoyable ball was held with a suitable stand-in for the hostess, people were satisfied. On several occasions balls were so well attended that the rooms were 'literally filled to suffocation', according to local journalists—'Came away about 2 o'clock heartily tired with the bad supper—bad dancing Stupid people and the clouds of dust', was George Boyes' comment. But 'A brilliant assemblage of well dressed people', wrote visitor Elizabeth Gould.[21]

Jane Franklin did not enjoy these entertainments, but clearly did her best and appeared pleased and charming. Balls were a great deal of hard work, with many details to supervise—and she was a perfectionist. In 1840, she wrote, 1150 invitations were sent out and about 500 people attended. Her cook, Charles Napoleon, had mixed success with the supper. He disguised the poultry as creams and blancmanges, so she had to put tickets on them to identify them; two sprawling pigs and a sprawling kid lacked refinement; there were so many rounds of beef, ribs of beef, saddles of mutton, hams and large poultry pies (one made in the shape of a bastion mounted with guns) that the leftovers would last the whole family a week. Sir John in his toast to the Queen forgot to mention Prince Albert; a tipsy man had to be escorted outside; but otherwise all went well.[22]

Jane Franklin's main problems with balls rose when the question of guests' 'want of character' arose—and she had high standards of behaviour. Mrs Elliott was the wife of Colonel Elliott, the colony's senior army officer and a person of importance—but Lady Franklin was told that Mrs Elliott was not worthy of being admitted into society, and Colonel Elliott only married her for her money, to escape a debtor's prison. Mrs Elliott was not invited to the Queen's Birthday ball. Colonel Elliott protested that this reflected badly on him and the regiment, that his wife had been received everywhere else they went; but Mrs Elliott stayed excluded. He resented this strongly, and there were several newspaper criticisms.[23]

Even more offence was caused by rescinding invitations after people had accepted them. Surely it would have been better to check people's acceptability in the first place, and ignore information received after invitations were sent out? In 1840 a clergyman's wife informed Jane Franklin of a scandalous event: a lady had given birth to a child five months after she was married. The couple had been invited to the Queen's Birthday ball, and Lady Franklin directed that the husband be given a hint not to attend.[24] Similarly, a Mrs Browne accepted an invitation to a ball before Lady Franklin found that she was 'unfit to be visited': as Miss Gregg, she had followed Mr Browne from the West Indies to Hobart, and the archdeacon reported that a marriage licence was procured in a great hurry. Mr Browne was requested to send back the invitation, and another with his name alone was sent out; he declined it. These unfortunate occurrences were at least kept private, but another made the newspapers. A letter complained that on the morning of a ball, 'a lady as unexceptionable as Lady Franklin herself' who had accepted an invitation received a note from Government House rescinding it. Lady Franklin's system of female exclusion 'has been constructed upon a very uncertain, and therefore obnoxious basis'—gossip, implied the writer.[25]

Even more unwise was rescinding an invitation to Robert Lathrop Murray, an upper-class ex-convict, a Cambridge graduate, now a newspaper editor. Though he had been pro-government in recent issues, as an ex-convict he was not welcome (why was he invited in the first place?). Standards have changed, and we cannot judge Jane Franklin by what the governor's wife, or we ourselves, might do today. However, Eliza Arthur and Caroline Denison, governors' wives before and after her, were more lenient in similar circumstances[26]—and Murray became a bitter critic of the Franklins.

Balls and soirees were large, complex affairs which Jane Franklin showed little sign of enjoying. Dinners were different. She loved them, with their varied guests and stimulating conversation. Even if guests were on the boring side, she enjoyed interrogating them. In later years in London, Jane became famous for her dinners, and in Van Diemen's Land she honed her skills as a hostess. Both she and Sir John were indefatigable inviters, not just in advance but on the spur of the moment. 'On my way home Sir John Franklin with his Aide-de-Camp passed me', wrote George Boyes in his diary. 'After proceeding about 60 yards he stopped turned about and rode up to me shook hands &c and asked me to take a dinner with them in the family way at 6½. I went and passed a very pleasant social evening.'[27]

The Franklins' dinner book shows that in six and a half years they gave 162 dinners, one a fortnight—not as many as the Arthurs, but a good effort. (There were in fact more, for Jane Franklin's diary and other sources mention many not included in the dinner book, perhaps casual affairs like family dinner the Boyes attended.) The number of guests ranged from two to 23, with an average of ten. The guest list was heavily masculine, 85 per cent men; but given the island's strong male numerical superiority, this was not surprising. Husbands were often asked without their wives, but this also occurred in other colonies, and was perhaps some contemporary custom. Ships' captains, other visitors, naval and army officers, and civil servants predominated.[28]

Even critical George Boyes enjoyed most dinners. Not all: 'Dined at Gov^t House—a large party of second rate people who appeared but too happy at getting their legs under Sir John's [illegible] and tasting his pemmican and Snow Water', he wrote once, and on another occasion, 'I am now obliged to dress for a Gov^t House dinner, where I am to meet Sir James Dowling and then ride back about midnight cold, tired and disgusted'. On most occasions, however, he spent 'a pleasant evening', 'a very pleasant merry evening'. He enjoyed talking to Jane Franklin: 'I had a good deal of conversation with Lady Franklin—I handed her in to the dining Room and sat near her.'[29]

Jane Franklin recorded many different aspects of her dinners. 'D^r. T. sat by M^{rs}. Pedder, & they flirted away delightfully.' 'There was much conversation after dinner about Wheatstone's electric Telegraph & Harris's Lightning Conductor.' 'The party to day, tho' rather a noisy or strong one, … was upon the whole interesting & agreeable.' 'I had the greatest difficulty in understanding M^r. Mackillop, from his Scotch accent & his mumbling way of speaking.' 'I found in the course of conversation with M^r Wm. Henty that he was a great lover of the Fine Arts & had some practical knowledge himself.' And to illustrate how she interrogated people:

I asked [Mr Lawrence] some questions about M^r. Ashburner, who, he said, was much recovered & talked of going immediately to England.—He has 11 children, the eldest of whom, a son, he leaves in charge of the estate, assisted by an overseer.—His 2^d son is already in England.—The next 5 of the children he takes with him to England to place at school, & the 4 youngest he leaves under the care of a governess here.—His property, it appears, tho' considerable, has never been quite free from embarrassment.— M^r. Lawrence did not reply to my query whether he considered M^r. A. to be a man of any talent—but replied he was a man of education & a gentleman.

Sometimes there was music: 'We were in full musical force this evening, M^rs. Smith at last consenting to add to the number by singing some pretty little French airs.' A dinner for the Quaker missionaries, James Backhouse and George Walker, was more sober. After the meal they all joined Eleanor and the young Maconochies, who were sitting round the drawing-room table busy with sewing and books. 'The absence of all ostentation or display, and the exhibition of social and domestic comfort in the family which ranks highest in the land, struck me as particularly pleasing', wrote Backhouse. At nine o'clock the servants appeared and everyone joined in prayers led by Sir John. The missionaries were impressed with his sincerity.[30]

Another duty Jane Franklin enjoyed was putting up visitors. She loved having guests, new people to find out about, often important ones such as the Bishop of Australia. She also accompanied Sir John on public occasions like laying foundation stones, opening bridges and visiting institutions. Martin Cash, a convict in the prisoners' barracks, expected important visitors when he saw the buildings being whitewashed. Sure enough, along came Sir John and Lady Franklin, chaperoned by the superintendent. The visitors only stayed briefly and declined making enquiries that might have resulted in troublesome answers, said Cash cynically, but at least after the visit prisoners were allowed to use knives at their meals.[31]

A second duty of the governor's wife was supporting community activities. Jane Franklin was less enthusiastic about this, especially attending meetings, 'a great bore'. An efficient organiser herself, perhaps she could not bear to sit through other people's incompetent efforts. Eliza Arthur had been patroness of two women's groups, the Infant School Society and the Dorcas Society, attending their functions and annual meetings (her husband was the patron). Jane Franklin also became their patroness. She went to some of the Infant School Society's fairs, and she and Sir John attended one examination of the children.[32] The Dorcas Society assisted poor respectable married women at their confinements by giving them baby clothes, oatmeal, soap and a Bible. Jane attended one committee meeting. The society asked her to attend their annual meeting, but she was received with no attention, given a hard wooden chair, and had to listen to five speeches. That was it for the Dorcas Society. This minimal support of charities seemed to be enough, for there was little adverse comment.[33]

It was just as well journalists did not know Lady Franklin's real opinion: that charitable associations did mischief, helping the poor who should be supporting themselves, since there was plenty of work for industrious men. 'Can any thing be so contrary to common sense, as because the times are hard ... that the poor shd be fed for nothing?'[34] At least she kept this opinion to herself.

More to her taste were the Horticultural Societies in Hobart and Launceston, which she could encourage without attending meetings. She and Sir John enjoyed inspecting their exhibitions, and she gave prizes for the neatest cottage gardens. She also patronised Daniel Bunce's publication, *A guide to the flora of Van Diemen's Land*— evidently Bunce thought her name would help sell copies—and presented a silver cup to the Southern Agricultural Show, for the three ewes producing the most useful fleece.[35]

Occasionally Lady Franklin visited the Queen's Orphan Schools for boys and girls, where orphans and children of convicts under sentence were cared for and educated. The schools were notoriously harsh, but she did not comment on this, merely approving when the girls looked 'cleanly & orderly as usual'. She did not attempt to change anything, and her only positive action was to attend one annual examination and present prizes to the children. Sometimes she took visitors to see the schools, or went there to obtain servants: 'I proceeded to the Orphan School to see if I could procure a girl to take a little of the house-work & wait on Miss Williamson.' On Jane's voyage from Sydney the death of a woman passenger left her daughter orphaned, and Jane placed her in the Female Orphan School. She once visited the girl, who 'seemed pleased to see me, but flung herself round a little when I gave her some good advice'.[36]

Easier than attending events was providing money, and Lady Franklin supported a variety of worthy causes, ranging from St Mary's charitable hospital to a woman with a 'carious jaw' and a memorial to a deceased clergyman. In 1841 Hobart was treated to an exhibition of 'Feegeean curiosities [which] show clearly the rude habits of the people'. It was thronged with spectators, mainly women—heaven knows what they were goggling at—but few of them signed the book of subscriptions for Fijian missionaries, it was noted, even though Lady Franklin set a laudable example.[37]

Altogether, Jane Franklin performed her duties as governor's wife acceptably, if not quite as fully as Eliza Arthur. She might not have enjoyed many aspects, but she did her duty: balls were fine, dinners excellent, and support of local causes passable. She scored better than Mrs Arthur in her demeanour, often described as affable, welcoming and charming.

The reward for this virtue was the prestige of being governor's wife. Lady Franklin was the leading lady among 50 000 people, receiving due deference. If this was not forthcoming, she noticed—as at the Dorcas Society meeting. She deplored the way people straight from England did not realise the governor's exalted position. They had an attitude of confidence and equality, 'so different from that which is habitual with those around us', whom she expected to kowtow. She was given the best seat, the best service, and if it was not offered, she took it: 'I bespoke the best locality however for myself' (sleeping quarters on a ship). Her cynical brother-in-law Frank Simpkinson called her 'The Queen of Van Diemen's Land'—his 'jocular mode of denigrating me'—but she took such things seriously. So did Sophy, who noted, without irony, that a woman visited by Lady Franklin and suite was 'shy in our august presence'.[38] Frank was not so far out.

There was another, entirely unofficial, role of the vice-regal couple, which the Franklins surely fulfilled to perfection. Most people enjoy discussing the activities of the famous, the more unusual and noteworthy the better. With few entertainment stars or other famous people, the vice-regal couple provided the best gossip-column material in Van Diemen's Land. And with Lady Franklin, there was always something to talk about. Whatever would she be up to next? She's not *really* paying a shilling a head for snakes, is she? Climbing the mountain? And why haven't they any children? Do you suppose ... ? Readers will be amazed at Jane Franklin's activities, as described in the following chapters: how much more amazed must colonists have been, nearly two centuries ago.

6

THE HOME FRONT

What was she like, this woman who became governor's lady of Van Diemen's Land in 1837? For a start, she was middle-aged: no pretty young thing, as sometimes depicted, but 45 on arrival and almost 52 when she left. Though not vain, she did not want to look too old; she admitted that her hair was greying, but a portrait that showed her with 'a sickly, worn, aged look' has disappeared. Still slim, she was graceful and elegant—'sylph-like', one newspaper claimed. Her admirer James Calder described her face as full of expression, a mixture of the intellectual and amiable, with a sweet smile. She had a 'morbidly nervous and sensitive temperament', this 'delicate, fragile lady who was overcome by the fatigues of a ball'; but out in the bush she was strong and brave, 'a perfect heroine; danger never deterred her'. An astonishing mixture, said Calder.[1]

Jane Franklin was fit enough to climb Mount Gawler in the heat of a South Australian January, walking 20 miles (32 kilometres), according to Eleanor. 'Mama was bruised, our feet swollen & the skin off in many places ... we were tired out'—and next day, 'Went up another steep hill'. But Jane also suffered from debilitating sick headaches, probably migraines, which confined her to bed for several days at a time. Being Jane Franklin, she never gave in. 'I had a very bad sick head-ach to day, which did not however prevent my seeing Mr. Gell'—and then more people; 'I kept my room with sick headach, but in the evening got thro' Boone's Educational Economy in England, & the printed evidence in Council on the Bothwell Church Case.'[2] Eleanor attributed the head-aches to fatigue, Sir John to housekeeping, and Jane herself to 'mental excitement', fatigue and, once, a letter from Captain Maconochie.[3]

Occasionally she suffered from other illnesses, such as severe stomach pains and a dreadful attack of piles, for which she underwent the hideous-sounding operation of having the piles extracted, without anaesthetic. In March 1841 an injury to her leg meant she could barely walk for six months, though by October 'I manage to shuffle about pretty well'.[4] After a worrying year, in late 1842 she came down with a mysterious disease in which she lost feeling in her left side. Paralysis, said the doctors, which terrified her, but John and Eleanor put it down to 'great nervous debility'. Sir John himself enjoyed good health, despite being overweight, though once for a severe fit of lumbago he was 'cupped upon the loins'—a painful-sounding treatment.[5]

Jane Franklin showed little interest in the usual female diversions of food, cooking, clothes and fashion, though a surviving dress of hers (in the Auckland Museum), which she generously gave to a missionary's wife in New Zealand, looks elegant. Made of a fine woollen–cotton mixture in a red and green paisley design with green silk piping on the seams, it has a tight V-fronted, boned bodice, a small waist, three-quarter-length sleeves with a deep lace frill to the wrist, and a full skirt. At the Queen's Birthday ball of 1843, Jane 'was dressed in my Constantinople embroidered muslin green & gold, which I wore at the last Drawing room in 1836', so she was hardly a model of up-to-the-minute fashion, though there were few criticisms of her being dowdy. As far as food tastes went, 'They are by no means epicures in diet', wrote George Robinson after a visit by the Franklins. 'Intellectual feasting, viz. food for the mind, is what they appear to covet.' Not that this was necessarily elevating. Jane Franklin liked reading, writing and talking to people about current events and news ('Write me a letter of gossip with all the news of the day'), finding out and relaying facts. She loved learning something new: routine made her dull, and she praised 'the amazingly tonic power of great excitement; the danger is the being at rest again after it is over'. Above all she loved a lively dinner with entertaining conversation—and she refused to keep to women's traditional role, listening to the superior male. Furious when a French ship threatened to bombard the Queen of Tahiti, Jane 'was determined to let [a French visitor] know my mind about it ... we nearly quarrelled on the subject, for he made but a lame defence'. As Calder said, it was a rare person who defeated Jane Franklin in debate.[6]

Her husband and stepdaughter were deeply religious, but Jane did not seem to share their consuming personal faith. She had much the same attitude to religion as to science and art: civilising influences that she encouraged, but which did not much affect her personally. She described herself as 'very low Church'—a no-frills Protestant—and was so vehemently anti-Catholic that she once checked a bookshop to see if it was selling Catholic translations of the Bible bound to resemble Protestant ones ('I was not able to detect this trick however'). Several people noted her lack of belief, from Johann Lieder who tried to convert her in 1834, to a Franklin sister-in-law who pitied her for having no faith to sustain her in hard times.[7] Outwardly she conformed, however, and that was enough. She was certainly respectable, only dealing with respectable people, and even prudish in her dislike of coarse language or anything at all risqué.

It is difficult to glean much about Jane Franklin's inner life from her writings. She was not introspective, and in any case only a fraction of her output survives. Her extant writing from Van Diemen's Land comprises 650 000 words, but includes diary entries for only 28 months out of 82, and 41 of the 71 letters she wrote to her sister Mary—and many of these have been copied with omissions, the originals destroyed. But enough remains to give some idea.

Jane Franklin was determined, capable and intelligent. She was self-absorbed—one day's diary entry about herself and her interests could run to several thousand words—and self-confident to the point of arrogance, but she knew she was apt to feel 'holier than thou' and worried about whether people liked her (of a male visitor, 'We got on somewhat better than on our former visit—he did not avoid me so much & seemed to like me better'). She felt some emotions passionately—'scorn & loathing & indignation are ever rising in my mind ... I long for something to venerate & love', 'I am so constituted as to be intolerant of injustice & falsehood'—and she enjoyed the enlivening sensation controversy brought. At other times she could appear quite cold. A mix of characteristics, as she said.[8]

Her admirer Calder tried to analyse her. He felt that this excellent woman was 'one of the best and kindest of her sex', with an inexhaustible stock of good humour; but she had her eccentricities, and insisted on having her own way in everything. Calder summed her up as 'accomplished, adventurous, and eccentric'. Philip Gell, her step-grandson, noted her 'incessant restlessness and Spartan indifference to hardships and discomforts', her delight in 'rough journeys of exploration', her lack of interest in making a home. 'She knew where she wanted to get, & she got there.'[9]

What drove her? John Montagu and Frank Simpkinson claimed it was a love of fame, of achieving what no one else did—but neither of them liked her. Others claimed she wanted power; perhaps she did, though not so much for its own sake as to enable her to carry out her aims. She relished achievement, and was the sort of person who has to have a project. She was always busy with something, and if it enhanced her husband's career, so much the better.

If she had been frustrated when younger at the lack of opportunities society offered intelligent women (though her surviving writings do not show this), Van Diemen's Land gave her more openings and, unlike almost all women, she was in the enviable position of being able to do much as she pleased. Her position as governor's wife provided prestige. She had her own money. She had no children, which made a huge difference—no tiring months of pregnancy, no years of care. Ignoring domestic duties meant she had spare time. Above all, she had an admiring husband who never tried to limit her. She took full advantage of this, while keeping up the facade of a dutiful wife who obeyed her husband: 'we are summoned back to Hobarton by Sir John', she wrote on one expedition, when they were returning in any case.[10] She always asked his permission—and he always gave it.

However, even Jane Franklin had her limitations, and she was frustrated at the difficulty of helping her husband in politics, as she wrote to her sister—not being able to act openly, having to keep her actions secret. Frustration might have accentuated her less sympathetic characteristics. Competently bossy, rather precious and socially snobbish, she took herself very seriously, and lacked both sympathy for people generally and a sense of humour. She knew best, saying, for example: 'I wished people would come to me to ask whom they should marry—I should make a better choice for them than they wd themselves'. Yet there was nothing she would not do to help someone she liked, or even, sometimes, someone she did not particularly like, as when she invited a widow to stay even though her presence would be 'a great trial'. On her return from her New Zealand trip, she sent gifts to people she thought would benefit: the dress to the missionary's wife, a miscroscope to an amateur botanist and to other people books, cheeses and 'a few trifles'—a good deal of trouble for people often only met by chance. Many liked her, even those who fell out with her often coming round again. She was not genial like Sir John, but she could turn on the charm. She realised this, noting when travelling in New South Wales that there was 'something in our very selves, which captivates all who come within our influence': for 'our' read 'my', since it was very much her party. In particular she was charming to men. 'Les hommes vous adorent',[11] a French visitor told her—'men adore you'. Many did, though not all, and perhaps 'admire' would be more accurate than 'adore'; but she was certainly a man's woman.

Jane might charm many men, but the most important man in her life was definitely her husband. She was devoted to him, or at least to furthering his career. Sir John was not physically attractive. On his arrival, one newspaper described him as short and rather corpulent, his appearance speaking of the hardships he had suffered; however, he was active for his age, almost sixty. (He was fifty.) 'I was surprised to find him so infirm,' wrote a visitor in 1842. 'He is rather deaf, his hand shakes and he looks nearly seventy though I believe he is not sixty [he was 55].' The size of his stomach was a family joke. An American convict, who hated Sir John as the personification of the loathed British Empire, was 'honoured with a visit from his bulkiness, the *great* Sir John Franklin ... of all men I ever saw, none ever gloried in such breadth of waistband. I was told he had devoured a whole sheep at a meal.' When 'old granny' made a speech, continued the American, he hemmed and hawed, stuttered and blundered.[12]

Whatever they thought of Sir John's appearance, almost everyone liked him. Henry Elliot, his aide-de-camp, described him:

> *Franklin's great characteristic was his thoughtfulness for others and his complete absence of thought for himself ... Of a singularly simple and affectionate nature, identifying himself with the interests and welfare of those over whom he was placed, he won their love in an extraordinary degree, and although of highly sensitive feelings, he was never known to be provoked to use a harsh or hasty word.*[13]

To what degree he won his wife's love is not clear. She always started letters with 'My dearest love' (as did he to her), but she did not mind being away from him, with two long trips of four and five months, many shorter ones, and a planned return to England without him. Back home in Hobart, she sometimes slept at a cottage in the Government House grounds, or went to a holiday home bought for vice-regal use at New Norfolk, 35 kilometres northwest of Hobart. As in the early 1830s, her desire to be with her husband was not overpowering.

When they were living in the same house, they did not spend a great deal of time together, and were seldom alone. He was busy with work, she with her interests. Besides, she liked solitude, working in her room, and often had dinner by herself. 'I dined below at Sir John's hour not liking to leave him alone with Mr. Elliot & Sophy' was quite a concession. Only one diary entry in 28 months comments, 'We were quite alone to day'—'we' meaning Jane and John. She had her own bedroom, so they no longer shared a bed, and there were gossipy imputations that he was, if not impotent, at least challenged in that regard. A newspaper hinted, 'We had heard that Sir John's *extremities* had suffered much from the frost at the Pole', and at a dinner party some ladies were more forthright:

> *The ladies when they retired after dinner were wondering why Sir John had no family, "Dear me," said one of them, "don't you know! I always heard his members got frostbitten when he went to the North pole."*[14]

In a parody on a ball, a newspaper reported the song sung for Lady Franklin as 'Virgins are like the fair flower in its lustre'.[15] But this was the Victorian period, when women were not expected to enjoy sex, and considerate men did not force unwanted attentions on their wives. Perhaps Sir John had his problems, perhaps one or both were lukewarm about sex, perhaps Jane was going through menopause and had to cope with hot flushes—but there is little evidence to give body to any such speculation.

Whatever their sexual activities, John and Jane were a companionable couple. One day Jane stayed in bed all day, ill. Towards evening she felt better, '& Sir John coming in to sit with me, and we set about composing an answer to Capt Mac[onochie]'[16]—a cosy vignette which typified her way of writing about their relationship. She felt that he relied on her for everything and supported him, boosting him when he was low and trying to increase his self-confidence. This dependence might have made her feel maternal towards him, rather than passionate.

Her desire to protect him drove her to great lengths, even intercepting his mail. His friend and patron John Barrow, civil head of the Admiralty, had asked Franklin to take his unsatisfactory son Peter with him and find him something to do, but Peter was dissatisfied, resigned, and returned to England, complaining bitterly. Jane was afraid that a critical letter from Barrow senior would upset her sensitive husband, and when a ship arrived which she thought carried it, she arranged for Sir John's secretary to give it to her. It did not appear. 'Baffled', she wrote in her diary—and it took a great deal to baffle Jane Franklin. But she was an outstanding organiser, and had another ally on the alert, her niece Sophy. Unexpectedly, next morning the butler brought in the feared letter with the local mail. Sir John took his letters in to breakfast and was about to read the one from the Admiralty— but Sophy saw it, snatched it, and rushed it upstairs to her aunt. Jane nodded, Sophy applied a match and by the time stout Sir John made it up the stairs, the letter was a pile of ashes on the hearth.

'This was a sad & almost tragic scene', wrote Jane. John was violently agitated, groaning with distress, accusing her of ruining his relationship with his best friend. But Jane was adamant. She had acted for the best (definitely, for as the letter burnt she glimpsed the words, '... yr once faithful, now much injured ...'). She was sure she was right, and she would do it again, she told him. 'It was long however before he could be pacified'—but, of course, she succeeded. They had been married for a decade, and she knew how to manage him. Eventually he admitted she was right, and her explanatory letter to John Barrow convinced Barrow himself of the same.[17]

Sir John's attitude to Jane was straightforward. She was his wife, and he loved her. She could do no wrong, and he admired everything she did, even (eventually) destroying his mail. He relied on her, missed her when she was absent: 'You must not make any unnecessary delay for I want you back', 'come back as soon as you can & increase the happiness of our family circle'. He did give her advice occasionally— when she was in South Australia, he suggested she did not 'push the point farther than [the governor] willingly consents to'—but otherwise he was the perfect obedient husband. He had even stopped worrying about her: 'I was glad to find that he expressed no impatient or uneasy apprehensions about us'.[18] His love for her was absolute, and no contemporary accused him of the slightest interest in any other woman.

Jane on the other hand, continued to enjoy warm friendships with men, as she always had. When Bishop Broughton from Sydney stayed with them, she found him delightful, she told her sister Mary: 'unassuming, amiable, attaching, and engaging in a most remarkable degree as a man', with his 'large and beautiful dark grey eyes shaded with black eyelashes'. They had long discussions about church matters, and before the bishop left he requested a private interview, in which he asked if there was anything he could do for her, and whether they could correspond. Jane was moved by his extreme kindness, she wrote, 'yet not in my heart desiring any such formidable correspondence'. He was so serious that she did not intend seeing him again, even to say goodbye—though there was an accidental meeting, in which he pleaded for one more shake of her hand. He was married, she added, with two teenage daughters.[19] Jane clearly enjoyed telling her sister about this hint of romance—but nothing happened, nothing more physical than a handshake. Indeed, perhaps the attraction was all on Jane's side—those eyelashes—and she was just magnifying the ordinary attentions of a guest to his hostess.

She was not above using her sexuality (in a mild form) to get her own way:

> had a very long interview with Mr. Spode according to appointment. I admitted him into my present working & bed room (the ante-room) where he found my tables & sofa & chairs & even the floor, covered with papers.—I have no doubt he thought this a privilege & an honor & I had some intention that he should do so.

A gentleman admitted to a lady's bedroom! Most unusual, but she wanted his support in forming a ladies' committee to visit female convicts. 'Mr. Spode highly approved': he could hardly do anything else.[20]

These attentions to and from gentlemen could be seen as romantic interest, and one woman accused Jane of being flirtatious. Captain King took Lady Franklin's party to Recherche Bay to the south, with his wife also on the ship. Mrs King already felt slighted by Hobart society and accused Jane Franklin of seducing her husband, citing 'various circumstances on board the schooner, & my own letters', wrote Jane. 'She alludes to my possessing the applause of the community & to my "genius" & "talents" & "fascinating deportment" all as instruments of infatuation ... That half crazy, demoniac woman.' Jane sent Mrs King's accusatory letter to Captain King and refused to invite her to Government House, though he was welcome.[21] Apparently this worked, for no more problems were mentioned.

Not every man succumbed to Jane's charm. In his novel-cum-memoir written in the 1880s, Robert Crooke thought it unlikely that she had any affairs. 'She certainly possessed considerable conversational powers, but the author could never quite divest himself of the idea that she was a man in petticoats.' Some gentlemen partial to bluestockings found her agreeable, 'and insinuations were thrown out that her intimacy with more than one was of rather a particular character', but Crooke thought her chastity remained immaculate, for 'a more undesirable person than her Ladyship for any such amusement could with difficulty be met with'.[22]

As well as admirers, Jane Franklin had five or six protégés, mostly younger men. She never did things by halves, and once a man was her protégé, she thought him able to do anything. She urged him on to more achievement, sometimes finding him a job beyond his powers; then she could be let down. (Her outstanding protégé was, of course, her husband.) Some did not relish being taken up by Lady Franklin, but most either genuinely appreciated her attentions, accepted them for their practical value, or kept quiet; she was (or passed herself off as) a great lady, so her attentions could be flattering, and well-bred gentlemen must be polite.

However, the men Jane Franklin appreciated were far outnumbered by ones in which she took little or scathing interest. Her diary is full of pithy remarks. Captain S. would keep sober for a time, but at the first temptation would 'give himself up to a course of prolonged & brutalizing intoxication'. Another man was 'rather an interesting person when once one can succeed in overcoming the disgust which his first appearance excites' (he disfigured himself trying to blow out his brains after a disappointment in love, she noted). One diary entry reads, 'Dr Jeanneret called—has false teeth'.[23]

Jane Franklin might have found some men attractive—but not women. They bored her. She liked only a few, unthreatening ones she could dominate or found useful, such as her sister Mary and niece Sophy, and she made no friends among women in the colony. This was not because they were all inferior in intelligence, education or cultural interests. There were several clever women of similar tastes, such as artists Louisa Meredith and Mary Allport, literary Elizabeth Fenton and, above all, Lady Pedder, a member of Lady Franklin's social circle and also a reader, one so charmed by a scientific paper she wished it were longer. Surely nothing could have been more promising, but no friendship developed. The French visitor who said men adored Jane continued: 'women do not like you. You are too superior.' Robert Crooke agreed:

> *Above the weakness of her sex, she cared little for dress or amusements, scarce ever associated with ladies, and her time was divided between politics and science ... By her own sex she was universally disliked. She took no pleasure in balls or parties though from her position compelled to attend them, and made it a point to be rude and uncivil to ladies.*[24]

Crooke exaggerated, but there is no evidence that Van Diemen's Land womenfolk did like this lady who obviously thought herself their superior, though they might have admired her activities. Her opinion of them was poor:

> *A great proportion of the women of this country live in much seclusion. They ought to have a love of reading and of improving study.—Their time is divided between housekeeping and their*

Jane Griffin aged 24, painted in Geneva by Amélie Romilly. Jane thought it 'very like', though Fanny did not (Edward Simpkinson)

Above: The Griffin coat of arms and motto, on a window in the Goldsmiths' Hall (The Goldsmiths' Company, photography Richard Valencia)

Left: The Griffin children, Jane, Fanny, Mary and John, painted by Benjamin Burnell in 1798 when Jane was six (Edward Simpkinson)

Facing page, top: Government House, Hobart (centre), with St David's church left, the wharf in front and Mount Wellington behind, 1844 (John Skinner Prout, ALMFA, Tasmanian Archive and Heritage Office); *centre*: Rossbank Observatory, by Thomas Bock, with John Franklin, Francis Crozier and James Ross centre. Jane Franklin sent this to London to show her husband developing Science in the Antipodes (Tasmanian Museum and Art Gallery); *bottom*: The 1842 Hobart Regatta, by Mary Morton Allport (ALMFA, Tasmanian Archive and Heritage Office)

Above: Mathinna, by Thomas Bock, commissioned by Jane Franklin. She thought the portrait 'extremely like … the attitude is exactly hers', though it made Mathinna look as if she were about twelve, when she was in fact seven (Tasmanian Museum and Art Gallery)

A Hobart street scene, 1843 by T.E. Chapman: a far cry from fashionable London (ALMFA, Tasmanian Archive and Heritage Office)

Right: Figurehead from the missionary ship *Frankfort*, said to be based on Lady Franklin, installed in a boathouse in Bantham, England. Its plaque claims that Lady Franklin bought and equipped the ship in memory of her husband (Richard and Charles Barber)

Below, centre: Ancanthe Museum, in its present-day suburban setting in Lenah Valley, Hobart (Alison Alexander); *bottom*: Chris Goodacre and Jean Elder recreating Jane Franklin's ascent of Mount Wellington, 2012 (James Alexander)

*children and the being able to read with enjoyment and profit,
the best works of the wise and good, would be of inestimable
advantage to them.*[25]

Jane Franklin had no sympathy for or interest in the domestic occu-
pations that kept most women busy from dawn to dusk and beyond.
She rarely mentioned such duties in her writings, except when they
were more than ordinarily trying: 'I was disagreeably occupied all the
morning with house-hold vexations'; 'Our household establishment is
in a most disjointed state & gives me a deal of daily anxiety which I
could well dispense with.' An unusually domestic occasion occurred
when she spent three hours in 'Margaret's confectionary room'
(Margaret was a servant), learning

> *the art of making sponge cakes, Naples or finger biscuits & drops,
> cheese-cakes, tartlets & puffs—With a white muslin apron on,
> prepared for me by Margaret, I practised some of the manual
> arts of her profession, half-smothered & smoked however by the
> oven of this ill-constructed room.*

There was always a fly in the ointment in domestic matters. She
attended two more demonstrations but, when interrupted by a gentleman's arrival, forgot herself and went to him still wearing her apron—a
faux pas which had to be hurriedly explained, for ladies never wore
aprons.[26] That was the end of cake-making.

Despite Jane Franklin's lack of enthusiasm, Government House
ran smoothly, for she was a competent organiser. She did worry, sometimes. 'Pray do not make yourself nervous or unnecessarily anxious
about the provision or Lodging of the party', Sir John once wrote to
her: if there were no ladies there would be lodgings enough, and as for
dinner, the main guest always talked too much and would not notice
any deficiency.[27] (Sir John was right when he said he always looked on
the bright side—annoying sometimes.)

Jane's daily routine began with breakfast in bed, and she spent the morning reading, writing notes or letters, or copying documents. Sir John had an hour's walk in the garden with Eleanor before prayers and breakfast at nine o'clock. He went to his office, everyone met for luncheon, and in the afternoon Sir John returned to work and Lady Franklin took a drive, paid calls or, more often, saw people she summoned to Government House. Dinner was at 6.30 p.m. for adults only, and afterwards there was conversation, music or, if they were alone, reading or writing: 'employed the greater part of the evening in copying into a blank book the description's of Goulds V.D. Land birds'. The day ended with tea and household prayers, but Jane often worked late into the night, up to 4 a.m., writing her diary, copying out papers and writing letters, which were often long (once 8506 words to her sister Mary). Or else she read: 'read <u>Vicar of Wakefield</u>', 'I read a good deal to day in a beautiful book, the "Christian Life" of D^r. Arnold', 'read Channings slavery'. Novels were rare, though she once recorded enjoying 'a light amusing book', a princess's memoirs.[28]

Seldom in her daily routine did Jane go for a walk. Though she became famous for walking through the bush, this was due to a love of exploration, not either walking or the bush. If there was another way of travelling, such as being carried, she took it. Instead of native forest she preferred European-style landscapes, such as the 'beautiful scenery' of the Coal River valley near Hobart, with its green fields, fine crops and neat fences. On one trip, 'After being confined for a short time to bush scenery, we emerged upon another lovely part of the Coal valley, where the brightest verdure spreads over the valley ... with great beauty'.[29]

Family life at Government House seems to have been harmonious. The core group consisted of John and Jane Franklin, Sophy Cracroft, Eleanor Franklin and her governess Miss Williamson. At various times they were joined by Sir John's relatives Mary Franklin and Tom Cracroft (Sophy's younger brother who became Sir John's clerk), the Aboriginal children Timemernidic and Mathinna (see Chapter 9), the eight Maconochies and their three servants, other private secretaries and aides-de-camp and their families, and a huge range of visitors, some staying for lengthy periods. At most, over thirty people, probably averaging well over a dozen. As well there were servants. On census night in 1842 there were 42 people in Government House: 28 free people and 12 convict servants; 35 adults and 7 children.[30]

This is a large group to live in harmony for seven years, and there are several possible reasons for the lack of conflict. Jane Franklin was in charge, and no one challenged her. In such a large, rambling house the group was dispersed, not living on top of one another. Guests knew they had to be polite. But much of the harmony came from Sir John. He was a conciliator, so decent, so thoroughly *nice,* and believing everyone else the same, that it would have been unkind, even cruel, to let him down by bad behaviour. Sophy described her uncle as 'the life of our party', and one guest greatly admired Sir John's excellence: 'he might well be judged by the manners of all around him towards himself, and to see the Breakfast table of a morning was beautiful'.[31]

Jane Franklin was in charge of the indoor staff of Government House, which usually numbered about nine, typically a butler, a housekeeper, a cook, a lady's maid for herself, three housemaids and two laundresses. Sophy reported the 'inexpressible trouble of servants', and Jane told her father it was difficult finding trustworthy ones but, as with domesticity generally, she usually only mentioned servants when they were at fault, staying out late when they were meant to be in church, insisting on marrying and leaving, being impertinent ... 'The constant ill-health & therefore inefficiency of my housekeeper' meant, for Jane, that 'I have much anxiety of a kind for which I am very unfitted'—no sympathy for the sick woman. She sounds a severe mistress, finding fault and meagre with praise, though this was a typical attitude among employers. Servants came and went, none remaining the full seven years.[32]

The butlers and lady's maids were free immigrants, but the rest were mostly convicts. Convict servants were often untrained and unenthusiastic, and relations between them and their mistresses tended to be fraught. At least 27 convict women worked for Jane Franklin.[33] As usual, almost all were transported for theft, but they averaged five years older than the general female convict average age of 26, and more were married and widowed: so Government House was allocated more mature women, with some actually trained servants. All came from the British Isles though Jane Wilson, a cook, was born in Paris—which sounds promising for a cook. Sadly she was deeply pockpitted, 'stout made' with a retreating forehead. Half the women had children, mostly left behind in Britain; six had been prostitutes and Margaret Murray had made a living in England by hawking stolen goods and passing base coin, hardly likely backgrounds for efficient servants. (She was not the Margaret of the confectionary room.)

Convicts' behaviour varied from excellent to wayward. Susan Adams, a cook with a cheerful temper, arrived in the colony in 1834 and worked in Government House until she received a pardon in 1839, committing no offences. At the other end of the spectrum, in her seven-year term in Van Diemen's Land Mary Harper committed 31 offences under seventeen masters. All her offences involved being absent without leave, drunk or both. She repeated the offences at Government House after three months there, and was sentence to a month's hard labour at the wash tub. Overall, of the 27 convicts, a third were very well behaved in the colony, punished for no offences, or only one or two; another third behaved moderately well, averaging one offence per year of their sentences; and the remaining third committed between 11 and 31 offences—so Government House had its share of turbulent servants. Most convicts left Government House after committing an offence such as drunkenness, unauthorised absence or taking a man into the laundry; there was no serious crime. Still, trying to obtain solid work from a servant like Ann Balfour, found drunk with two bottles of rum in her possession, would be challenging.

Presumably the housekeeper had immediate control of these women, for Jane Franklin rarely mentioned them. She expected them to behave poorly, and saw them fulfilling her expectations. When well-behaved Susan Adams gained a much-desired pardon and wanted to marry and leave, Jane observed that her pardon would do Susan little good, and now she, Jane, had to find another cook. In 1841 Jane

Wilson was sentenced for misconduct to three days' solitary confinement on bread and water, to be served at Hobart's Cascades Female
Factory, the institution that housed female convicts not working as
servants for colonists. Like many employers at the time, Jane Franklin
was contemptuous of convicts:

> *I drove to the Factory to prepare [the superintendent] to receive*
> *Margaret Callaghan, the Laundress who immediately on hearing*
> *of Wilson's return from the Factory, determined that she would*
> *do what she could to earn a visit to it also, & is now in the Watch-*
> *house preparatory to being brought into court for her sentence.*

Another trip to the factory was the result of Jane Franklin's reaction
when she learnt that one of her laundresses had been transported for
'an atrocious case of child murder'. This was Mary Braid, sentenced to
death for incest with her brother and murder of the subsequent baby—
the two having been dobbed in by their sister. Presumably because
Mary appeared penitent, the sentence was commuted to transportation
for life. In Hobart Mary was generally well behaved, though in 1840,
working at Government House, she was punished for being drunk:
thirty days in the cells on bread and water. Then she was returned
to Government House. Jane Franklin somehow found out about her
original crime, and drove to the factory to tell the superintendent she
did not want such a woman under her roof—understandably, really,
especially in a stickler for morality like Jane. The superintendent
said that he took no notice of women's original crimes, and refused.
But Jane did manage to get rid of Mary Braid, for when she was next
mentioned, in 1841, she was working elsewhere.[34]

The only convict servant Jane Franklin did praise was Marianne
Galey, a trained cook who had worked for Lord Townshend. She was
literate, and described as extremely well behaved. After Jane's French
cook Charles Napoleon resigned, Galey took his place: 'Galey is busy
making cakes unassisted, for Thursday's party'. Charles Napoleon
asked to return, but Jane decided not to take him back because he

was expensive, and Galey 'has contrived to send us up some very fair dinners, & in an ordinary way does better than Charles'. But despite Galey's cooking skills, soon she was found guilty of misconduct, and was returned to the factory for assignment elsewhere.[35]

The servant closest to Jane Franklin was Christiana Stewart, her lady's maid from 1840 to 1842. Aged about thirty, Christiana was a free immigrant. Jane often reported information from her, and seemed to rely on her: Christiana accompanied her on her arduous travels to South Australia, New Zealand and the west coast of Van Diemen's Land. Unusually, Jane never found fault with her.[36] Yet even this paragon does not come to life in Jane's writings. She is merely Stewart, in the background, taken for granted—the usual attitude to servants. Her marriage and departure from Jane's service do not rate a mention. (It was mutual: Christiana called two of her children John and Eleanor, but there was no Jane.)

In fact, Jane Franklin had little time for most of Van Diemen's Land's inhabitants, convict, ex-convict or free settler. 'Everyone on the first arrival ... almost makes an involuntary shudder at the bare thought of being side by side in the street with convicts', she wrote home. 'Yet the feeling of security and the knowledge of good order and vigilance soon dissipate this feeling.' But she did not like living with felons. Though many people thought ex-convicts should be able to resume their place in society after serving their sentences, she did not, believing they were forever tainted with their crimes. She dealt with ex-convicts only when she had to, and could not understand how Governor Arthur's family allowed a member to marry the daughter of a convict, even though she was wealthy, pretty and modest. But even Jane Franklin had to make some concessions. Because of their social position, she had to invite the young Arthurs to Government House; she commissioned ex-convict artist Thomas Bock rather than a free artist, presumably because she thought him more talented; and she bought notebooks at an ex-convict's shop, writing that he was pious and well conducted, and 'must have erred from weakness rather than depravity'.[37]

She did not think much better of free colonists. She was snobbish, and they almost all came from middle-class or, worse, working-class backgrounds. They were 'petulant, excitable, passionate, malicious, revengeful, like a set of wicked children, who have never yet had their natural & inherited corruptions whipped out of them'—all this criticism because they insisted on helping the poor in hard times. There were plenty of jobs, and assistance only encouraged the poor not to work, said Jane firmly. She also claimed that 'the stupid cowardly colonists' never defended themselves against bushrangers.[38] This was nonsense, but shows how prejudice could blinker her vision: she accepted information she liked, and did not question its accuracy. The only people she would admit as her social equals were a few upper-class settlers and officials, and the only people she approved were those who responded well to the opportunity she gave them.

Family life, domesticity and her role as governor's wife did not take up more than a fraction of Jane Franklin's formidable energy. Her real interests and commitments were elsewhere.

7

FEMALE CONVICTS

Jane Franklin was not restricted by conventional ideas of the role of a governor's wife, though one of her interests could be seen as a suitable activity along traditional charitable lines: trying to reform female convicts. Before she left England, in 1832, she had observed philanthropist Elizabeth Fry working with women prisoners in London, reforming them by kindness and material help. Fry and a ladies' committee helped female convicts in England, providing them with requisites for the journey to Australia. Before Jane Franklin left for Van Diemen's Land she contacted Fry, who commissioned her to report on female convicts, and assist them at the other end of their voyage.

In Van Diemen's Land, Jane found that 'the subject of the women has never been considered or touched upon that I am aware of except as a hopeless evil'.[1] Women convicts were assigned to settlers as domestic servants. Many had no training and were not particularly good at this work, but the majority were keen to end their sentences and behaved well enough, only occasionally committing offences such as drunkenness or insolence. For the authorities, these women were not the problem. The 'hopeless evil' was the obstreperous minority who committed further crimes, mostly theft, and were sent to female factories for punishment. The (male) authorities found them more difficult to deal with than the men. Female insolence and rowdiness—and sexuality?—were more disturbing than male misbehaviour, and control was harder, especially since the harsher punishments of former years, like cutting off their hair or flogging, were no longer approved. At female factories, offenders served sentences of solitary confinement or hard labour. Also there were women waiting to be assigned, and those who were pregnant or nursing babies.

In 1838 Jane Franklin confessed to her sister Mary that she had not written to Fry, because it seemed impossible to do anything with the female convicts,

> *huddled as they all are together, and such impudent creatures, almost all of them ... I think the whole system of female transportation,—and particularly, of female assignment in service,—so faulty and vicious, that to attempt to deal with the women who are the subjects of it, seems waste time and labour.*[2]

Jane did want to do something for female convicts, but did not know what: 'if I could see a right system at work for their humiliation, I [would] work morning, noon & night in the cause'. She discussed their treatment with officials but received no encouragement, perhaps because they did not want an outsider interfering, perhaps because her ideas were more severe than theirs. Ignoring Fry, who advocated more humane treatment of convicts, Jane Franklin believed firmly in the value of punishment, of bringing the women to a sense of their sin, 'their humiliation'. She was appalled that officials encouraged the women to marry, which removed them from the system into their husbands' care—merely rewarding them for sin.[3]

She finally wrote to Elizabeth Fry in 1841, saying she had delayed because she shrank from reporting evil and confessing she had done nothing, though she did not feel she was to blame. Influences on female convicts were not favourable to reform, she continued. Landed from the ship, they were assigned to families as servants—to all families, including ex-convicts (no hope of reform there, she implied). There they corrupted children (a popular myth for which there is little evidence) and were seduced by male servants. When as a result a woman was 'likely to become a Mother', she was cared for in the factory, looked after her child for nine months, and was then punished only by being kept in the factory among her friends, nothing else, not even the very effective punishment of shaving her head. Then she was assigned to another household. The child was sent to the orphan school but allowed to see its depraved mother—and if she married, she could reclaim it. This system only encouraged immorality: convicts' children should have no contact with their corrupt parents, wrote Jane.[4]

'I do not expect that the manner in which I have treated the subject will suit M[rs]. Fry's views', Jane wrote to Mary, and doubtless she was correct—Fry was probably aghast on reading these severe strictures. But she replied tactfully. Could Lady Franklin suggest a better system than assignment? She herself found cutting off the hair only hardened the victim, and she thought the laws of God opposed separating mothers from their children. She ended positively: 'I am glad indeed to find the interest you take in the poor Convicts.'[5]

The reason Jane Franklin reluctantly put pen to paper was the arrival in May 1841 of the ship *Rajah*. It brought 180 female convicts under the supervision of 23-year-old Kezia Elizabeth Hayter, sent out by Fry—and she was reporting to Fry, so Jane was forced into similar action. Fry's ladies' committee gave the convicts materials to make a quilt, and Hayter supervised this mammoth sewing effort. The Rajah Quilt is now a prized work of art in the National Gallery of Australia. Hayter followed Fry's treatment of prisoners: sympathising, helping practically, reading the Bible, encouraging. 'If I have been nothing else I have been a comforter to many a sad and sorrowing heart', she wrote.[6]

Jane Franklin liked Kezia Hayter, finding her sensible, ladylike and intelligent. She suggested that Hayter live at Government House, work not just at the Cascades Female Factory but at a Sunday school, and help with Eleanor's education—at a salary, but it is not surprising that

Hayter declined. She found herself a job teaching at a school. Irate, Jane wrote her a nasty letter with bullying undertones: 'I presume still to think that you are wrong in your view of things—that with your own principles you shd place yourself where you can do most good ... has not the finger of God pointed out to you the path that was destined for you—you think otherwise.' They compromised: they would visit the factory together twice a week. Kezia Hayter was her right hand and guide, wrote Jane Franklin. 'She is wise beyond her years & possesed of much more experience in that particular department [assisting female convicts] than I have yet attained.' Kezia Hayter wrote to a friend that she found Lady Franklin 'rather an eccentric character devoid of religious principle'.[7]

For six weeks they visited the factory, Hayter addressing the women, saying prayers and setting lessons. What Jane Franklin did is not clear, though she did hear a woman repeat a lesson. Once she was advised not to go to the factory because the women were convinced Miss Hayter was going to put them in solitary confinement and cut off their hair, and were determined to tear her to pieces. Seldom afraid of physical danger, Jane went, to show that the report was absurd. The superintendent agreed, saying that 'except in occasional moments' the women were very quiet.[8]

As often happens when an outsider enters an institution, the authorities resented it, and the superintendents of the factory and of convicts generally accused Kezia Hayter of being a mischief-maker. Upset, she said she could only work in the factory with a ladies' committee, and Jane Franklin established one, comprising about ten women with herself at the head. They were to visit the convicts, making every effort to bring about moral and religious improvement. Newspapers thought this a good idea, but several criticised the committee—it should contain middle-aged married ladies used to colonial life, not young single women newly arrived in the colony. Horrified, Hayter resigned and the committee evaporated. Jane Franklin remonstrated indignantly, but for these women, private citizens, being criticised in the press was appalling. One newspaper actually apologised for offending them.[9]

Meanwhile, John Franklin instituted an enquiry into female convicts. 'Such disclosures!' wrote Jane—they proved things were far worse than she had described to Fry, with such abominations (meaning lesbianism) that the enquiry's report was described as unfit for her to read. In 1842 a branch factory was opened for women waiting for assignment, so they were separated from the criminals undergoing punishment. Jane Franklin had wanted this and newspapers gave her credit for it, but she herself did not claim it, and it is not clear how much influence she had. Hayter approved, but was irritated with Sir John's 'vacillating undecided conduct' about the new factory. 'I very candidly told him my mind nay almost quarrelled with him and threatened to withdraw', she wrote. He renewed his promises of action and tried to laugh it off, but 'I was heart sick with his irresolution and certainly spoke much more warmly than I had ever done'. She did not say what Sir John omitted to do, but she was not the only one to find him vacillating—and he was not the only Franklin from whom she differed. 'What do you think dearest Charles of a proposition Lady F made to me today to accompany her to Sydney and Norfolk Island to report upon the Factory & discipline there', she wrote to her fiancé. 'I should as soon think of attempting a flight to the moon.'[10]

Jane Franklin's factory visits ceased, but Hayter's continued. She felt welcomed by the 'poor women', the 'wretched outcasts', describing her work among them as arduous but delightful. However, in April 1842 the superintendent accused her of something—she did not say what. But 'your Lizzie stood erect in conscious innocence and made her accusers quail beneath her true statements', she told Charles. She told Jane Franklin that she felt thwarted in everything at the Female Factory and did not go there again, possibly refused entry by the superintendent. She worked as a governess, and in 1843 married her Charles.[11]

Jane Franklin turned to an activity far more to her taste: reading everything she could about female convicts, gathering opinions and writing a long despatch summarising all views, which was sent to England. She said she wanted to help female convicts, that 'it has been the one object I have thought most about, & cared for most, since

I have been in this Colony', that she would willingly spend her life in the women's service: but unless she had authority from England to act as she thought fit, she would do nothing. 'There are many good but weak people who think if you only read to & pray with them, they must be amended by it', for instance Miss Hayter and Mrs Fry, she told Mary. But 'will it do any good to pray amidst the howling & blasphemy of a brothel or what is worse hushed for the moment you are there, but recommencing before you are out of hearing?' In 1843 she was 'beset', she said, by members of the former ladies' committee wanting her to revive it, but she refused to act without power.[12]

For women like Fry and Hayter, helping women prisoners was straightforward: sympathising, praying, trying to bring out the best in them. Jane Franklin did not believe in this method: but what did she believe in? She said she wanted to help the women, but what did she plan to do, failing actually being in charge herself, which is what being given authority ultimately implies? It is not clear, perhaps was not clear even to Jane herself, whether she really wanted to act, or took shelter in saying she would if she were given authority. She must have known there was no chance of this.

She showed little interest in male convicts, but had much the same attitude to them as to women: their punishment should be harsher, control over them more effective. She wrote a 62 000-word description, 'Notes on the Convict System of V.D.L.', which summarised the system and opinions of it, but did not give her own views.[13]

Though Jane Franklin thought, talked and wrote a great deal about female convicts, she actually did little to help them—but it is hard to blame her. Reformers such as Fry and Hayter felt able to work with female prisoners, but Jane Franklin would not be the only one to quail at the prospect.

In 1843 the women who had 'beset' her did form a committee to visit female convicts. It included Sarah Hopkins, a middle-aged, married woman twenty years in the colony, just as the newspapers recommended. 'The women listen with attention, and apparent gratitude', she wrote in her diary, 'but thou, O Lord, art the searcher of hearts, and knowest whether they are sincere. I feel totally unfit for such a work.' She persevered, but it was hard going. In 1844 she wrote:

> *I have now visited the female prisoners for nearly twelve months past. I have endeavoured to convince them they are sinners, and need a Saviour ... endeavouring to discover the easy besetting sin of every individual I conversed with, that I might give them suitable advice ... yet little good appears to have been effected; their minds are still hardened.*[14]

Another well-meaning effort to help female convicts failed—not surprisingly, at least from the female convicts' point of view.

In 1844 a probation station was set up to train female convicts before they were sent out as servants. Dr and Mrs Bowden were in charge, and newspapers gave glowing reports of neat, clean, well-behaved and industrious convicts learning household skills, singing hymns and appreciating the Bowdens; but eventually the Bowdens ran foul of the authorities, and the probation station was disbanded. Were they incompetent, or did they show up others? The history of female convicts had too many villains, real and imaginary, convict and free.

A favourite story in popular accounts tells of female convicts smacking their bottoms in front of Jane Franklin, but it has no basis in fact. It originated in a novel-cum-memoir written in the 1880s by Robert Crooke, entitled, *The Convict: a fragment of history*. He enjoyed writing it so much he penned several versions. They mixed interesting comment on the aspects of life in Van Diemen's Land Crooke experienced with wild exaggerations, to make a dramatic story.

Crooke described Van Diemen's Land as a terrible place. Universal profligacy prevailed, each home contained its quota of prostitutes, convicts were white slaves, their situation wretched to the last degree (wild exaggeration). His story opens with Sally, a convict, corrupting her employer's daughters (that myth Jane Franklin mentioned).

Sally is sent to the Female Factory, whose dreadful facets include the chaplain:

> The women at the factory knew the Chaplain's character well. They were quite aware that he loved roast turkey and ham with a good bottle of port to wash them down, far more than he loved his Bible … His ministrations were of no value whatever … on one occasion as he was crossing the courtyard of the female [factory], some dozen or twenty women seized upon him, took off his trousers and deliberately endeavoured to deprive him of his manhood.

They were stopped by constables 'who seized the fair ladies and placed them in durance vile'—Crooke enjoyed novelistic flourishes.

On another occasion he described a visit by the governor, his wife and the chaplain to the factory:

> The women, numbering some 300 or 400, were mustered to receive his Excellency who made them a sort of stereotyped speech containing a large amount of commonplace with a quantity of the good talk interspersed. So long as the Governor spoke he was listened to with respect. His character was at least good. He was the fine hearty old sailor, his disposition was kind and humane and though under the influence of evil advisers, he was induced to do many evil deeds, yet for the most part bond as well as free men liked him.
>
> Her Ladyship, however, a man in petticoats … was disliked by all. Her talents were admitted to be of a very high order, but her love of power and her spirit of meddling and intriguing rendered her a dangerous enemy, and an unsafe friend. Her character was well known in the factory, and when she stood up to address the prisoners and talked to them of homes of refuge, Mrs. Fry, etc, murmurs of dissent and a few hisses were heard. Still she was enabled to finish her speech and display her eloquence which she was but too fond of doing …

The Reverend Gentleman however wished to have his say and commenced to preach to the women … when they had listened to the platitudes of the Governor and his lady for upwards of an hour, were in no humour for a sermon from the Parson, as he was termed, and determined to check his eloquence … on a sudden the three hundred women turned right round and at one impulse pulled up their clothes shewing their naked posteriors which they simultaneously smacked with their hands making a loud and not very musical noise …

The feelings of the Governor and her Ladyship may well be conceived … They were more than shocked, they were horrified and astounded. The Governor held up his hands to heaven, the Parson looked unutterable things, her Ladyship pretended to faint (it was but pretence) and the Aidecamp … burst out laughing.

In other versions the Franklins laughed too.

Sally's story continues, but it is hardly a narrative, more a tirade against the Anglican church, the authorities, wealthy settlers, Jane Franklin—everyone who had not appreciated Robert Crooke.[15]

Crooke was born in 1818 in Ireland, gained an Arts degree, and in 1840 emigrated to Van Diemen's Land, becoming assistant master at the Queen's School under John Gell, Jane Franklin's protégé. Gell took Crooke to dine at Government House—once. He was never asked again, so it seems that Jane Franklin, that indefatigable dinner-inviter, did not think much of him. In 1843 Gell dismissed him, as he 'has not succeeded in making himself either obeyed or liked by the boys'.

Crooke wanted to be ordained, but the church refused, and he became a religious instructor at a distant convict station. Finally in 1855 he was ordained and sent to the remote Huon, but sued a resident who accused him of loose behaviour: asking people if they thought Mr Nation 'is man enough' for Mrs Nation, and whether a girl's bonnet was torn when she was in a vertical or horizontal position; becoming so drunk at a ball that he danced home along the road singing 'Pop goes the weasel'. Parishioners refused to go to church, and witnesses

accused him of lying in court. From Crooke's evidence he sounds a
silly man, melodramatic and vain. The jury could not agree on a
verdict, but the church dismissed him. The Crookes went to Victoria,
where Robert returned to teaching and in old age wrote *The Convict*.[16]

In the 1940s Professor Kathleen Fitzpatrick was writing a study
of John Franklin's governorship. Her cousin, Crooke's granddaughter,
showed her *The Convict*. In her otherwise scholarly study, Fitzpatrick
quoted Crooke twice, narrating the 'ribald tale' of the smacking
bottoms as fact, though admitting that *The Convict* was fiction.[17]

Ever since this salacious story appeared, people have loved it.
Virtually everyone who wrote about the Franklins reproduced it. With
such an eminent historian as Kathleen Fitzpatrick as the source, who
could doubt it? Feminist historians seized on it as showing female
convicts' vitality, independence and lack of conventionality. I narrated
it in my book about governors' womenfolk, *Governors' ladies* (1986).
Male historians also cannot resist quoting this ribald story; Professor
Andrew Lambert included it in his 2010 biography of Franklin. He
knew its authenticity was questioned, 'but it is too good to omit'.[18]

By the time a second version of *Governors' ladies* was published
in 1999, my attention had been drawn to the lack of evidence for the
story. There is no contemporary corroboration: no mention in convict
records, though surely such horrifying behaviour would have been
punished; nothing in the press; nothing in any diary or memoir;
nothing in Jane Franklin's writing. And she never gave speeches
in public.

There are three possibilities. Firstly, the smacking bottoms story
happened: unlikely. Secondly, Crooke made it up: possible. Or, thirdly,
it had some basis in fact: the most likely. Ellen Scott was transported
in 1830 for theft. She was a rebel, part of the Flash Mob in the female
factories—'flash' meaning savvy, streetwise, wide-awake. The Flash
Mob had no reverence for authority, dominated other women, traf-
ficked in forbidden goods such as tobacco and slept together. Ellen was
punished for 48 offences while she was a convict, including violently
assaulting the factory superintendent with intent to kill and, in 1833,

'indecent behaviour during the performance of divine service by the Revd Wm Bedford', the factory chaplain.[19] It is possible that she pulled up her skirt and smacked her bottom at him—it would fit the rest of her story. Perhaps she did, and perhaps this tale was told over and over again, growing into the story of all the women smacking their bottoms at Bedford.

In another twist, in 1892 'G.P.' published a memoir of living in the Female Factory from 1828 to 1831 (he seems to have been the super-intendent's young nephew). As a rule, he wrote, the women were submissive and orderly, but not always. When Bedford arrived he was full of zeal, and gave Governor Arthur a list of men who were cohab-iting with their assigned servants. Arthur sent these women back to the factory. They were furious, and on Bedford's next visit, he 'was savagely attacked as soon as he entered the yard by a large mob of women who, with demoniacal howls and yells subjected him to the most gross and outrageous personal maltreatment'. Sure enough, the records show that in 1825 two women were punished for abusing and being insolent to Bedford.[20]

Two small but definite attacks on Bedford, magnified by gossip into the manhood-depriving and smacking bottoms stories? By the time Crooke arrived in 1840 there was plenty of time for the stories to have been exaggerated, and they were just the sort of smutty innuendo he enjoyed, just what he wanted to show up the detested Anglican church and Jane Franklin. Easy to move the dates to the Franklin period in which his story was set.

Whatever did occur, it seems certain that the smacking bottoms episode never happened as Crooke described it. Jane Franklin saw plenty to shock and disgust her in Van Diemen's Land, but not this particular event.

8

IMPROVING

THE COLONY

A great believer in the Victorian drive for improvement, Jane Franklin tried to improve Van Diemen's Land in a number of ways. She had the requirements to achieve this: not only ideas and energy, but also money. She was willing to put thousands of pounds and endless effort into improving Van Diemen's Land, in her own way. The finances of many of her projects such as the *Tasmanian Journal* are not explained, but there is little doubt that her money backed them.

Encouraging education was obvious, a favourite method of reformers. John Franklin was genuinely interested, and greatly extended the system of primary schools, his major achievement in the colony. Jane Franklin was just as determined. She was not particularly interested in existing schools, or girls' education. She had an excellent opportunity to put any ideas into practice with her stepdaughter, but the governess who was considered academically inadequate when Eleanor was twelve remained until she was nineteen. Jane deplored the low standard of girls' education in Van Diemen's Land and sketched a plan for a superior school for young ladies, but did nothing about it.[1]

As usual, she was far more interested in the male side, boys' education—not just any boys, but sons of gentlemen. Some private schools in the colony offered some secondary education, but from the 1820s a few people suggested a superior school to, as John Franklin said, 'train up Christian youth in the faith as well as the learning of Christian gentlemen'. Governor Arthur tried to found one, but it sank on the rocks of religious division—Anglicans versus Presbyterians versus Methodists, Catholics, Baptists and Congregationalists, all asserting their claims.[2]

Jane Franklin said her 'hobby of hobbies' was establishing such a college—why, she never even hinted. Sir John was also enthusiastic. He applied for a headmaster to Dr Arnold of Rugby School, who sent John Gell, one of his prize pupils and a Cambridge graduate. Gell arrived in 1840, aged 24. Scholarly, tolerant, slightly diffident, he had a quizzical sense of humour. 'I cannot tell you how much I like him', wrote Jane Franklin. 'He has a profound and original mind and pure and noble feelings. It does me good to be with him.' He became one of her favourites, often at Government House for dinner, though he provoked her by being unflappable: 'he will not go into a passion when I think he ought; will not feel a due indignation. He laughs & reasons.'[3] That was not her way.

In 1840 Jane was busy writing a minute for Sir John to put before the Legislative Council, to convince them to vote money for the project. This succeeded, and Sir John duly laid the foundation stone of Christ College at New Norfolk. In theory, plans would now be drawn up and the college built.

Meanwhile, Gell set up the Queen's School in Hobart as a preparatory institution, with government funding. The hostile newspapers opposed it bitterly, with some reason. Similar schools received no financial aid; why should Gell? He charged high enough fees.[4] Jane Franklin provided all the encouragement she could, lending Gell money, urging fathers to enrol their sons (even from South Australia and New Zealand), urging Gell on ('I always ask minutely after his school') and asking the boys to Government House:

*I have M*ʳ*. Gell & his 30 boys every Thursday evening to tea &*
a chemical lecture—a long table covered with a cloth, & plates

of cake & jam, & preserved fruits or jellies, with tea & coffee is
attended by 2 or 3 of the maids & the boys come & go to their
hearts' content—I have offered them 2 prizes for the best account
of the lectures.[5]

But the Queen's School ran into problems: too few pupils, unsuccessful
assistant masters and difficulties with Gell himself. One boy 'set upon
Mr. Gell just as if Mr. Gell had been one of the boys, kicking, biting &
scratching him & threatening him that his father wd take him away'.
The father told Gell he did not flog the boy enough. This disheartened
Gell, who, wrote Jane Franklin in one of her rare witticisms, did not
much like 'the manual part of his profession'.[6] Even her support waned,
with lectures petering out, though the school continued.

Her enthusiasm for establishing Christ College did not wane,
however, and her writing contains tens of thousands of words on
every possible aspect of it, from architectural plans to gaining the
charter from England that Gell thought essential for its independence.
There was opposition to combat, from non-Anglicans who opposed
her ideas of Anglican dominance, and from those who disapproved
of the College because they thought existing schools sufficient. Jane
could never accept that their argument was legitimate, that a colony of
50 000 people, three-quarters convicts or their descendants, could not
support a semi-university college (and when the Anglicans did establish their own Christ College a few years later, it failed). No: anyone
who opposed her must be an intriguing mischief-maker.[7]

Delay followed delay, but in 1843 the British government sent
out the charter. It was too late. Sir John did not have time to put the
question to the Legislative Council before his successor arrived.

Despite her efforts, Jane Franklin achieved little for education in Van
Diemen's Land, at least partly because she had no direct power. Science
was another matter. It was private, not public, and she could act for
herself, or at least through Sir John (which was much the same thing).

Science led to revolutionary new discoveries, and enabled Europe to dominate the world. Britain and France sent scientific exploring expeditions, universities studied science, and by the time the Franklins arrived in Van Diemen's Land it was accepted that gentlemen, and ladies, might have a scientific interest like studying birds, or collecting rocks or seaweeds. Jane was not always impressed with local efforts, noting that one woman 'occupies herself with botany, or at least with collecting & preserving flowers'.[8]

Interest started in Van Diemen's Land in 1827, when the Hobart Mechanics' Institute was founded to promote 'useful and scientific knowledge', by holding lectures and setting up a library, and a museum to display the island's natural products. Activity, mainly lectures, came and went.[9] In 1829 the Van Diemen's Land Society was started, with much the same aims. Members were told that the island was scientifically a land of mystery, abounding with anomalies like the platypus that might illuminate unanswered questions. 'No botanist has trodden your fields', it was all there waiting to be discovered—out they should go! They should avoid theories, just observe, collect and describe, then send the results to England for analysis, so the veil would be withdrawn and man could understand creation. This was promising, but the society faded.[10]

In the mid-1830s Hobart saw several scientific visitors, notably the *Beagle* on its voyage of scientific discovery, with Charles Darwin on board. John Franklin was welcomed not just as a hero but as a scientific man. However, when he arrived a newspaper bemoaned that 'nothing of a literary or scientific character exists among us'.[11]

Franklin had been interested in science ever since his voyage with Flinders in 1801. He loved it, regretting that he had no time to undertake research. He did send specimens to England, such as skeletons of the thylacine (Tasmanian tiger). Jane Franklin was not particularly gripped herself: 'I am hardly even a dabbler in science'. She was interested in observing nature—a fine hedge of boobialla whose berries were eaten by the Aborigines, the susceptibility of pines to dry rot, not however found in the curly gum, and so on, endlessly—but her writings contain no exclamations of joy at, say, recognising a rare bird or rock. She did collect specimens, but a visiting scientist found them neglected, her stuffed birds dirty and moth-eaten. More than collecting she enjoyed reading about science, and had the latest journals and books sent from England—a visitor was astonished when she gave him a copy of his latest book, which he himself had not yet seen.[12] In this spirit, Jane Franklin approved greatly of science, and encouraged other people's activity as much as she could.

One of John Franklin's first actions was to instruct his private secretary to revive the moribund Mechanics' Institute. It held lectures every winter, with Franklin as patron. But the family rarely attended, and this was criticised.[13] Doubtless these meetings were not up to London standards, but the colonists' disappointment is understandable. Instead, one or both of the Franklins decided to act on their own.

'We are about forming a small private scientific society', wrote Jane Franklin in February 1839. John Franklin is generally credited with founding the Tasmanian Society, but from her writings there is no doubt that it was his wife who thought of it, set it up and kept it going, and Joseph Hooker, a visiting botanist, gave her the credit for founding it. However, to fulfil her self-imposed role of boosting Sir John, she wanted credit for any achievement to go to him. The society had the same aims and activities as the earlier Van Diemen's Land Society—but that had lacked the advantage of a Jane Franklin to organise it.[14]

It was eight months between that initial statement and the first meeting, what with working out who could join (membership was by Lady Franklin's invitation, though members were then 'elected'), refuting prophecies of doom, and Jane's prolonged absence in New South Wales. On her return she set events in motion, and the first meeting was held in October. At one early meeting Dr Hobson, a naturalist, read a paper on the blood of the platypus, and showed members a drop under his microscope; Sir John read letters about Aboriginal vocabulary, tidal phenomena and the value of large meshes for keeping off mosquitoes; and then the meeting descended to discussing 'offensive particulars' about some gossip. Over the next four years many topics were discussed: for example, Captain Cotton talked on his rotatory steam engine, which was installed in the drawing room for the occasion; Henry Kay spoke on magnetism; and Dr Bedford prepared some drawings of young inside the pouches of marsupial animals. The gentlemen withdrew to the library to look at these; were they considered indelicate for ladies? There was a palpable feeling that members were making new discoveries in a strange place. Their motto, 'Quocunque aspicias, hic paradoxus erit' ('Whichever way you look at it, this is baffling', in rather wobbly Latin) was translated by one witty member as 'All things are queer And opposite here'.[15]

Over seventy people joined the society, and in 1842 there were 32 resident members in Van Diemen's Land and 39 corresponding members overseas. Jane Franklin was indefatigable in recruiting them. Locally most came from the officer-and-gentlemen class, with a sprinkling of clergymen and colonists. Corresponding members included people of scientific importance in neighbouring colonies or England, and notables like governors who were expected to be interested. There were two female members, artist Mary Allport who 'is going to etch for the Society' and Mrs Whitefoord Smith, but neither attended meetings. Jane, Eleanor, Sophy and Miss Williamson were not members but did attend meetings. 'Mr Gell read a very good paper on the language of the Aborigines of S Australia', Eleanor wrote in her diary, and, less enthusiastically, 'Dr Hooker on some sort of rock'.[16]

Meetings flagged in Jane Franklin's absence. In 1840 she returned from one of her travels to find the society inactive, and with some effort revived it, with dinner meetings to encourage attendance. Meetings were enlivened by officers from visiting ships, and Jane described a very successful one:

> There was a great deal of animation & excitement, knots & groups of talkers intently engaged, & every body apparently amused & interested. Mr. Lawrence observed that it was long since he had seen any thing like it—Mr. Lillie seemed in a high state of enjoyment—Mr. Gell remarked that these meetings were

decidedly pleasanter than any other parties we had at Govt. House[17]

—a double-edged compliment.

Some meetings were less lively. 'Papa read Sir John Herschel's very interesting paper on Terrestrial Magnetism', wrote Eleanor. 'It lasted till past midnight, and some, not to say many of the gentlemen were charming us with the delightful noise of snoring; we were nevertheless much interested.'[18]

Jane Franklin decided to publish the papers, and the first issue of the *Tasmanian Journal of Natural Science, Agriculture, Statistics &c* appeared in 1841. She sent copies to anyone who might be interested and impressed, in Australia and England, particularly the Colonial Office in London. By 1846 the society had published eleven issues containing 128 articles in 878 pages, an impressive achievement. They were reprinted in handsome volumes, in Van Diemen's Land and London. Officially Jane had no role in this, but the journal would not have existed without her. She organised papers, editing at least one, and roped in family members to help—'engaged today in correcting press for Journal', wrote Eleanor.[19] Jane also organised a small museum for the society, which she displayed in Government House. She looked on the Tasmanian Society as hers, only reluctantly deferring to members' wishes not to invite strangers all the time—'I am bound in all honor & good faith not to introduce them slily'. She solicited both members and papers for the journal without consulting existing members, 'considering myself invested with a general commission'.[20]

Museum, meetings, the journal—the Tasmanian Society was most successful, even though (perhaps because) it remained private, not open to the public. To succeed, such a society in a small community probably needed to be tightly run. A few problems did arise. George Boyes, the colonial auditor, was only moderately enthusiastic. He thought the first issue of the journal 'a so-so publication'; and when visiting French scientists were elected members, 'I have no doubt they made merry with the honer conferred upon them, as soon as they left us'. Sir John was not always a keen listener: 'Bradbury read a paper on New Zealand he read it very badly and so prosily that he sent Sir John to sleep who snored like a hog and blew like a grampus'. Boyes also recorded a dispute between two members, which resulted in resignations.[21]

However, virtually everyone else thought the society and the journal 'exceedingly creditable' to the colony. High praise came when the President of the Geological Society of London stated that Franklin was rendering Van Diemen's Land a school of natural knowledge, with a journal which would do credit to any London society.[22]

As well as aiding the Tasmanian Society to forward science, Jane Franklin encouraged visiting scientists—with enormous enthusiasm, sometimes more than the recipients actually wanted. Gentlemen interested in science were urged to dine, stay in Government House, present papers to the Tasmanian Society, and generally add to the lustre of Sir John's rule.

Among her favourites were two botanists, Ronald Gunn and Joseph Milligan. Gunn was a police magistrate in the north, where he collected specimens and corresponded with the distinguished botanist William Hooker in London. Visiting Hobart, he was impressed by the Franklins, who 'are sincerely desirous of forwarding the Cause of Natural History in this Colony'. Jane Franklin was particularly encouraging: 'She is a most amiable & estimable Lady—and has certainly secured my best feelings.'

In 1838 Gunn was promoted to police magistrate in Hobart, where the Franklins showed him 'the greatest possible kindness & attention'. He accompanied Lady Franklin's party to Recherche Bay, where he collected many specimens, and in early 1840 he became Sir John's private secretary, as well as secretary of the Tasmanian Society and overseer of Jane Franklin's botanic garden. However, she was always inclined to overwork a willing person, and this 'incessant official drudgery' left Gunn no time for botany. He resigned, moving north again. Jane also encouraged his friend Dr Joseph Milligan. In 1842 he accompanied the Franklins to Macquarie Harbour on the west coast, and he was appointed to a senior government position in Hobart for which he had no obvious qualifications.[23] But she did not encourage everyone. She ignored Francis Abbott, a distinguished astronomer who also corresponded with English experts—but was an ex-convict.

John Gould, a taxidermist with the Zoological Society of London, was famous for his books about birds, finely illustrated by his wife Elizabeth. They arrived in Hobart in 1838. 'He is an exceeding good-natured, kind-hearted & amiable man, but knowing & caring for little beyond his birds', Jane told Mary. 'She is a correct minded, amiable, nice person, with a very observant eye & clever hand.' Henry Elliot, sprig of the aristocracy, thought middle-class Gould too conscious of his fame, but Jane Franklin did not see why 'a bird fancier should come all the way to the Antipodes in pursuit of his peculiar fame, and not think the better of himself for it'.

Jane was extremely hospitable to the Goulds, having them to stay in Government House for nine months. The Franklins were kind beyond measure, Elizabeth Gould wrote home. They gave many dinner parties, but otherwise 'live in a very regular, quiet way', which suited her. When Jane Franklin and John Gould left for mainland Australia, Jane insisted Elizabeth remain with John and Eleanor, to avoid loneliness in her pregnancy. Elizabeth called the baby Franklin, and Jane was so taken with him, she wanted to adopt him:

> that sweet little Franklin, whom I think you ought to make over to me ... Come, what say you to such an arrangement? Must the youngest be ever the one from whom you can least bear to part? They have all the privilege of having been the youngest once.

A strange offer, apparently serious, from a non-maternal woman: the child remained with his parents. However, Elizabeth was most grateful to the Franklins, thanking them for converting a strange land into a pleasant home. She was one woman Jane seemed friendly with, and the Franklins were thrilled with the Goulds' magnificent eight-volume *The Birds of Australia*, which praised their assistance.[24]

In September 1840 Paul Edmund de Strzelecki arrived in Hobart. Ambitious, capable, handsome, aristocratic, Strzelecki was a self-taught geologist and self-appointed Count. He travelled widely, analysing soil and examining minerals, and spent much time in Van Diemen's Land. Both the Franklins admired his work and liked him as a person. 'He is one of the most accomplished and agreeable men I ever met with', wrote Jane. Mary would be enchanted with him: 'everybody is without exception, he is so gentlemanly, elegant, so very clever, so accomplished, so full of fire and vivacity, and withal so amiable, only a little bit satirical'. His best gift was his wonderful tact. He almost became one of the Franklin family, staying with them whenever he was in Hobart, thinking everything they did a good idea, advising Jane on her garden ... It paid off, for the Franklins helped finance his book on the physical geography of New South Wales and Van Diemen's Land, which he dedicated to Sir John.[25] It laid the basis for Australian palaeontology.

Jane Franklin enjoyed offering hospitality to officers from visiting ships, particularly scientists. The most exciting, not only for the Franklins but for all Hobart, were the *Erebus* and *Terror* expedition. In 1839 the British Admiralty turned its exploring interests south, and appointed Captain James Ross in charge of an expedition to explore Antarctica and make magnetic observations at a chain of observatories, including one to be built in Van Diemen's Land. The nephew of explorer John Ross, James had been on six Arctic expeditions, having spent most of his adult life there. Captain Francis Crozier, also with Arctic experience, was his second-in-command. The expedition arrived in Hobart in August 1840. Also on board were botanist Joseph Hooker and Lieutenant Henry Kay, John Franklin's nephew, in charge of the observatory, which Jane named Rossbank. It was quickly built—Ross was impressed when convict workers wanted to continue their efforts on a Saturday night, to get it finished in time—and the expedition stayed for three months to establish it and wait for warmer weather before sailing south. The officers were often at Government House, and 'the captains' (as Jane called them) and Henry Kay stayed there, part of the Franklin family party.

Jane Franklin's hospitality could be overwhelming, even unwelcome. Ross and Crozier never complained, but Jane Franklin commented that, one evening at dinner, 'There was much & overmuch discussion of the Bothwell Church Act, which poor Captn Ross is fain to listen to whether he will or no'. Surely as hostess she could have changed the subject from such boring local trivia? Joseph Hooker wanted to find specimens, not socialise. 'Lady Franklin ... would like to show me every kindness, but does not understand how, and I hate dancing attendance at Government House', he wrote. He was grateful when she asked him to accompany the party to Port Arthur, but they were only there for Sunday and Monday morning. 'I got about 500 specimens on Monday, and a few after service on Sunday, though Lady F. did not like it, and very properly, but I thought it excusable as being my only chance of gathering *Anopterus glandulosus*.' However, like all the officers he loved the visit: 'Van Diemen's Land was quite a home to us and a most attractive place.'[26] (It seems hypocritical that Jane Franklin disapproved of Hooker collecting plants on Sunday when she travelled through the bush on many Sundays without even religious observance. Perhaps her change of heart was due to her husband's presence.)

James Ross, intelligent, sympathetic and handsome, became a close friend of both John and Jane Franklin. A fellow Arctic explorer, he spoke the same language as Sir John, the first person in Van Diemen's Land who really understood. Crozier, less outgoing, remained in Ross's shadow. 'The arrival of Captain Ross and Crozier has since added much to Sir John's happiness', wrote Jane to her father. 'They all feel towards one another as friends and brothers and it is the remark of people here that Sir John appears to them quite in a new light, so bustling and frisky and merry with his new companions.' He loved assisting in the observatory, visiting it daily to inspect progress.[27]

Jane herself was not particularly interested in magnetism—'We were all about as wise when we came away as when we went in', she wrote after having it explained in the observatory—but James Ross was just the sort of man she appreciated. Like her other favourites, he was clever, personable, younger; sympathetic to her, willing to play up to her in the lively, amusing way that could be seen as flirtation, but which surely had no active sexual side, certainly not on her part. It was Jane Franklin continuing to enjoy masculine admiration, not to mention enticing gossip. 'Captn Ross talked to me of the Minto family … I told Captn Ross of Sir John's letter from Parry …'. After the expedition left in November, Jane became ill.[28]

She was irate that she was in New Zealand when Ross and Crozier returned to Hobart in April 1841. Everyone else had a marvellous time. The local theatre capitalised on the general enthusiasm with a nautical drama, *The South Polar Expedition*, whose characters included the captains and the Franklins, one actress playing the parts of both Jane Franklin and Britannia. Eleanor heard all about it:

> One of the scenes was the taking leave at Government House previous to the expedition's departure, in which her Ladyship proposed to drink a bumper of wine with Captain Ross and this <u>highly</u> <u>characteristic</u> act she is said to have performed admirably. Two other ladies, said to have been meant for Sophy and myself, were also not slow to fill their glasses. We of course did not go to this grand performance, as Papa does not encourage the theatre, but it is said to have been ridiculous in the extreme, from its extreme dissimilarity. Sir John Franklin, for instance, had a head full of hair.[29]

The one effort Jane Franklin herself made towards practical science was her botanic garden. Governor Arthur had tried this, but it developed as an ordinary garden only. In her turn, Jane bought land, eventually 410 acres (almost 166 hectares), in a beautiful mountain glen at Sassafras Valley (now Lenah Valley) near Hobart. Wanting a suitably classical title for 'my mountain garden', she asked members of the Tasmanian Society to provide one. Dictionaries were consulted, words discussed, and finally Ancanthe, meaning 'vale of flowers', was made up—'unexceptionable in its derivation & not amiss in sound'.[30]

Jane put botanist Ronald Gunn in charge of developing the garden. He aimed to lay out 'the Natural Orders of our indigenous plants', not just from Van Diemen's Land but from the whole southern world, so that they could be introduced to Britain. However, he only had time to lay out a few tracks.[31] Joseph Hooker, a botanist on Ross and Crozier's 1840 expedition, enjoyed seeing local plants growing vigorously instead of just dried specimens. One day Jane Franklin took him and others to the garden. They climbed Gunn's path up nearby Prospect Hill, but mist obscured the view. On the way down, Jane heard a scream and thought someone had seen a snake, but 'it was only a new orchis which Mr H. had not seen before'—note her personal lack of interest in botany.[32]

Soon Gunn moved north and Jane Franklin's vision of a botanic garden faded, for no other botanist was available. The garden became a pretty picnic site—and still is.

In much the same spirit as she was interested in science—a beneficial and civilising influence she should encourage—so Jane Franklin was interested in art. Horrified to find there was no art gallery in any Australian colony, she planned to establish one in Hobart. In 1842 she collected money from about seventy people and asked her sister Mary to organise purchases through an art union. Some pictures arrived, but for some unknown reason it all fell through. Jane was also interested in commissioning paintings of Australian topics. In Sydney in 1839 she ordered a painting from Conrad Martens, beating him down to a quarter the price he suggested. She paid his account, but it is not clear what the painting was.[33]

Back in Hobart she commissioned copies of Thomas Bock's paintings of Aborigines, paying him what she described as a formidable sum, though it was average for the time. She also commissioned him to paint a portrait of her Aboriginal protégée Mathinna, a view of Rossbank observatory, and (unwillingly, to please Mary Maconochie) a sketch of Jane Franklin herself, the only clear depiction of her as a mature adult (she later avoided having her photograph taken). Although she disapproved of convicts on principle, she patronised Bock, a convict but an excellent artist, in preference to Benjamin Duterrau, a free immigrant but an inferior artist. Another immigrant artist was John Glover, but she disapproved of him, even though he was an old acquaintance. She was relieved when he did not recognise her, for she heard he was a cruel husband, a bad father, a sordid lover of money, and worst of all, 'a pretended Atheist'. She did not like his art either—it would 'disgrace a signpost'.[34] (Glover is now admired as a leading artist of the period.)

Jane sent most of these paintings back to England, to show people there that Van Diemen's Land under Sir John was a centre of culture. The painting of Rossbank was especially notable, with Sir John, the central figure, presiding over developments in science in this remote outpost.

The Franklins had little interest in other branches of the arts. Neither was musical, but there was music at Government House, performed by guests, Sophy or, on grand occasions, local bands. Sir John patronised a concert by visiting French musicians, but he did not approve of the theatre and the Franklins never attended.[35]

In 1841 Jane Franklin made a major attempt to encourage art, asking her sister Mary for 'a pretty little design for a Glyptothek'. She was probably thinking of the Munich Glyptothek, a Greek-style temple Ludwig I designed in 1815 to house his Greek and Roman sculptures. 'I mean nothing more than 1, 2 or 3 rooms, of small size tho' good proportions, to hold a small number of pictures, and a dozen of casts of the Elgin and Vatican marbles', Jane continued. She suggested suitable architects and reproductions of classical sculptures, but Mary did not fulfil these orders, and the two-roomed glyptothek, temple or museum (it was called all three, but usually museum) was designed locally by the well-known convict architect James Blackburn. It is in fact more Roman than Greek in style, and resembles the Sessions House in Spilsby, Sir John's birthplace, far more than King Ludwig's building. Failing sculptures, Jane Franklin fell back on science: the museum was to contain examples of Tasmanian natural productions and books about Tasmania, and Jane thought it could be perfect of its kind.[36]

For the site, she bought land near her garden, Ancanthe, 'a lovely spot in the lower & more cheerful part of the valley'—now in suburban

Lenah Valley. She planned the museum carefully to sit in a hollow with a small hill behind, and Mount Wellington rising high in the background, a beautiful setting for an exquisite building. In March 1842 fifty people attended the laying of the foundation stone. The invitation was written in English, Latin, Greek, Italian, German and French[37]— definitely High Culture.

Eleanor enjoyed the day. 'Papa laid 1st stone of Tasmanian Museum at Ancanthe', she wrote in her diary:

> *Went to top of hill at U[pper] Ancanthe & dined. Large table cloth spread on ground, & 2 fallen trees as seats or backs of seats. After dinner in wh[ich] 'Success to Museum' was drunk, coffee stirred with parasols or other sticks & Hill named 'Nieka' by Mr Gunn & wine poured out. From native Nieka Hill. After wh[ich] returned home in cart much jolted ... All appeared pleased.[38]*

There is no clue as to how much the museum cost, but no expense seemed spared, and it was built of excellent-quality sandstone. Progress in building was slow, and Jane Franklin kept a supervisory eye on it, making Blackburn rectify any mistakes. The museum was finally opened in October 1843.[39]

Jane wrote nothing extant about the finished product, her jewel of a museum. We do not know whether she was pleased, if she thought her vision had been fulfilled. She was never one to rave about such things. But she remains the only woman in world history to build a glyptothek.

As well as her extensive efforts to encourage science and art, Jane Franklin improved Van Diemen's Land in a number of other ways. One was by encouraging the development of a sturdy yeomanry, the backbone of Britain. Ever since British colonisation began in the seventeenth century there had been discussion about how best to establish communities on distant soil. In the 1830s systematic settlement of free immigrants was the rage, with the British government trying the complicated Wakefield system in South Australia. In Van Diemen's Land, Lady Franklin tried her own version, 'my emigrant colony' as she called it. Many colonising schemes failed, but Jane Franklin's succeeded. She was no academic analyst and her colony did not get bogged down in theory; instead she was an excellent organiser, which proved more practically helpful to her settlers.

It was not a novel idea to divide land into allotments and lease it to farmers; many landowners in Van Diemen's Land did this, gaining rents and tenant labour. Jane Franklin gained little from her scheme, except the satisfaction of assisting worthy people and helping develop Van Diemen's Land, bringing lustre to Sir John's rule.[40]

It is doubtful if she arrived in Van Diemen's Land aiming to do this, but in mid-1837 she met John Price, who owned land by the Huon River. The area was known as a source of Huon pine, excellent for shipbuilding, and a handful of people lived at Port Cygnet on the east bank. In 1835 the area was surveyed, and land was put up for sale. By 1837 John Clark, the first permanent settler on the west bank, was farming there, and John Price bought land beside him, where the town of Franklin now stands. He started clearing it with convict labour.[41]

The son of a baronet, Price was welcome at Government House. The story went that, finding his land unprofitable, he managed to unload it on to Lady Franklin. She decided to help immigrants by renting it to them. In early 1838 she discussed 'my emigrant colony' with a government official who thought it would not work, so she decided to organise it herself. Soon she was renting land to two farmers. One, George Walter, came from Lincolnshire and the Franklins seem to have known him already. Jane helped the family in other ways, having the two daughters to stay in Government House, where Miss William-son gave them lessons to help them earn a living as governesses.[42]

In September 1838 Jane Franklin visited the Huon. Eleanor described how she, Mama and Mary landed: 'Heavy hail drove us to Clarke's place, where we dined under a shed. Rowed to a river. Mr Price made a fire and we warmed ourselves. Got home [their ship] about 6.'

The next day they visited George Walter's one-roomed bark hut. He had cleared land and was growing potatoes, turnips and carrots—'and it is no trifle clearing the thick bush about the Huon', wrote Eleanor. John Price showed them how to fell a tree, and they saw other huts—'up to our ankles in mud'.

On the third day they inspected Port Cygnet, across the river. 'Both today and yesterday Mama was talking in French that she might not be understood when she afterwards discovered that those about here were French' (a Frenchwoman convicted in England and transported). The visitors admired the neat bark huts, and when the settlers complained that meat was dear, Lady Franklin promised to send down cheaper provisions on the barge she was building for settlers, *Huon Pine*. Newspapers praised her work: 'utility and philanthropy combined'.[43]

From 1839 Jane Franklin extended her scheme. She bought more land, as did several men in her circle, probably strongly encouraged by her. Some was kept for a village reserve, and Jane had her own farm run by an employee, but she leased the rest to respectable free settlers, rent-free for the first year, on condition that they buy the land within seven years. In August 1839 she was busy interviewing candidates for allotments. She was so particular about their steadiness, ran a later reminiscence, that they had to be virtually teetotal. Christianity was essential too, but Jane did not want too many Methodists in case they swamped the Anglicans—though Methodists did form a bulwark against 'the encroachment of popery'. Occasional disputes among tenants were sent to her to solve, which she did competently. Otherwise everything went well. 'I was exceedingly gratified by this proof of the success of my schemes.'[44]

In October 1839 Jane and Eleanor visited the Huon again, taking the archdeacon with them to consecrate the chapel. They were pleased to see how much progress had been made. Land was cleared, huts were built, crops grown, timber sold, and the population numbered about sixty. When the Walters set up a Sunday School, Jane provided books and slates.[45]

Less successful was another immigrant, Horatio Tennyson (related to the poet), wild and indolent at home, who was sent to the colonies to see if anyone could improve him. He was Sir John's niece's brother-in-law, a connection remote enough that Jane could be excused from asking him to dinner (not with that reputation!). His family sent him to the Walters to learn agriculture. He was amiable, Jane told Mary, but wasted a couple of years shooting ducks, with no desire to work.[46] A poor specimen beside her hard-working yeomen.

The Huon settlement progressed well. Jane Franklin did not employ a manager but organised everything herself directly with the farmers, keeping a firm hand on the tiller. She continued to recruit settlers and employees, going in person to the immigration quarters (where newly arrived immigrants were housed) to invite married men to go to the Huon. In 1842, for example, she recruited the extended Geeves family of ten people to clear land for her, and took them herself to the Huon to start work. There was brisk demand for allotments and almost all were occupied. A town was laid out, and 'the spot is all activity and industry', a newspaper reported. Jane was thrilled when a settler visited her and pulled out crumpled notes to pay the first instalment of his rent, telling her of his progress.[47]

Jane visited her colony annually, and when the Franklins left the colony in 1843 they paid a farewell visit, taking the new bishop. As they landed at the township jetty, the chapel bell was ringing. They were welcomed, given refreshments, and entered the crowded chapel. The bishop conducted a service and christened four children, one named Jane Franklin Louisa. Jane presented her namesake her with a handsome Bible and prayer book.

The party stayed in the Clarks' cottage and dined on roast pork and plum pudding. The next day they explored the settlement, despite rain and mosquitoes. The neatest cottage, wrote Jane, consisted of a kitchen and parlour, a bedroom, and a third room containing a table and benches 'which I thought looked like a drinking room, but which Mr Coleman informed me was used for praying'. One tenant who owed rent 'had as usual such a woful, threadbare appearance that I could not find fault with him'. The inhabitants, now numbering over 120, seemed enthusiastic and hardworking.[48]

After the Franklins left the colony, the government named the small township Franklin in their honour. Potatoes and timber brought the settlers prosperity. Lady Franklin was highly praised for encouraging migrants in this way, and her memory was revered, 'a source of grateful remembrance among the Franklin population'.[49]

So far Jane Franklin's improvements to Van Diemen's Land were more or less typical of contemporary activity, but with her ever-active mind she branched out into novel activities as well. She had a horror of snakes, and was amazed that colonists did not try to get rid of them. People told her such an idea was foolish—and in fact, Van Diemonians did not seem particularly worried about snakes. No one mentions them as a problem, and, despite a dearth of local activity to report, in the Franklin period newspapers mentioned only two cases of snakebite. Both victims survived.

Undeterred, Jane Franklin set up her own scheme, paying a shilling for each snake killed. In a year she paid out over £600, for more than 12 000 snakes. But employers objected, as their assigned convicts pursued snakes instead of working; and the police, who had to handle paying the shillings, complained about the extra work. Officials wrote firmly that the scheme had to stop. Virtually everyone thought Lady Franklin's snake idea crazy, 'the most remarkable of her whims' according to her admirer James Calder; she even received an anonymous valentine comprising a red painted heart with a dead snake twisted through it.[50]

In later years, the activity for which Sir John Franklin was best remembered by Tasmanians was establishing the Hobart regatta—though it would not have happened without his wife's support, and she could have started the whole idea. But the regatta ended unhappily for the Franklins. In 1841 Jane presented a 'most elegant 5-oared gig' as a prize, but that year locals patronised the liquor booths too enthusiastically, and the Franklins withdrew their support of the event.[51] Locals ran it instead, and it still flourishes.

Not really an attempt to improve Van Diemen's Land, but a quirky activity that was part of Jane Franklin's wide range, was her purchase of Betsey Island. She thought she might build a country retreat on this starkly beautiful but barren and waterless islet at the mouth of the River Derwent, and bought it for £910 (its previous price a few months earlier was £600). The Franklins paid the island two, extremely expensive, visits.[52] This episode demonstrates an impractical, impulsive streak in Jane Franklin, which she usually kept under control.

Not only did Jane Franklin try to improve Van Diemen's Land, but she strongly defended it as the best colony possible. She was so insistent that Hobart was more impressive than Sydney (even then an unrealistic claim) that Sir John had to calm her down on her visit there: 'Bear in mind also my dear that Sydney people are jealous of VD Land'.[53]

What were Jane Franklin's motives for all her strenuous activities in Van Diemen's Land? As usual, she was aiming to fulfil her two ambitions. She lived life to the full, doing what she enjoyed: exploring (as seen in Chapter 10) and putting into practice schemes her fertile brain conjured up, such as trying to eradicate snakes and buying Betsey Island. At the same time, she wanted to boost her husband's career. She put much time and money into improving Van Diemen's Land, not because she liked the place—her writings show little if any fondness for the island or its inhabitants—but because it must be seen as successful under Sir John's rule. When she went to Sydney, she wrote, 'I shall be thinking of nothing so much as our own precious colony with whose prosperity Sir John's credit is also inseparably connected'.[54] Jane Franklin was continuing her fight to make her husband and everything he did a success. If it was sometimes an uphill battle, she only became more determined.

9

THE ABORIGINES

As their exploration penetrated into more and more areas of the world, Europeans came into contact with many other races. Their attitude varied from contempt to sympathy, but almost all believed that Europeans were superior. The 'great chain of being', a pre-evolutionary belief, ranked races, with Europeans at the top and everyone else in descending order according to their degree of observable 'civilisation'. Native people were seen as scientific curios, to be inspected, studied and taken back to Europe for display, with their weapons, ornaments and any other artefacts. Two seen as the most 'primitive' were the Tierra del Fuegians and the Tasmanians.

When British settlement began in Van Diemen's Land, the island was inhabited by the Tasmanian Aborigines. They were nomads, hunter-gatherers, and Europeans ranked them low in the great chain of being, as they had little by way of visible culture or possessions and Europeans placed no value on a society of nomads, however well they had adapted themselves to their environment. Though some British newcomers pitied the Aborigines, their arrival meant the end of the Aboriginal way of life. They took over Aboriginal land; with their hunting grounds and food supplies vanishing, the Aborigines retaliated; settlers fought back; and the uneven conflict ended in the Aborigines' defeat. Many British people saw this as inevitable: a 'primitive' race had to give way to a 'higher' one. A few were sympathetic. At a meeting of the Van Diemen's Land Society in 1830, George Frankland, the surveyor-general, suggested members study the Aborigines. British newcomers, he said:

> have heaped ruin and destruction upon those children of misfortune, the Aboriginal owners of the soil—a people naturally amiable and intelligent, who with better treatment on the part of those who have come in contact with them, might have been rendered valuable friends, and have continued a happy nation! ... surely no more glorious object could this Society propose to itself than that of acquiring a more intimate acquaintance with this much wronged people, with a view of ameliorating their condition, and of saving them from being extirpated from the face of that earth on which the Almighty had placed them![1]

This was a rare view, and even those like Frankland who sympathised with Aborigines did nothing practical to help them. Jane Franklin had a less exalted and more usual view, seeing native people as scientific curiosities. Wherever she travelled, she wanted to learn as much as she could about them, and watch them throwing boomerangs, dancing at corroborees, climbing tall trees and so on. She admired some aspects and criticised others, but her attitude was not particularly positive or negative—she was just intensely interested, as she was interested in all aspects of the new world.

By the time the Franklins arrived in Hobart, the remaining Tasmanian Aborigines had been moved to Wybalenna on Flinders Island, where white officials tried to turn them into Christian peasants. This was part of an Empire-wide move to 'protect' native people after they had been evicted from their country; but as so often happened, at Wybalenna government support, staff, finance and equipment were insufficient. The Aborigines pined for their homes and their traditional way of life, and deaths were frequent.

The attitude towards native people exemplified by Jane Franklin is distressing to modern eyes, as it was to contemporaries like Frankland. In 1841 a Dr Sinclair was a guest at a Government House dinner. 'I had some very interesting conversation in the evening ... with Dr. Sinclair about races of men', wrote Jane Franklin:

> We came to the Aborigines & I entirely agreed with him in his want of sympathy with those people who think it so very shocking that these inferior races of men should be gradually disappearing from the earth to make room for a higher race—I thought it was more as specimens of natural history that they were regretted than for any thing else.

Some people did not even show regret. Captain Smith, one of the commandants at Wybalenna, told her that 'when he had mentioned the sad state of things to M^r. Forster & how [the Aborigines] were dying off, M^r. F. replied that he thought it would be a very happy thing when they were all comfortably buried'. When Charles Darwin visited Van Diemen's Land in 1836, he commented that the island 'enjoys the great advantage of being free from a native population'.[2]

Jane and John Franklin were interested in the Tasmanian Aborigines, and were keen to visit Wybalenna. They arrived in January 1838, as the superintendent, George Robinson, recorded in his diary. It was difficult, as Robinson's wife was ill and he was desperate to make a good impression, for the sake of the settlement and his own career. As soon as the governor's ship was sighted, Robinson had everything cleaned, instructed the Aborigines to put on new clothes, and told the guards to present arms ('it had a good effect'). The vice-regal party arrived at 7 p.m., watched the Aborigines dance, visited their cottages, then slept in the Robinsons' bedrooms (poor Mrs Robinson!). The next day the party inspected the settlement. The Aborigines performed a mock battle, and the Franklins presented them with gifts of beads, knives, handkerchiefs and harmonicas. All went well except for a little fuss at the store, when Lady Franklin became indignant at something and walked off in a huff.

At 3 p.m. eighteen people (no Aborigines, of course) sat down to a grand dinner, which included a sucking pig, a goose, a leg of mutton and two fowls. Then the party climbed Grass Tree Hill. Jane Franklin insisted on going, though the others tried to persuade her not to. Robinson walked with her at a gentle pace, while Eleanor, Henry Elliot and botanist Ronald Gunn went ahead. They waited for the slower party, Robinson wrote, but started again as soon as they appeared. Irritated, Jane told them they were unkind—it reminded her of her father who did the same thing when she was a girl. 'The gentlemen took the hint and in future kept in the rear.' Gunn's version was that 'the accomplished lady displayed her usual energy, walking most cheerfully over trees and bushes in a manner which astonished and delighted me'.

It was getting dark and Sir John thought they should turn back, but 'Lady F had made up her mind on the subject and the only notice she took was to increase her speed'. They arrived at the summit at sunset. Halfway home, in the dark, they were met by Robinson's son and a party of Aborigines with flaming torches, which 'had a pleasing effect', wrote Robinson. 'The company were in high spirits.' The Franklins asked him to procure them an Aboriginal skull for their collection, which he did. Back at the settlement, at the Franklins' request the Aborigines sang, and at 10 p.m. the visitors left. Robinson thought the visit successful, with the Franklins and the Aborigines highly pleased with everything. He summed Jane Franklin up favourably: intelligent, benevolent, kind-hearted, observant and 'very persevering in all her undertakings'.[3]

As well as collecting relics of Aborigines, Jane Franklin was interested in collecting Aboriginal children. By the 1830s native children had been adopted by Europeans in many areas, for example when the *Beagle* officers took a Fuegian, Jemmy Button, back to London as a scientific curio, his name coming from the pearl button they paid for him. In Van Diemen's Land, the first Aboriginal child was taken by Europeans in 1804 shortly after settlement, and the practice continued. Settlers' motives were a mixture of gaining a servant, bestowing charity and trying to extend the benefits of civilisation.

Jane Franklin did not treat her Aboriginal protégés as servants, and there is no evidence that she wanted to help them. She did not like children generally, and showed little maternal or personal interest in them. Instead, she wanted to see what effect civilisation had on them. In London orang-outangs were being given English clothes and taught the English language to see how far they could be trained towards behaving like English people, and Jane Franklin's actions were uncomfortably similar.[4]

Later in 1838 Robinson visited Hobart, and Lady Franklin asked him to send her a black boy and examples of different snakes. Timemernidic, aged about nine, arrived in January 1839. He had been given the English name of Adolphus, and was the only son of Wymurric, a chief of a northwestern people. Timemernidic was, wrote Robinson, 'some what volatile in disposition'. He recommended that the boy's studies should not be prolix, though he should be kept in order and given athletic exercise for his health.[5] Jane Franklin called him Timeo, a shortened version of his Aboriginal name—she did not seem to approve of giving Aborigines European names. There is no account of what Timemernidic felt, taken from family and friends to the confines of Government House, where he was expected to speak English, do what he was told and learn an alien way of life, cut off from his own people and culture.

A few months later, when Jane Franklin was leaving for Port Phillip, she wrote to Eleanor, 'If you see Timeo, tell him I hope he is a good boy & that I shall find him improved—Tell him that I do not forget him'. Eleanor sometimes noted in her diary that she was teaching Timy, as she called him, and wrote in October that 'he is anxious to be able to read and write well. He waits at table and does other little things. But unfortunately he is very idle and obstinate, so that it is difficult to keep him to his duty, unless he is constantly watched'.

A month later Jane asked the headmaster of the orphan school to take him, because he was idle and disobedient, and might improve under better discipline. The headmaster was discouraging, saying he found it impossible to keep the other Aboriginal boys in the school indoors, or teach them anything.

When the French explorer Dumont d'Urville was dining at Government House, wrote Jane Franklin, 'Timeo was sent for—& the drawings of natives looked at, with the books'. But Timemernidic proved too unresponsive, so she sent him back to Flinders Island. 'You have heard of my unsuccessful experiment to civilize a native boy', she wrote to her sister Mary. 'If my servants had helped me better in the matter, I might perhaps have been more lucky'—so she blamed lack of supervision, rather than Timemernidic's nature. Later he worked as a seaman on a ship, where in 1842 the Franklins met him, aged twelve. Eleanor noted that he was very dirty but made himself useful, knew something about ropes, took his turn on watch and kept up his reading a little with the other boys; but she feared that when the novelty was over, Timemernidic would be tired of work. Jane wrote that the boy behaved pretty well, 'answered as if he understood' and seemed much improved in intelligence. Timemernidic later joined a vessel bound for England, and no more is known of him.[6]

Jane Franklin also wanted to try the civilising experiment on an Aboriginal girl. Robinson was going to send one with Timemernidic, but decided she was too old. He left Wybalenna in 1839 and the arrangements made are unknown, but in 1841 Mathinna was living in Government House. Jane later wrote:

Mathinna Wanganip Flinders [was] a little native girl whom I brought up for 2 or 3 years in Government House in VD Land. I could not learn her native name when she was sent to me, so I called her Mathinna after the name of a necklace made of shells which the natives string together & put on their neck. After some time I learnt the name of Mathinna's deceased mother, and then I added Wanganip to the little girl's name, and lastly, as she was still without a surname, I called her Flinders because she was born on the island of that name.[7]

In 1841 Jane obtained more information about Mathinna from a Flinders Island official:

The girl at Gov[t]. House, meaning Mathinna, is supposed to be about 6 years old. Her father's name is Palle, *of the Port Sorell Tribe, "considered wild by the other tribes"—The mother's name, Eveline of the same tribe—she died last Sept[br] or Oct[er] ... Mathinna has no brothers nor sisters alive.*

From this information and George Robinson's writings, it appears that Mathinna's parents were Wanganip (or Wongerneep) and Towterer, who were brought to Wybalenna in 1832 or 1833. Mathinna was born about 1835. Towterer died in 1837, and Wanganip married Palle, but died in 1840.[8]

As with Timemernidic and her other scientific interests, Jane Franklin did not become involved in day-to-day activities herself. Mathinna lived in the schoolroom area with Miss Williamson and seventeen-year-old Eleanor, who was given the task of educating her. In May 1841, writing to a cousin, Eleanor said she must end her letter 'as my little pupil Methinna (a native girl) is waiting for her lesson, and every few minutes interrupting me to shew me her work'. Eleanor also noted that Mathinna dictated an unprompted letter to her stepfather Palle, back at Flinders Island:

I am good little girl, I have pen & ink cause I am good little girl. I do love my father. I have got a doll & shift & petticoat. I read My Father. I thank thee for sleep. I have got red frock. Like my father come here to see my father. I have got sore feet & shoes & stockings & am very glad.[9]

'Said one day I do love my God', added Eleanor. 'She is affect[ion][ate] & intelligent.' At least in Eleanor she had a kind and warm-hearted carer. Eleanor arranged a European playmate for Mathinna, and John Gell, a frequent visitor at Government House, described her as 'a very nice intelligent child and a great favourite. She … has the manners of a wellborn child.'[10]

Mathinna adapted to European civilisation more compliantly than Timemernidic. When Jane Franklin saw Timemernidic in 1842 she noted that, though he had developed, 'he is vastly inferior however to Mathinna in intelligence & sweetness of expression—& is much blacker in complexion than Mathinna who appears to us to be daily growing more copper-coloured as she advances in civilization' (another uncomfortable observation for modern readers). The child certainly encountered many European institutions. John Gell even asked her for a subscription to some worthy cause, which she gave, so she must have had pocket money.[11]

Jane Franklin had little to do with Mathinna, seldom mentioning her in her writing, though she did take her to visit the wife of a former superintendent at Wybalenna. She did not sound particularly fond of her (but neither did she of Eleanor, Sophy or any other female in Government House). However, she was interested in how Mathinna was developing, and paid Thomas Bock to paint her portrait, writing 'She is dressed in a scarlet frock with a black leather girdle which sets off her naked black arms & legs to great advantage'. Jane sent the portrait to London, and wrote to her sister Mary:

> Mathinna's portrait is extremely like, but the figure is too large & tall—she looks there like a girl of 12, but is only 7—the attitude is exactly hers, & she always wears the dress you see her in—when she goes out, she wears red stockings & black shoes—I think you will find people much interested in this portrait & the hair—She is one of the remnant of a people about to disappear from the face of the earth.

Jane sent Mary some of Mathinna's 'woolly hair', as well as a Port Phillip squirrel. Later she instructed Mary to ask Count Strzelecki to have Mathinna's portrait engraved:

I have given him the portraits of two Tasmanian natives for the same purpose, they were quite savages; Mathinna's will show the influence of some degree of civilization upon a child of as pure a race as they, and who in spite of every endeavour, and though entirely apart from her own people, retains much of the unconquerable nature of the savage; extreme uncertainty of will and temper, great want of perseverance and attention, little if any, self controle, and great acuteness of the senses and facility of imitation.[12]

Eleanor was more positive, telling her cousin that 'our little native girl … is improving, I think, though it will probably be a long time before she becomes quite civilised'. John Gell explained why: 'the little one proved a good girl, though her tempestuous passions sometimes shook the order of the schoolroom at Government House.' John Franklin loved strolling with his daughter in the garden before breakfast, continued Gell. 'As they walked together, Methinna would be darting about, or climbing the trees with hand and toe, native fashion, peering down with wild bright eyes out of the lofty foliage upon the two best friends she had in the world.'[13] He did not include Jane Franklin in this category.

So Mathinna received kindness and attention at Government House but, like Timemernidic, she was expected to adopt European ways, with no concessions to her heritage. It was not only Jane Franklin who treated her as a scientific specimen. Robert Crooke described Lady Franklin's room as

more like a museum or menagerie than the boudoir of a lady. Snakes, toads, stuffed birds and animals, weapons of savages, specimen of wood and stone, and last, though not least, a juvenile lubra [Aboriginal woman] arrayed in bright scarlet, being the staple articles of furniture.[14]

No other contemporary mentions Mathinna; not George Boyes in his long association with Government House, no visitors in their diaries, no newspapers. Perhaps because she lived in the schoolroom they did not see her—no one mentions Eleanor much, either—but her presence was not kept a secret. Obviously she was not a fascinating novelty worthy of comment.

In 1869, in a romanticised, sentimental and often incorrect article, 'Old Boomer' described Mathinna as 'a princess of the purest of lineage'. She was, 'when I saw her last', a tall, graceful girl,

> *very erect, with a quick, thoughtless, or perhaps, thinking, if you please, toss about her head now and then. Her hair still curled short as before, but seemed to struggle into length, and was blacker than black, bright, glossy, and oh! so beautiful! Her features were well chiseled, and singularly regular, while her voice was light, quick, yet sighed like, and somewhat plaintive. Whenever she spoke to you, her thoughts seemed to be somewhere else.*[15]

This reminiscence, unreliable as it is, is the only surviving description of Mathinna.

In February 1843 the Franklins visited Launceston. Mathinna was left behind in the charge of a visitor, who refused to have anything to do with her, 'or at least as little as possible—the child is also very troublesome & disobedient', wrote Jane Franklin.[16] Mathinna was aged eight.

By now the Franklins knew they would soon be returning to England, and in July Jane sent Mathinna to the orphan school. There is no contemporary comment on this. Old Boomer gave the only explanation in 1869: Lady Franklin wanted to take Mathinna to England, but was warned by Dr Bedford that as the girl had a weak chest (the first mention of this) and was perhaps inclined to be consumptive, it might lead to fatal results. It might be true; at any rate, it has been repeated ever since. But the Franklins might also have considered it better to leave Mathinna among her own people, or wondered what they would do with her in England. In a letter Jane Franklin wrote about Mathinna in 1844, she took it for granted that she should have left the girl in Van Diemen's Land.[17]

Fanny Griffin, Jane's eldest sister
(Edward Simpkinson)

A typical silkweaver's house in Spitalfields:
three windows wide, with the shop on the
ground floor, two floors of living quarters,
and the weaving looms on the top floor
(James Alexander)

A sampler sewn by Jane Griffin as a child—not very neat, with a mistake in the alphabetical
order. Jane never did like sewing (National Trust of Australia (Tasmania) Runnymede,
New Town; photography Kim Eidjenberg)

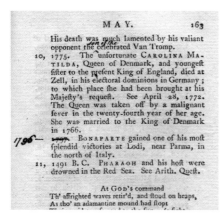

This correction to the schoolbook in Jane's writing shows at least some level of intellectual activity (Brian Rieusset)

Mary Griffin, acknowledged as Jane's pretty sister (Edward Simpkinson)

John Franklin, naval hero (Edward Simpkinson)

Jane Franklin's handwriting, in a stern letter to Kezia Hayter, 1841. 'I presume still to think that you are wrong in your view of things …' (University of Tasmania Library, Royal Society Special Collection, http://eprints.utas.edu.au/8434)

Jane Franklin by Thomas Bock, chalk on paper, 1838 (Queen Victoria Museum and Art Gallery, Launceston)

Wybalenna, the Aborigines' residence on Flinders Island, which Jane Franklin visited in 1838 and 1843 (Tasmanian Archive and Heritage Office)

Frenchman's Cap by W.C. Piguenit, showing the terrain the Franklins visited on their West Coast journey (Tasmanian Archive and Heritage Office)

Port Arthur, superficially charming, as painted in 1848 by Jane's nephew Frank Simpkinson (Tasmanian Archive and Heritage Office)

Jane Franklin's carrying chair, a dining chair with an added footrest and rings for the bearers' poles (Tasmanian Museum and Art Gallery)

Crossing the Picton by W.C. Piguenit: how Jane Franklin crossed most of the rivers in her West Coast journey (Tasmanian Archive and Heritage Office)

Beautiful but barren, Jane Franklin's purchase of Betsey Island, centre back in picture (Tasmanian Archive and Heritage Office)

John Montagu, 'that snake in the grass, sleek, smooth, & slippery' (from *Sir John Franklin in Tasmania 1837–1843* by Kathleen Fitzpatrick, Melbourne University Press, 1949)

Watched by an enormous crowd, Jane Franklin's ship *Prince Albert* leaves the docks at Aberdeen in 1851 to search for John Franklin. It flies the French flag in honour of Joseph Bellot, its second-in-command (*Illustrated London News*, 1851)

Jane's ship *Isabel* searching for John Franklin in Baffin Bay, 1852
(*Illustrated London News*, 1852)

Jane's final Search ship *Fox* 'steaming out of the rolling pack' in the
Canadian Arctic (*Illustrated London News*, 1859)

McClintock's men dismantling the cairn which contained the only written
record of the Franklin expedition (*Illustrated London News*, 1859)

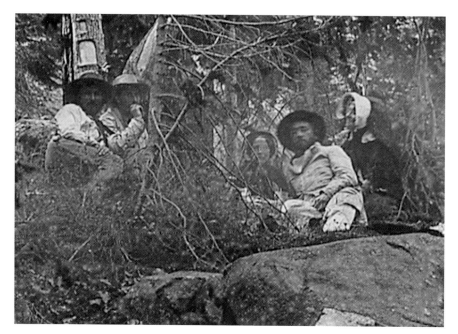

Jane Franklin (far right) triumphant, having been carried up to Moss Rock in Yosemite National Park, 1861. Sophy, centre, looks rather tired—she had to walk (George Eastman House, International Museum of Photography and Film)

Perhaps the only commemoration of Jane Franklin in Britain, on the outskirts of Spilsby—noted as 'Birthplace of Sir John Franklin' (James Alexander)

The Franklins left in late 1843, and in February 1844 Mathinna was returned to the Aboriginal settlement on Flinders Island, probably one of three unnamed Aboriginal children the new superintendent, Joseph Milligan, took with him from the orphan school. The following year she was reported to be attending the scripture class and learning her tasks. There was dissension among white staff at the settlement, and either as a result, or simply in Mathinna's interest, in 1847 Mrs Jeanneret, wife of the superintendent, asked the governor's wife, Caroline Denison, to help 'poor Mathinna', now aged twelve. She had no friend or relative to care for her '& appears to be particularly the object of the vindictiveness of those from whom these poor children have suffered so much ill treatment'—the other white staff. They denied the charge. Mrs Jeanneret wrote to the bishop's wife, saying that she had been caring for Mathinna, but other staff ordered the girl away. She was wretched, dirty and miserable, and afflicted with some unnamed disease. The catechist had pushed her down 'and ordered her to go whence she came', then pulled her up by the ear, even though she was carrying a little child at the time. Mathinna started several letters to John Gell asking for help, but did not finish them.[18]

By this time the Aboriginal establishment was being moved to Oyster Cove, south of Hobart. The four girls, including Mathinna, were sent to the orphan school in Hobart 'for protection against persons who have made them the unconscious instruments of fighting', and to educate and train them in preparation for the time when the older Aborigines died and the girls joined the wider community. Governor Denison and his wife took an interest in the Aborigines, and at Christmas 1848 invited fourteen, including Mathinna, to festivities at New Norfolk. The Denisons shook hands with them, and helped serve their lunch of beef and plum pudding, with fruit and lollipops for the children, and tobacco for adults. The Aborigines played rounders and swung on a rope, while the white inhabitants of New Norfolk crowded round to watch—politely, Caroline Denison wrote. She thought the guests thoroughly enjoyed themselves.

A fortnight later the Denisons visited the Aboriginal children at the orphan school. The four girls were happy to see them, showed them a native dance, and sang an Aboriginal song and an English hymn. The matron said she treated them with indulgence, allowing them to follow their own devices more than other children, because they could only be brought into civilised habits by gradual degrees. But the Denisons' interest petered out, and there is no more mention of Mathinna in Caroline Denison's diary.[19]

Mathinna spent four years at the orphan school, which might have been happy enough, but in 1851, when she was fifteen, the authorities decided 'Mitthynna' was too old for the school, and should be removed to Oyster Cove or taken into domestic service 'should anyone be willing to receive her'. No one was, apparently, so she went to Oyster Cove. This is the last definite mention of Mathinna.[20] Her name does not appear in any later record of the Aborigines. This might indicate that the authorities were embarrassed or ashamed at the fate of Lady Franklin's protégée under their care. Jane Franklin herself is not known to have enquired after Mathinna.

There are barely any records from Oyster Cove until 1855, when a list of Aborigines living there does not include Mathinna or any young woman of her age (about twenty). The station was a sad, dilapidated place, where the Aborigines received few advantages. The superintendent until 1855, Jane Franklin's protégé Joseph Milligan, who must have known of Mathinna from his frequent visits to Government House, apparently did nothing for her despite Lady Franklin's kindness to him.

Mathinna's exact fate is not known, but she died young. Either of two recorded deaths at Oyster Cove could refer to her. In their despair many Aborigines took to drink, and in 1855 the visiting magistrate noted that four of them were helplessly drunk at the nearby Kingston inn. This was a dangerous habit. Three years earlier in 1852, Aminia (or Amenia, or Armenia), 'a Native Aboriginal woman', became drunk at a local inn, and while walking home fell on the road with her face in a puddle. She was found dead the next morning.[21] Was this young woman Mathinna, who would have been sixteen or seventeen at the time? Aminia is never mentioned anywhere else, not at the orphan school or on Flinders Island.

The other possibility is that an unnamed Aborigine who died in 1857 of an unspecified cause was Mathinna. Omitting the name of the deceased would fit the cover-up theory—the records name all other Aborigines who died after 1855. This would mean that Mathinna was also omitted from the 1855 list, and would agree with a tradition that she was 22 when she died. But whatever the date and cause, she did die young, in sad circumstances. Old Boomer wrote that at Oyster Cove 'she fell into the habits of the rest'—drunkenness—'amongst sawyers, splitters, and characters of the deepest depravity'. One night she was missing, and a search found that she 'had died, abandoned by every virtue, and—in the river': suicide. Another writer agreed that Mathinna was 'found drowned'.[22]

The result of Jane Franklin's intervention in Mathinna's life was negative. As an Aborigine in Tasmania at this time, her life would have been difficult in any case. But Mathinna also had a challenging two years in Government House where, though she was treated with kindness, she had to conform to an alien way of life in which because of her race she would never be accepted. It was long enough to alienate her from her own people, and back in the Aboriginal community she had problems fitting in. From the age of nine she had no effective protector. Jane Franklin can never have thought of her intervention from Mathinna's point of view, since for the girl there could be no positive result.

From the 1850s George Frankland's attitude of pity and sympathy for Aborigines became more common, and it was usual to depict the Aborigines' fate as tragic, hunted to extinction by brutal whites. Mathinna's story was seen to embody the whole terrible tale. It gained fame in 1869 when Old Boomer published his reminiscence. (He was apparently John Graves, author of the song 'D'ye ken John Peel', a man described as not only inventive but erratic and eccentric, confined for a time in the lunatic asylum—an unreliable historical source.) The story was widely reprinted, and James Bonwick included it in his 1870 book, *The last Tasmanians*, for decades the standard history of the Aboriginal race. 'No story can be sadder', he wrote of Mathinna's life.

Mathinna's story was seen as having great significance. As it was summed up in 1879: 'Mathinna, the unfortunate favourite of Lady Franklin, who, after her patroness left the colony, passed through so many sad trials, which terminated in her committing suicide, by throwing herself into the river Derwent, where she was drowned.' This sadness typified the whole Aboriginal experience, the young, innocent girl with such a tragic end. As well, Bonwick used Mathinna's progress at Government House to show that Aborigines were 'capable of reaching as high a tone of civilisation as the more favorably circumstanced Caucasian race'. More prosaically, he used her fate to illustrate the evils of alcohol.

No one criticised Jane Franklin for removing Mathinna from her own people. Old Boomer depicted 'dear old Lady Franklin'—whatever would she have thought of that—as kind, giving Mathinna 'the tender care of one who had always proved far more than a mother to her'. The weak chest story was seen as a perfectly adequate reason for leaving Mathinna behind, and there was no suggestion that she was abandoned, or that better arrangements should have been made for her care. The villains of the story were the bad company into which she fell at Oyster Cove, 'the untutored of her own race, the ignorant and vicious of ours', who led her astray.[23]

Over the last century and a half, Mathinna's story has been told and retold, in history, fiction, verse, dance, even light installation. The roles of both Jane and John Franklin have been questioned, and the villains are now the white usurpers, part of their wider guilt in destroying the Aboriginal community.

10

MOUNT WELLINGTON, SYDNEY AND BEYOND

The myriad activities already described might have been enough to fill an ordinary woman's life, but Jane Franklin was no ordinary woman. Relishing travel, she made the most of her years in the antipodes by seeing all she could. She made many short trips around Van Diemen's Land, but also made four major trips, all rugged and demanding. She always came back for more, but did take a different companion each time—Sophy, Eleanor, her governess Miss Williamson, and finally Sir John.

Only three weeks after the Franklins landed in Van Diemen's Land they went on a tour of the island. There were plenty of new sights, but also official functions, addresses, welcomes and so on, not the sort of travel Jane Franklin enjoyed. Her diary survives for her next visit, at Easter, to the penal station at Port Arthur. She noted down everything, starting with interesting items pointed out on the way by John Montagu, the colonial secretary: a bank where fishermen could catch several dozen flathead in an hour, a white stone house rented by a man called Johnson who was building a boat, a red public house kept by a twice-widowed woman both of whose husbands had drowned ...[1] She was interested in everything.

Captain Booth, the commandant at Port Arthur, was amazed by the visitors. After minutely examining everything at the coal mines, even a jetty—surely Jane Franklin was the only contemporary woman in Australia, perhaps the world, who would minutely examine a jetty— the party continued to Port Arthur. Booth recorded torrential rain, but Jane Franklin did not mention it. She never did mind this sort of physical discomfort, though she hated heat. In Port Arthur, she wrote, 'my Ld wanted fireplace—he is <u>so</u> noted for his great fires that among other directions given by signals to announce us was <u>not to have too large</u> fires, knowing my dislike to heated rooms'. So Sir John gave up his beloved roaring fire to please his wife. At Port Arthur she noted possibly her most trivial fact: that Booth's dog's grandfather was called Billy, which had no relevance to anything.

On Good Friday she examined the prisoners' huts, tasted their soup, inspected the school and visited the boys' establishment. On Saturday, despite blustering winds and frequent squalls of hail which kept Montagu indoors, she inspected the workshops, stores, solitary cells, water supply, gardens and dockyard. Not everyone would inspect a water supply in a squall of hail: Booth was surprised. This blistering pace continued, and the only negative note in Jane's diary bemoaned not the weather but Lieutenant Steel indulging in coarse conversation at dinner. She decided she had a headache and retired to apply leeches—but must have left tactfully, for Booth wrote in his diary that 'a more agreeable or pleasant visit could not have been passed'.[2]

In December 1837 Jane Franklin did something few white women had done: she climbed Mount Wellington. Dominating Hobart, this 1274-metre mountain is a long, hard, steep climb. The first European at the summit was explorer George Bass in 1798, and the first European woman was Salome Pitt in 1810, said to have been accompanied by an Aboriginal girl, Miss Story. Later climbers included naturalist Charles Darwin, whose first attempt failed due to dense vegetation. In 1871 climbing Mount Wellington was still described as a heroic feat.

By 1837 there was a rough track up the mountain, and a cairn and flagstaff at the top. Apparently in November Miss Wandley, whom Jane

Franklin knew well, climbed to the summit to see where her fiancé had drowned at distant Southport. Perhaps this inspired Jane, for on 14 December her party made the ascent: herself, Mary Maconochie, thirteen-year-old Eleanor and four gentlemen, including the surveyor-general, George Frankland.

The party left Government House at 4.30 a.m. on a calm, sunny morning, and travelled to the end of the Lenah Valley road, at the base of the mountain. Here they began their 'delightful walk', almost straight up, 1000 metres. From the end of the track, near today's Big Bend, they rock-hopped to the summit, over boulders which seemed impractical for the female foot, wrote Frankland, but were easier than the small, loose stones further down. 'The courage and activity of the ladies were however beyond all praise', and they reached the summit at 11.30 after six hours' climbing. Everyone admired the wonderful view, and sat down to a 'merry breakfast' of cold chicken, tongue, bread, tea and claret, enjoying looking at the whole of Hobart through the handle of the teapot. Couches were placed under awnings and the ladies had a siesta, while the gentlemen set up a camp.

The travellers rose at 2.30 a.m. to see sunrise from the summit. Jane Franklin sat on the cairn with a map, and had someone point out every feature. At 5.30 a.m. they began the four-hour descent. Inspired, another group also containing three ladies set off the next day, but some of the party became lost, and were only found after a terrible night with nothing to eat for 36 hours.[3]

Climbing Mount Wellington was a major achievement—and Jane Franklin was 46, called 'elderly' at the time. Her description of the climb does not survive, and no one mentioned what the ladies wore. A long skirt sounds impractical, but in 1837 she certainly did not wear trousers by themselves. A newspaper hinted that ladies in the second party wore culottes, and Jane had worn trousers under her skirts when climbing mountains around the Mediterranean. Perhaps in 1837 she wore some form of legwear beneath her skirt. In 2012 Chris Goodacre and Jean Elder re-created the walk, wearing long skirts. They reported that skirts down to the ground were impossible as the feet caught in them, but skirts that cleared the shoes were quite comfortable and practical, except on very steep parts when the wearer had to hoist them up. A painting of a Hobart street in 1843 showed women wearing skirts clear of their shoes, so this is probably the answer. Chris and Jean finished the walk in three hours, with great respect for Jane Franklin—it was steep and tiring, they reported, even on a good track with easier gradients (the Old Hobartians track, for bushwalkers—her track straight up has been abandoned).

Frankland published a theatrical description of the walk, and a few people criticised it. All this fuss: had no one ever climbed Mount Wellington before? As for including the ladies' names: 'it is not in the broad glare of public notoriety that woman finds the sphere the best suited for the culture of her virtues, or the exhibition of her thousand graces.'[4] But no one criticised the actual climb, and the fact that other ladies copied Jane Franklin indicates admiration for her achievement (and that of Mary Maconochie and Eleanor, but they were given no credit).

Early in 1838 Jane Franklin made another trip north, and in December a trip south by boat. She intended to go to Port Davey on the west coast, but bad weather meant she had to turn back halfway, at Recherche Bay. 'This evening a great swell, and we were sick,' wrote Eleanor frankly. Jane and Eleanor enjoyed looking round Recherche Bay, with Jane particularly interested in the French garden begun by d'Entrecasteaux fifty years earlier. Intensive search did not find it, but they did see marks where he had nailed inscriptions to trees. The inscriptions had probably been carried off by Aborigines, Jane thought; she in turn carried off some of the nails. It was on this trip that she made the rare admission that there was nothing interesting to do or see—though only because it meant she had not missed anything when she was confined to her cabin with toothache.[5]

There were also trips to other parts of Van Diemen's Land, and in 1839 a party landed on Bruny Island in heavy surf. Eleanor had a teenager's eye for entertainment. As they landed, she wrote, 'Capt

M[oriarty] carrying Mama tumbled & she fell on top of him. This excited great mirth.'6

In 1839 Jane Franklin made an extremely ambitious trip: from Melbourne to Sydney overland, the first white woman to do so. The track had only just been opened, and it was still considered adventurous, even for men. Jane's party consisted of herself, Sophy Cracroft, Henry Elliot, Captain Moriarty (the Hobart port officer and a skilled bush traveller), Dr Hobson (a young naturalist) and three servants, Mr and Mrs Snashall and a convict driver. Sir John could not go, as he could not take the time off from his work.

The party left Launceston in March, and had a busy two days in Melbourne. Jane saw all the sights, met everyone of note, gained advice about the trip, wrote pages of detail about the new town, and escaped from callers by going for drives. George Robinson, now Protector of Aborigines at Port Phillip, organised the best corroboree he had ever seen, and was annoyed when the Franklin party arrived late, missing the first half. Fortunately the rest was excellent: painted men, naked but for apron-like bundles round their loins and ruffs of gum branches round their ankles, singing and dancing, and stretching their legs as far apart as possible, making them 'quiver with great rapidity'. 'Indescribable', wrote Jane Franklin, having described it.

To her ire, Melbourne's merchants presented her with a welcoming address, to which she had to compose a reply. Her party thought the whole thing ludicrous and behaved badly at the presentation, Henry Elliot making intentional blunders when reading out the reply, and others trying to look serious and obviously failing.7 Their reaction at having to associate with middle-class merchants?

Everything looked promising for the trip: 'as usual all difficulties vanished on a near approach', Jane wrote cheerfully—her husband rightly thought she was 'not a person to be overcome by ordinary difficulties'. They left Melbourne on 6 April with a heavy waggon for luggage (including Jane's bedstead) and a light though jolty one for the ladies. The gentlemen rode and the ladies shared a pony, and everyone walked at some stage. The scenery was monotonous, but every evening they reached a station (ranch), although the houses were so rough the party preferred to camp. The ladies had a tent, the men slept under tarpaulins, and a stretcher served as a table. There are no details about sanitary arrangements, which must have been challenging, especially for the women when they had their menstrual periods, in the bush with limited water. The whole party must have become grubby and smelly, but such things were never mentioned in diaries or letters.

Each morning they left camp about nine o'clock, travelled about 15 miles (24 kilometres), then set up camp in the afternoon. The gentlemen went shooting to gain birds both for the pot and as specimens; Hobson tried to teach Jane Franklin how to skin birds, but they gave up after one lesson. Dinner included not just ducks and swan, but cockatoos and magpies. Then Jane wrote up her voluminous diary; a typical day, 27 April, has 928 words, and there were tens of thousands altogether. They had the occasional rest day but travelled on Sundays, which would have horrified Sir John. In fact no religious observance was mentioned, which would have horrified him even more.[8]

On the fifth night they reached the Goulburn River, near modern Seymour. The scenery became more varied but also more dangerous, and they feared Aboriginal attacks. The travellers were alert for suspicious noises or shadows, but nothing happened, and the Aborigines they met were friendly. It was just as well, for they were not a practical party. One evening they were still travelling after dark in three groups, and Hobson became lost. A gunshot guided him to the others. Another night it rained so hard that the camp was awash, and Moriarty and Elliot carried the ladies to safety. Jane Franklin hints at elegant chivalry in her diary, but Hobson describes how he laughed at the other men staggering along with 'sundry and divers groans and puffs'. During the night Lady Franklin was alarmed by 'what she imagined was a shot succeeded by a cooey'. She woke the camp, and 'to quiet her Ladyship' the men fired guns and set up a sentry. Her alarm seems understandable—they were at the spot where shepherds had been murdered the year before.[9]

Jane enjoyed questioning anyone she met, from landed gentlemen to barefoot settlers. Once they camped near a hut belonging to a family called Smyth. Despite bad reports, Sophy and Jane visited them. Mrs Smyth, 'a disagreeable looking woman', did ask them to sit down, and Jane asked her about her life, learning many facts: the family moved there for the water; they had about 2500 sheep; her husband was away buying cattle at £3 a head ... Jane gave the little girl some biscuits, and Mrs Smyth softened enough to give her three eggs. 'Gents considered this quite a triumph over her ill humours.' It was also a practical victory, for the eggs were welcome. The party had run out of potatoes; the butter was uneatable except for strong stomachs; their Melbourne bread lasted only ten days, though the men so dreaded its replacement, hard biscuit, that they picked out the last bits untouched by mould. Finally only damper, rice and macaroni remained. Jane Franklin did not seem to mind, but was annoyed when Snashall broke her glass, and she had to drink from a pannikin.[10]

There were some dangerous incidents. Once a wild bull charged into the camp. The ladies and Henry Elliot took shelter while Moriarty hit it with a club, bringing it to its knees. Then Sophy's horse bolted and threw her. She landed on her head and Hobson admired her courage as he treated her for concussion, but Jane Franklin showed scant sympathy. Similarly, when Mrs Snashall was thrown off the carriage, Jane merely wrote, 'She fell most neatly & comfortably & was only bruised in the knees.' Travelling with Jane could be tough, though she herself never complained, ignoring for example the extreme cold overnight and oppressive daytime heat which irked Hobson.[11]

In these conditions, tempers frayed. Moriarty was cross with Hobson for wandering off; Hobson found Jane Franklin demanding; Mrs Snashall was out of sorts. At one breakfast, Hobson rose from a bench and Elliot, at the other end, was tipped off. Jane Franklin told Hobson firmly that when a man had university degrees and was married, it was time to leave off practical jokes. Sophy fell in love with

Henry Elliot, whose reaction is not clear—but it was a difficult situation, cooped up together. The journey had to continue. On 19 April they reached the Murray River, fortunately low and easily forded. They enjoyed a rest day, 'amusing' themselves looking at local Aborigines. Hobson described how a man climbed trees to look for possums clad, in Lady Franklin's presence, 'in shirt and jacket only!!!!' This did not feature in her description.[12]

From here on, settlement gradually increased. At Mullingandra there was a shop, where the party bought sugar and Snashall got drunk. Jane Franklin threatened to leave him at Goulburn, and he promised to reform. On 24 April came the 'wonderful sight' of another cart, the first for weeks, and even more astonishing was a smart conveyance containing three gentlemen who told them of arrangements to meet them at Yass. Jane did not welcome these 'signs of outskirts of civilization'. However, at Tarcutta she enjoyed the attractive scenery and visiting Aborigines, seeing them throw boomerangs.[13]

On 30 April civilisation struck. At a station, their host provided bread and a plum tart, and Jane Franklin accepted his offer of accommodation, her first bed since 5 April. It was a mistake: fleas made it a nightmare. Next day Mr Hardy, the local police magistrate took them into Yass in his carriage. There Jane changed from the older woman who had to be humoured into Lady Franklin, the governor's wife. She was honoured, introduced to the chief inhabitants, invited to stay in houses. These were not necessarily an improvement on tents. The Hardys gave up theirs to the party, but played with their four cats while they all had dinner together, and told Jane that two slept with them every night. Jane was not a cat-lover. 'We were very uncomfortable in our bedroom which was dirty, full of fleas, crowded & untidy—door never opened for a moment but in came the cats & when shut out came in at window.' Next day, 'plagued with cats coming in at breakfast'.[14] How attractive her cat-free tent must have seemed.

Most houses were comfortable, even luxurious, and borrowed carriages made for smoother travelling than the jolty cart. At Goulburn they sold their camping goods and split up. Jane Franklin, Sophy

Cracroft and Henry Elliot visited the Illawarra, which they found very interesting, with grand scenery, people, towns and buildings. 'Every body has been kind beyond example', Jane wrote to John.

On 18 May they arrived at Sydney before they were expected, and stayed at Government House with Sir George and Lady Gipps. Jane liked them, at first: Elizabeth Gipps was quiet and gentle, and Sir George, though brusque, was willing to talk to her on intellectual topics. She enjoyed sightseeing, shopping for books and maps, and meeting the 'best people'. At a bazaar where people bought rhymes about themselves, hers began 'Behold another Sheba comes', comparing her to that great biblical traveller. Jane claimed this was embarrassing, but seemed rather pleased (who would not be?). At one dinner she recorded laughing out loud, a rare event. Handing round the cheese, Snashall could not make one guest see it, so held it right in front of the guest's nose and kept it there. Jane Franklin and Sir George both burst into laughter.[15]

Sir John wanted her to return home, but she found many justifications for staying. The Gippses were organising dinners and it would be rude to miss them; her health was better; above all, by staying longer she could help her husband by finding out information for him. These all have the ring of rationalisations; she was thoroughly enjoying herself, but could not admit this as a motive for staying. Then Elizabeth Gipps fell ill, and surely Jane should have left; but she stayed, helping Sir George receive guests at the Queen's Birthday ball despite having a headache. As often when ill, she felt badly done by, something of a martyr—there was no dinner, she had to eat from a tray, her help was not appreciated.[16]

She continued to expect others to put themselves out for her. After nine days in Sydney, she, Sophy and Mrs Snashall boarded a steamer for Port Stephens. The cabin was too stuffy for sleep, so she had the servants bring mattresses on deck and erect a tarpaulin. Rain started, so she and Sophy went to the cabin and made Mrs Snashall give them her bed. Jane could not sleep for the smell of bilge water, so when the rain stopped she had the servants bring another mattress on deck—in the middle of the night. Later she invited herself to stay with a family where the wife had given birth just four days earlier.[17] But these were common upper-class attitudes.

Invited to breakfast at Newcastle, Jane was alarmed (her word) to see an Indian lady behind the tea tray, the wife of the commandant—a member of the elite, whom she had to treat as an equal. Having to dine with a drunken gentleman was merely deplorable, not so challenging to the social order. After a week they returned to Government House in Sydney, where Elizabeth Gipps was still ill. There were more dinners, sightseeing and telling people how superior Van Diemen's Land was, and then they left for an excursion to the Hawkesbury River region with the bishop. This was interesting, but relations in her party were becoming strained. Once more they arrived back in Sydney before they were expected, on both occasions, wrote Jane, because of

> the discontent expressed or implied rather by [my] companions who made me feel that they were being dragged along on my account & that in their eyes I was never satisfied with wander-ing—I felt with them as if an apology were necessary for all I did & as if I did not dare avow that curiosity had one thing to do with it.[18]

In Sydney they were going to stay with the bishop, but he had illness in the house and told them they could not come. So it was back to Government House, though Jane felt they were not wanted, and Eliza-beth Gipps treated her coldly.[19] She was in an awkward position, on bad terms with her party and hosts—but she could have gone to a hotel.

The Gippses put their best foot forward, and for a while all went well. Jane Franklin often went out, shopping, climbing a lighthouse with Captain Moriarty; the Gipps organised more dinners, with one guest surprised to find that Lady Franklin was 'by no means the Amazon proposed, but a gentle affable woman'. However, she again outstayed her welcome. Wanting to see Elizabeth Gipps, Jane tapped on her door. Sir George growled, 'What?' and she went in. He was lying on the bed, fully dressed (fortunately), and said she could come in if she did not mind seeing him there. Elizabeth was embarrassed—a gentleman should stand up when a lady enters the room.[20]

Worse, Jane took out the Gipps' carriage in the rain, and the upholstery was badly damaged. Sir George was furious. They ignored each other at dinner. Jane felt ashamed, but did not have the courage to apologise, 'for fear of [his] repulsive or offensive manner'. She did try with Elizabeth Gipps, who said it was very bad indeed. Jane started to cry, Elizabeth softened and hoped she would not distress herself, and Jane returned to the dining room with red eyes. She and Sir George continued to ignore each other. There was also a problem with Mrs Snashall, who was too ill for the voyage to Hobart. The Gippses offered to care for her in Government House, but after an enormous amount of fuss Jane Franklin took her to hospital.

Elizabeth Gipps, who had obviously talked sternly to herself about courtesy to a guest, made peace with her and, perhaps after a connubial talk, so did Sir George. Jane was about to leave, which helped. At evening prayers Sir George asked the Almighty to help him control his irritability, which Jane felt was a sort of apology. On their last day he was full of jokes, but on the morning of their departure Jane felt low and badly-done-by again. She ate nothing at breakfast, which nobody noticed; when she thanked the maid for her kindness to Mrs Snashall, the maid had an unmoved countenance (so the servants were on their employers' side). But Sir George gave her his arm to the boat, and they parted amicably. However, Jane was disappointed in his response to her thankyou letter. 'I should have thought he could not have failed to feel obliged if not touched by it—Perhaps I expressed myself with too much sensibility.'[21] One imagines him throwing it across the room, cursing.

Sydney newspapers covered the trip in detail, almost all praising Lady Franklin's 'difficult and extraordinary' trip—'Lady F. is too good a subject for a par[agraph], not to be recurred to as often as they can contrive to say any thing about her', wrote the *Sydney Colonist*. A lady undergoing such perils was depicted as a good example to others. There was discussion of her motive, but once commentators decided she was writing a book, they were happy. This was praiseworthy; the book would be valuable and interesting. A typical article commended Lady Franklin's simple habits and lack of ostentation in her 'spirited & enterprising tour'.[22]

Most Van Diemen's Land newspapers were just as enthusiastic, proud of their representative: 'Lady Franklin's reception at this Settlement has been most gratifying, as, of course, we might expect it would be'. Only a few hostile papers were critical. Why would Lady Franklin leave her comfortable home and subject herself to the 'toils and terrors of the bush', living among naked savages? (This annoyed her—they wore blankets, she wrote indignantly.) Instead of riding round New South Wales in a 'strange, eccentric manner' watching 'some frolicsome group of black fellows', the governor's wife should be fulfilling her official duties at home, hosting the Queen's Birthday ball. This was a valid point; a five-month absence could be seen as dereliction of duty. Other newspapers thought this criticism undeserved. Surely Lady Franklin could do as she pleased.[23]

The return home was trying. On 16 July the party left Sydney, on a voyage which could take as little as a week. Southerly gales made theirs terrible. Sophy suffered her usual seasickness, and even Jane often remained in bed all day, once because rain drenched her stays and she could not dress. Captain Moriarty and Mr Elliot spent hours holding Sophy's cot to spare her more motion, while Jane sat in a corner, occasionally grasping Moriarty's knee. She showed little sympathy for Sophy (she did read her a couple of sermons) and the others showed little for Jane—they had been together too long.

In calm periods Jane resorted to her usual routine, reading, writing and interrogating other passengers. At last the ship was almost round Cape Pillar—a few more hours would see them safe in the Derwent estuary, almost home in Hobart—but another southerly gale blew up, and they spent ten more days tossing around the ocean.

Food ran short. Tea was reduced to one cup a day, and the crew had to eat a cask of tripe and feet previously thought inedible. Water was running low, yet the gentlemen had ample spirits, Jane recorded crossly. Then a northerly breeze appeared. They made good progress, and the captain said they might as well have prayers. 'Glad to hear this', wrote Jane—then a passenger read the evening service too slowly. It was definitely time for home.

In Hobart people were worried that the ship had sunk, but finally on 19 August 1839, five weeks after leaving Sydney and five months after leaving Hobart, they sailed up the Derwent. Newspapers announced the arrival of Lady Franklin 'in excellent health and spirits'.[24]

For over a year Jane Franklin had to be content with short trips round Van Diemen's Land, but in December 1840 John Gell decided to visit his brother in South Australia. Jane decided to go too, taking Eleanor, Mr Bagot the aide-de-camp, and her maid Christiana Stewart.

Leaving Hobart on 13 December, they arrived in Adelaide on a very hot Christmas Day. Eleanor's diary described being eaten by mosquitoes, waiting two hours on the shore, then going to Governor Gawler's house, even though Mrs Gawler had recently given birth. 'What a Xmas day!' Like Gipps, Gawler pleased Jane Franklin by discussing politics with her, as well as fascinating gossip such as whether a certain lady was the natural daughter of a duke; but she did not like Adelaide, 'a most disagreeable place'.[25]

This trip was not as adventurous as the Melbourne–Sydney one, but Jane Franklin enjoyed herself, seeing everything and finding out an immense number of facts on a week-long excursion to Encounter Bay. Eleanor was excited by her first long camping trip: the Aborigines' interest in the 'white loubras'; the gentlemen having to pull the bullock dray out of the mud ('Mama & I held the horses'); sitting round a fire at night 'enjoying the Moonlight Evening'; eating mullet at an inn, '& for the fun of it we had a pot of porter handed round to us all'.[26]

Back in Adelaide it was chaos: the Franklin and Gawler ladies were ill from the terrible heat, the servants offered bad wine and refused to obey instructions, and the governor himself had to hunt away bugs to secure a night's sleep. But the Franklin party could not stay long, as Gell had to return to Hobart for work. On the way home they visited Port Lincoln and climbed Stamford Hill. Jane claimed that her husband wanted to set up a monument to Matthew Flinders, 'the discoverer of South Australia', though Eleanor's diary shows it was Jane's idea, and she gave her husband the credit. On the homeward voyage they ate minced porpoise and made up a game, writing questions about South Australia on cards. Did Jane Franklin invent Trivial Pursuit? She provided questions faster than the others could answer, and preferred asking questions to answering them—this is someone who hates being wrong. They arrived home on 22 January, after six weeks away.[27]

On her return, Jane Franklin found that a ship was about to sail to New Zealand. It was too good to miss. She emphasised that Sir John wanted her to go, enlisted her maid Christiana Stewart, Miss Williamson, Mr Bagot and his servant, and left on 21 February 1841.[28]

Inhabited by the Maori since about 1300, New Zealand was colonised in the 1820s by English missionaries, whalers and traders. In 1839 the New Zealand Company announced that it would buy land. Alarmed, missionaries called for British control; Britain annexed the islands; and in 1840 Maori chiefs signed the Treaty of Waitangi, whereby they kept their land but ceded overall power. In 1841 New Zealand became a colony, under Captain Hobson as governor. Quite different from the Australian colonies: how interesting for Jane Franklin to visit. 'Her desire is to see & to know every thing', wrote Hobson.[29]

Her first stop was Port Nicholson (Wellington), the New Zealand Company's headquarters. She could not avoid receiving an address from local merchants—as she was leaving, in her cabin, surrounded by luggage, everyone holding on to the table as the boat tossed in the waves. The two leading citizens insisted on reading the address, and for once Jane Franklin made a speech in reply. 'I watched sharply what they said to me, and according to prescriptive rule slightly alluded to all, or most of it', which sounds competent. In letters home she played it down: she had not wanted to receive the 'ludicrous' address, she made sure it was presented in private, 'there was nobody I cared about who was listening', and her speech was praised as 'a very proper one, like a good wife who

Jane Franklin's Travels: 1839–1842

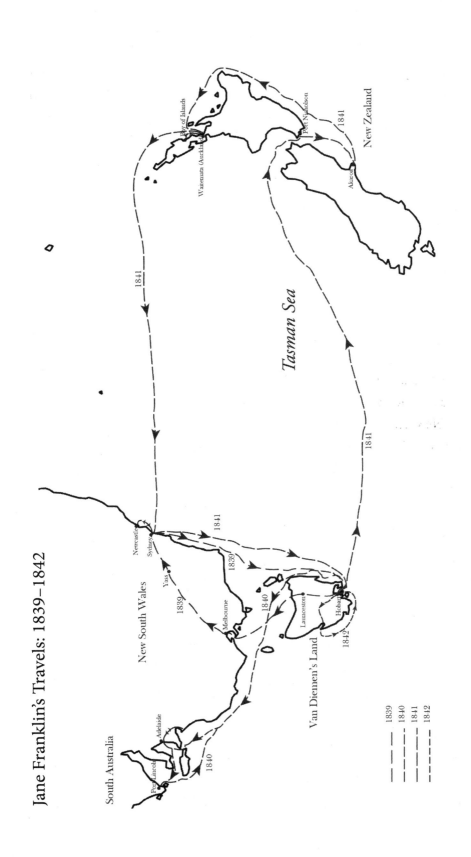

South Australia

New South Wales

Port Lincoln
Adelaide

Yass

Newcastle
Sydney

Melbourne

Van Diemen's Land

Launceston

Hobart

Tasman Sea

New Zealand

Bay of Islands
Waitemata (Auckland)
Port Nicholson
Akaroa

1839
1840
1841
1842

preferred her husband's praises to her own'. The merchants lamented her early departure, for with her admirable literary and scientific acquirements she could have turned their local treasures into knowledge. They asked her to assure her husband of their desire to maintain amicable intercourse. Later she realised that praise of her husband implied criticism of Hobson, for there was bad feeling between Port Nicholson and the seat of government at Waitemata (Auckland). She was embarrassed at having been used in this way.[30]

The party travelled to the small French settlement at Akaroa, near Christchurch. Jane enjoyed French manners and food, like vol-au-vent of crayfish, though she was sick afterwards. During a nocturnal excursion she missed a step and fell, lacerating the muscles in her leg. She could barely walk for months. Undaunted, the party continued to Waitemata, where Hobson suggested she view a large missionary meeting in the Waikato region. Typically, Jane Franklin preferred Hobson to his wife, who, rather than expressing sympathy about her injured leg, wondered (as one might) that she should want to travel forty miles (nearly 65 kilometres) to Waikato. Hobson organised a chair on poles carried by Maori porters, who, noted Jane, wore blankets round their shoulders, shirts which were much too short, and nothing else. She found the meeting curious and interesting, enjoyed a beach barbecue, and received presents of a bucket of lava and 'a few human bones'.[31]

The party visited missionary establishments at the Bay of Islands, but to Jane's intense irritation had to return to Waitemata before she had seen half what she wanted. Hobson arranged ships to suit himself, she wrote crossly; she criticised the way he appointed his officials, especially omitting one man she liked. Probably to general relief, the Franklin party left on 22 May and, after a four-month absence, returned home via Sydney, where the Gippses did their best. Only once did Sir George's nostrils curl in ill humour.[32]

The last major excursion was one the Franklins had planned for years: to Van Diemen's Land's wild, largely unexplored west coast. In 1842

the opportunity arose. They expected to take eight days, walking 66 miles (106 kilometres) from Lake St Clair to the Gordon River, along a track surveyor Calder had cut. Sir John announced that he was looking for sites for convict probation stations, but it was tacitly understood that this was a holiday, the sort both the Franklins relished.

The party collected near Lake St Clair: the Franklins and the maid Stewart; Mr Bagot; Dr Milligan as naturalist; David Burn, a romantic immigrant who pleaded to be included; Calder; their orderly, Sergeant O'Boyle; three constables and seventeen convicts, 28 people in all. Everyone revelled in the stupendous mountains, intense blue sky, picturesque scenery and dazzling brilliancy (wrote Burn).[33]

They started on 2 April. Calder organised the baggage, his task made more difficult by Lady Franklin, who insisted on taking an enormous amount despite 'all the persuasion in the world'. 'Though one of the best and kindest of her sex', wrote Calder, Lady Franklin insisted on having her own way in everything. 'There was positively no such thing as giving her the worst of the argument in any matter whatever.' If she could not persuade by reason, she would vanquish her opponent by 'some witty sally or exquisite rebuke, which no one ever wanted a second dose of', a satirical smile, or her 'peculiar and impressive' silence.

'Her peculiar talents for worsting everybody who opposed her were brought into full play on the morning of her departure from the lake', as she showed Calder how his men could carry double what he planned. 'I had not been five minutes under her tuition before I discovered that there was a good deal to learn yet, and that it only required a proper instructor, like Lady Franklin, to show how it was to be done both slick and quick.' Her method was to keep handing over bag after bag, bundle after bundle, ignoring Calder's remonstrances. Finally she walked away, leaving Calder to organise the men and their enormous swags.[34]

The party moved off, their spirits exhilarated: 'the fancy revelled, the bosom heaved, and the pulse thrilled with life and pleasure' (Burn again). Well, perhaps not the laden convicts, and not Jane Franklin either, for she was ill. She was carried by two convicts in a palanquin, a chair on poles, similar to those used at Port Arthur to carry visitors.

However, the path was so steep and rugged she could only be carried just under half the way, and once when Stewart was ill she gave up the palanquin to her. So she walked, with Burn all admiration: Lady Franklin had to 'wade through miry sludge, or scramble the mountain passes, encamping upon the damp cold ground, the green fern leaves her bedding,—blankets her seat,—and earth her table'. Stewart also did this, but Burn took no notice of a servant's achievement.

After the beautiful start, Burn's enthusiasm deteriorated, as did the weather. It rained for the next eighteen days. They struggled on, through 'impervious forests, rugged mountains, tremendous gullies, impetuous Rivers and torrents, and swamps and morasses', Jane wrote to Mary. Occasionally when the sky cleared they could admire the wonderful views, but their progress was far slower than anticipated, and Calder and the convicts had to keep returning for more provisions. Once Calder walked 77 kilometres in 54 hours, bringing back a 36-kilogram load. The provisions consisted of salt pork, flour which was made into cakes and baked in a frying pan, tea and brown sugar—for breakfast, dinner and tea, complained Burn.[35]

It rained, hailed, sleeted and snowed so hard that the party was stuck for a week at the base of the 1443–metre Frenchmans Cap, surrounded by water, with everything wet—the ground saturated, firewood damp, tents soaking, their beds made of damp ferns on sheets of sopping bark. It was so bad that Sir John did not even read the Sunday service. However, he and Lady Franklin remained unremittingly cheerful, and Calder found them such agreeable companions that it was next to impossible to feel any serious depression (only mild depression?). The convicts loved Sir John, and still praised him decades later. When food was running short and Milligan suggested convicts' rations be cut, Sir John insisted on everyone being treated the same, and he noticed one convict struggling to carry Milligan's rock specimens. 'You fool, why don't you rip the seam in the bottom of the bag?' he whispered. That night Milligan complained that few of his specimens were left, and Sir John suggested that smaller, lighter stones might stay in the bag. Even if these stories were apocryphal, they show the convicts' opinion of Sir John. They did not tell such stories about his wife, though her protégé Milligan described her as the life and soul of the party.

Finally the rain eased, and on 15 April they reached the Franklin River. It was so swollen with rain that they could not cross it on a fallen tree, as was usual, so one of the convicts, a shipwright, started to make a dugout canoe. Calder wrote of how, conscious of his importance, he behaved like the master of the camp, snubbing the others. Even the governor, trying to hurry the work, was told, 'You be off directly, and don't meddle with what you know nothing about'. Defeated, Sir John returned to his tent 'amidst the imperfectly suppressed titterings of all who were not too near him'. Meanwhile, food was short, and everyone was rationed to sugarless tea, biscuit and 80 grams of meat daily.

The canoe was finally finished on 19 April, the first fine day. They crossed the Franklin and walked to the Gordon River, though one of the convicts, clearing the path, was blinded in one eye by a sapling. John and Jane Franklin were all sympathy. This was unusual for her: was she forced into it by Sir John's genuine feeling? They reached their tiny vessel, *Breeze*, on 22 April. Calder and most of the men turned back—it was the happiest moment of his life, said Calder, after the most troublesome duty of his career—while the Franklin party explored the Gordon River and the old penal station, then were stuck in Macquarie Harbour by contrary winds. Provisions ran short again, one dinner consisting of seagull pie. Finally they sailed through Hell's Gates, and met a larger vessel sent to find them. Comfort at last! The ship's captain commiserated with Sir John on his trials. 'Not at all', was the hearty reply, everyone had been fine—except, he added jovially, poor Bagot, who ran out of eau de Cologne and scented soap. In fact the journey had been gruelling. Sergeant O'Boyle, the orderly, said he was so shattered by its hardships that he did not enjoy an hour's health for the rest of his life, and Jane referred to the Franklin as 'that frightful river'.[36]

Once on the larger ship, the Franklins were not going to waste their visit to the west coast: they explored Port Davey, established the exact location of South West Cape, and only arrived home on 24 May. Their long absence caused great anxiety. The only question in Sydney was whether they had drowned or starved, and in Hobart Eleanor was in despair. 'O that dear Papa & Mama were come, every thing seems to go wrong whenever they are away.' George Boyes, acting colonial secretary, was not worried, but Sir John's secretary, Francis Henslowe, drove him mad, fussing, 'boring me again about Sir John', sending him irritating letters just when he was sitting down to dinner. Finally, to soothe him and family members, Boyes ordered another boat to the west coast—it would do no good, he thought, but it looked helpful.[37]

Most colonists admired the vice-regal trek, and at the levee held shortly afterwards to celebrate the Queen's Birthday, many came especially to congratulate the Franklins, while the people of George Town presented Sir John with a congratulatory address on his safe return. The pro-Franklin newspapers agreed, but there was the usual criticism from their opponents: an utterly absurd journey, expensive, leaving the colony with no governor, and Government House not illuminated at the birth of the Prince of Wales. 'We do not want a Governor to go blundering through the bush ... in search of the picturesque.' However, it is doubtful whether the public took much notice. The *Hobart Town Advertiser* praised Lady Franklin to the skies: it was feared she would not be able to cope with the difficulties of the trip, but the same spirit of enterprise which bore her through the deserts of Syria and the wilds of New Zealand gave her energy to bear up with more than a woman's strength, and unflinching resolution.[38]

Jane Franklin's final expedition in Australia was an excursion from Melbourne to Mount Macedon in December 1843, on her way back to England. This involved discomfort, according to Sophy: extreme heat; Aunt being thrown from a cart when it overturned, which frightened her though she was not hurt; makeshift camping in the bush, Aunt sleeping on the ground under the cart; getting lost in the bush and only reaching their hotel at 2 a.m. Sophy found all this very trying, but on past performances Jane Franklin would have noted the interesting aspects and ignored the discomfort. Out of curiosity the party visited a 'lady squatter': she was not unfeminine or unladylike, wrote Sophy, surprised, though she was very stout and red-faced, while her female overseer and stockkeeper was plain and wiry.[39] Jane Franklin's opinion of these independent women has not survived.

The only experience Jane Franklin admitted scared her occurred not in distant parts, but just across the river from Hobart. She, Miss Williamson and Eleanor were staying in John Price's lonely house there, when one evening they heard that bushrangers—escaped convicts who lived by theft—might attack. Jane was lying on the sofa ill, but started to her feet and insisted they go to Hobart immediately, though it was dark and the boat small. 'Oh how I hurried the placid-motioned Miss Williamson and poor Eleanor', as well as her maid, 'a timid quiet middle aged person'. They must all leave at once, urged Jane, but the maid would not be hurried:

> *"What are you fidgetting about"? I sd to her impatiently—"only getting your ladyship's pillows—yr ladyship can't go without your pillows"—"Never <u>mind</u> the pillows"! I said. "But your ladyship's <u>lime water</u>! said she, "I <u>must</u> take the <u>lime water</u> –" "Fiddle <u>dee dee</u>, of the lime water," said I—don't you know the bushrangers may be here directly"! … I who had hitherto walked with very feeble and staggering steps, almost ran down the hill from Mr. Price's house, to the boat.*

Within five minutes of receiving the news they were in the boat, the maid grasping the limewater. In twenty minutes they were safely across the river, and the next day they heard that the bushrangers had been miles away.[40] It made an amusing story to tell Mary.

What was the result of all these travels? Much enjoyment for Jane Franklin, despite the hardships; a mixture of pleasure and difficulties for her companions and hosts. She learnt a vast amount of information that she could have passed to Sir John, but there is no indication that she did. She recorded tens of thousands of words about the places she visited, but never used this information either.

Today, historians value her journals. She left wonderfully detailed descriptions of parts of Australia and New Zealand, and her interrogations of everyone, rich or poor, of whatever social class, provide a rare picture of all types of people—almost all other travellers only recorded what the gentry thought. Jane Franklin might have been socially snobbish, but she was unique in her interest in everybody's experiences and opinions.

11

THREE WOMEN'S LIVES

To set Jane Franklin's life in context, this chapter describes the experiences of three other women in her family, who accompanied her and Sir John to Van Diemen's Land: Mary Franklin, Sophy Cracroft and Eleanor Franklin. John Franklin was the guardian of his orphaned niece Mary, and in 1836, aged 22, she joined his family. 'We form a very merry party—and none more merry than Mary Franklin who is the universal favourite', John wrote, while Jane chose Mary as her companion on a trip to the east coast.[1]

Pretty, popular Mary was soon engaged to be married. John Price, born in 1809, was a handsome, haughty, monocled English adventurer. The third son of an eccentric and impoverished Cornish baronet, Price sought his fortune in Van Diemen's Land. Arriving in 1836, aged 26, he bought land in the remote Huon district and started working it. Soon a better opportunity appeared. This aristocratic young man was invited to Government House, and by December 1837 he was engaged to Mary. 'We all like him', Sir John wrote; he had no fortune, but youth, perseverance and steady conduct were to his credit.[2] Neither John nor Jane had the perspicacity to see any darker side.

As described in Chapter 8, Price sold his Huon land to Jane Franklin and leased a farm across the Derwent from Hobart, a 'sweetly pretty' place with a four-roomed cottage—'he and Mary will not live in <u>great</u> style', wrote Eleanor. The wedding took place in June 1838, and John Price looked 'as happy and as loving as one could wish', according to Jane.[3] In 1839 he reaped the reward for marrying the governor's niece, becoming assistant police magistrate. His superior thought highly of him. Jane Franklin did not. 'I did much fear about them soon after their marriage', she wrote:

> *They were constantly sparring and Sophy assures me that Mary confessed to her great dissatisfaction with her married state. Mary's present delicate situation [pregnancy] has caused a truce at least to these unpleasant proceedings & it is to be hoped it will last.—Mr Price is a mixture of what is gentlemanly & what is rude.—There is a great deal in him of that odious coarse joking about conjugal supremacy & obedience which so often sickens one in domestic life.—He makes personal observations also, or passes personal judgments on ones habits—(for instance he will have the impertinence to say to his wife that she is later of a morning than any one in the colony except one, meaning me, which I either do not hear or pretend not to understand, in order to save myself the necessity of expressing my sense of his rudeness which being so unlike any thing else that I meet with from any other person, that I did not well know how to bear it.—With all this he is scrupulously observant of certain etiquettes of manner, (such as opening the door for you & acting the waiter).[4]*

Mary's first baby was born in October 1839. 'Child born at 12—Mr. Price hysterical', wrote Jane curtly. Eleanor's version was that Mary 'gave birth to a son after having suffered great agony for 24 hours'. Mary's later relations with her husband are not described, but at least she was a happy mother. 'Master Fredy Price is a dear little fellow', wrote Eleanor. 'He is not a very pretty boy, only a very good one, and a great pet of us all. Mary doats upon him.' She bore more sons in 1841 and 1842, and in total eight children, two dying young. Price built a handsome villa and the family lived in some style.[5]

Despite her fears, Jane Franklin appreciated John Price's usefulness to her. He supported Sir John, succeeded as a magistrate and a farmer, and provided financial advice and gossipy information, but he was annoying—'I was by no means so foolish as M[r]. Price imagined', she had to tell Sophy. Others detested him for his harshness and arrogance, his biographer describing him as brutally overbearing, perhaps a psychopath. Convicts hated him, and at the 1841 Hobart regatta a mob seized and ill-treated him. He does not sound like an easy husband, and Mary was almost certainly caught in an abusive relationship. When the Franklins left Van Diemen's Land in 1843 she was much distressed, wrote Jane, '& her emotion was almost violent'.[6] No wonder: now she had no one to protect her, and with little money and a growing family, had no option but to stay with her husband.

In 1846 John Price was appointed commandant at Norfolk Island. He became a byword for cruelty, the original of the brutal Maurice Frere in *For the term of his natural life*. A fellow officer described him as a fine man who loved devising games for his children—his public face? Mary's letters to family in England gave a picture of harmonious family life. However, a convict who called him 'the Demon' wrote: 'Prisoners, warders and his own children felt and spoke of him alike, and from prisoner servants we learnt that his wife feared him worst of all. The same sternness ruled the home as the barracks.' In *His natural life*, Mrs Frere has an affair with a clergyman, but how far this fiction copied life is not known.

John Price's health was poor and in 1853 the family returned to Hobart. Then he was appointed inspector-general of Victoria's penal establishments. The Prices lived at Pentridge Gaol in Melbourne, where Mary was known for her kindness to sick prisoners. Her husband was not. Vitriolic newspaper articles criticised Price's tyrannical rule, an inquiry was set up, and a select committee was hearing evidence—some terrible—when on 26 March 1857 a group of convicts set on Price, striking him with fists, stones and shovels. He died of his injuries.

There was widespread sympathy for the widow and six children, and, most unusually, 104 prisoners at Pentridge sent Mary a letter of condolence. She had little money, but the Victorian government gave her a payout, and the children did well, mostly. Frederick attended the new University of Melbourne and prospered in the Indian civil service, Thomas served with distinction in the British Army, but James, his father's son, died by violence in charge of a boat crewed by Aboriginal pearl divers. The daughters married, and some children and grand-children lived near Mary in Melbourne—as did the clergyman from Norfolk Island. She died aged eighty.[7]

John Franklin's niece Sophy Cracroft was in her twenties when she lived in Van Diemen's Land. At first she found life challenging, coming from genteel poverty to Government House, second in popularity to her cousin Mary. But Mary married and Sophy learned to cope, losing 'that appearance of affectation which she undoubtedly possessed', wrote her uncle. 'She is very much improved in manner and is really an amiable girl.'[8]

Intelligent, cooperative Sophy became invaluable to Aunt Franklin as secretary, lady-in-waiting and colleague. She wrote letters and copied out documents, relayed messages, passed on gossip, received visitors and acted as hostess when Jane was absent or ill. She was her companion and confidante, as they discussed the implication of letters or their reaction to political events. But Jane remained dominant, Sophy secondary. She knew her role as poor relation. A nod was enough for her to leave the room so Jane could talk confidentially to a visitor; when travelling, she naturally sat facing backwards in the carriage, and slept on the sofa or even the floor while Lady Franklin had the comfortable bed. 'For first time slept in same bed as Sophy, there being no 2d mattress, no sacking to bedstead, nor sofa', wrote Jane—so these were Sophy's usual alternatives.[9]

Sophy had more traditional feminine interests than her aunt, like embroidery, art and music. She was a sympathetic listener. 'I left him to the patient sympathy of Sophy', wrote Jane of a visitor; 'Dear sweet Miss Cracroft soothed and sympathised with me', wrote Kezia Hayter. The bishop's wife thought her 'a very pleasing person who seems to be the right hand of her aunt and uncle in all domestic matters'—so Sophy also helped run the household.[10]

She did not enjoy good health. 'You know she is at all times a great invalid', wrote Eleanor; 'Poor Miss Cracroft looks wretchedly ill', noted Kezia. 'Sophy caught a bad cold yesterday', Eleanor's diary ran in 1841, and five days later, 'Sophy still continues very ill. She is sick about every half hour & yesterday much oftener. [Dr] Bedford says it is an attack of the spine.' Months later, 'Dear Sophy's birthday. I wish she were in better health to enjoy it.' But like Jane Franklin, Sophy managed the arduous overland trip to Sydney with no obvious problems.[11]

Sophy's writing shows a complex character, and her diary of the voyage back to England depicts a nervous, emotional, self-centred bundle of anxiety who could be a martyr, insisting on copying documents for her uncle to the point of ill health. Typical diary entries run: 'when without occupation, I am certain to become anxious and full of care'; 'feeling very anxious and unsettled and depressed and perhaps in consequence extremely unwell and nervous'; 'have almost constant headach, fever, languor, tic douloureux'. One evening Sophy accused a fellow passenger, Mr Weston, of opposition to bishops, becoming quite hysterical. 'Mr W. was a little taken aback—for I was getting warm ... my heightened complexion was the source of much amusement.' Later Sophy remarked that if she were Queen she would enjoy tormenting her ministers. 'Mr W said "he had no doubt whatever of that." '[12]

A photograph of Sophy when she was 46 shows an attractive woman, and men certainly found her so. In Van Diemen's Land she was romantically involved (or wished to be) with at least seven, Jane Franklin calling her a 'sad flirt'—the pot calling the kettle black? First, Sophy fell in love with Henry Elliot, son of an earl, but in 1839 his mother ordered him home. Sophy, from the barely-gentry Franklins with no money, was not a suitable wife for an aristocrat. Sophy and Jane were most upset, and Henry said he was, but home he had to go.

In other cases, Sophy did not reciprocate men's passion. Major Ainsworth, an army officer, proposed marriage, entreating Jane Franklin to procure him an interview with Sophy. 'I succeeded in this & a promise of friendly feeling on Sophy's part & of resignation on his was the result.' 'Poor Major A. is indeed weak almost to imbecility', she wrote of his love for Sophy.[13]

Captain Francis Crozier, second-in-command of the *Erebus* and *Terror* expedition, also fell in love with Sophy. Nearly twenty years older, he was from a similar background to her with little money, and Sophy described him as 'a horrid radical and an indifferent speller'. He had no chance. Sophy said she would never marry into the navy: had Jane complained of a naval husband's endless absences? But this determination did not stop Sophy flirting enthusiastically with naval officers, such as Captain Owen Stanley. He fell desperately in love with her and proposed, but she replied evasively. Glumly, he accompanied Sir John on a trip to the Tasman Peninsula, only cheered by the fact that Ainsworth and Count Strzelecki, another suitor, were in the party and could not steal a march on him.[14]

John Gell became close enough to Sophy for someone to believe a rumour that they were married. In 1842 Jane Franklin told her sister Mary the current, complicated, situation. Sophy was taken with John Gell, and was trying to subdue his interest in Eleanor. Crozier was smitten with Sophy, and would have betrayed it had he not seen her obvious preference for James Ross. Jane thought Sophy was still attached to Henry Elliot, but she made herself agreeable to Strzelecki then flirted with Ross, even though he had just culminated an intense romance with an engagement, his fiancée waiting for him in England. Jane was indulgent. 'I don't believe [Sophy] takes the trouble of making herself bewitching except in cases where she would have no objection to marry the individual.'[15]

Sophy's flirtatious nature was even mentioned by the hostile press: speculation whether Dr Milligan, Jane Franklin's protégé, was going to marry into the family can only have referred to Sophy. But, as Sophy wrote, she did not want to marry the men who proposed to her, and she left Van Diemen's Land still single.[16] She remained so, eventually becoming Jane Franklin's devoted companion.

'A short square little thing', ridiculously like her father and with his sweet temper, was Sophy's summary of her cousin Eleanor. Aged from twelve to nineteen in Van Diemen's Land, Eleanor lived in the schoolroom with her governess, Miss Williamson, who sounds difficult. In 1839 John Franklin noted that Eleanor 'gets on better now with Miss Williamson', so there had been problems, and Sophy described 'the old Lady' as grumpy and querulous—'I really never saw so disagreeable a companion as she is'. Eleanor was stuck with her but, guided by Christian charity, never complained about people in her letters. Eleanor loved dancing and enjoyed botany, collecting insects, plants and seeds to send to relatives in England. Unlike her stepmother, she wrote rhapsodic letters about the beauty of Van Diemen's Land—its pretty flowers, magnificent trees, the tinge of lilac and yellow on Mount Wellington at sunset ...[17]

'Eleanor is in excellent spirits—but she cannot help being merry', wrote Sophy. A cheerful, kind girl, Eleanor seemed happy. She adored her father, who reciprocated, describing her as affectionate, lively and amiable, 'a great comfort to me'. Perhaps she reminded him of her mother, also cheerful, affectionate and lively—but no one ever mentioned Eleanor senior in thousands of words of writing. Still, in the interests of a good upbringing, Sir John could be severe. In 1837 he upbraided Eleanor (in a messy letter himself) for writing a letter so messy and blotted that it could not be sent, and even worse, ending its replacement only 'Yours affectionately'. She should have added an expression of duty, writing 'Your affectionate and dutiful daughter'. 'I do not suppose you are wanting a sense of duty—but the not putting it forth in your letters is a part of the same system of haste and inconsiderateness which is manifested in your bad writing and much blotting.' Nice, kind Sir John had his stern side—but Eleanor still loved him.[18]

Generally, Eleanor saw little of her stepmother, except possibly at the daily family luncheon, and Jane seldom mentioned her in diaries or letters. Yet their relationship seems friendly enough. Jane's surviving letters to Eleanor sound affectionate, and Eleanor, brought up to love and obey her parents as a duty, did not rebel. Jane took the girl with her on trips to South Australia, Recherche Bay and other local places, and as Eleanor grew older she sometimes acted as her stepmother's companion and secretary, copying documents, running messages and seeing people when Jane was ill—though not to the same extent as Sophy. But despite the surface amicability, Jane never sounds really fond of Eleanor, and Eleanor's son wrote that though Jane 'bestowed much detached and intermittent kindness upon [Eleanor], for her Father's sake ... the link of Mother & Daughter remained undeveloped'.[19]

Jane did not permit Eleanor the social activities of her own youth. When Eleanor turned fifteen, as a concession Jane allowed her to visit people with only Miss Williamson as chaperone, writing, 'It will always be the greatest satisfaction to me to allow you as much liberty as you can bear', as long as she used it with modesty, forbearance and meekness. And Eleanor did. She did not even complain, apparently, when she was not allowed to dine with adults or attend balls at the age of eighteen.[20]

Despite these restrictions, Eleanor's diaries and letters sound happy. She loved Mary and her babies, as well as pets such as a kookaburra, a canary and a wallaby. She and Sophy, the two single young women, became particularly close, Sophy writing that they were each other's best friend. Much courted, with an assured position at her aunt's right hand, Sophy had no need to be jealous of plain little Eleanor, still in the schoolroom. Eleanor was adventurous; she climbed Mount Wellington, and when on the voyage back to England the captain proposed sending the ladies up the mast, Eleanor jumped at the chance. Like her father, she was deeply religious, with a strongly felt, personal relationship with God. Piety did not stop her sense of fun, and she enjoyed jokes, giggling at Sophy to make her laugh when she was trying to repress a forward man.[21]

Unlike Sophy and Jane, Eleanor was no flirt. She fell in love once, and it was for life. John Gell arrived when she was sixteen: 'very agreeable, lively and clever', she told a cousin. Two years later Jane noticed that Eleanor greeted him 'unknown to herself with the most radiant looks', though jealous Sophy watched the pair like a lynx. Jane wanted Eleanor to marry a Simpkinson nephew, but 'I am well aware that Eleanor has no great attractions or personal accomplishments beyond the charms of youth & vivacity of expression', and perhaps John Gell would make her a good husband, for he 'is not over fastidious in small matters', and would overlook Eleanor's defects (probably meaning messiness).[22] Eleanor's cheerfulness, good temper and affectionate nature were so different from Jane's character that she placed no particular value on them.

Eleanor Franklin and John Gell had shared interests—the church, mainly, but he sent her a volume of history lectures, assuming her enthusiasm—and they became engaged in late 1843 when Eleanor was nineteen. She had to part with him almost immediately to return to England and their prospects of being reunited were doubtful, Jane thought.[23] Eleanor had to wait six years, but did marry her John, as described in later chapters.

Victorian novels were not always accurate. Marriage did not necessarily bring women happiness and security: the most reliable indicator of these was money. Beauty did not always bring bliss, either, for Mary Price, the most admired of these women, had one of the more difficult lives, while Eleanor, probably the plainest, enjoyed a happy marriage. However, all women could face difficulties, such as finding a husband; adjusting to him; the problems of childbirth and the sadness of childhood deaths; financial problems; domestic violence; difficult family members; lack of control of the future; coping with society's restrictions on women. And health: three of these women lived to old age, but health problems were endemic for Jane and Sophy.

If women disobeyed society's moral rules, punishment could be severe. In 1840 Alexander Maconochie, enthusiastic reformer of the convict system, was appointed commandant of the penal colony on Norfolk Island. There his nineteen-year-old daughter Mary Ann Maconochie was detected in an affair with a convict tutor. He was thrown in prison, and she was shut in her room, then sent to Sydney where she was housed by the Gippses in utmost seclusion until she could be sent, alone, to England, to live with her father's despised illegitimate sister, in disgrace, her life ruined. (Jane Franklin was not surprised. This was what came of indulging both convicts and children.)[24] However, the other women discussed in this chapter avoided such pitfalls.

Compared with the other three, Jane Franklin had much more control of her life. Money helped greatly, but so did her character, her determination, her choice of a high-status and easygoing husband. She was the one who made the most of the cards fate dealt her.

12

THE POLITICAL

QUESTION

Jane Franklin's activities as described in previous chapters were uncontroversial, and often admired. The odd opponent might carp, but almost everyone accepted them as the sort of things a wealthy, energetic, eccentric lady might do. Another activity was more questionable: engaging in politics.

Some general historians claim that the Franklins' problems in Van Diemen's Land occurred because they were unpopular, too elevated for parochial colonists to appreciate.[1] This was not so. The colonists liked them, as shown by their general support, warm memories, and the huge sum they donated to Lady Franklin a decade later to help her look for her husband. The Franklins' problems were political. John Franklin was a weak governor who depended on advisers, and a power struggle developed for this role. London had a poor opinion of him, and complaints against him in 1842 were the last straw. He had to go. Assessments of Jane Franklin's part in this vary from none to major responsibility.

Franklin can hardly be blamed for finding the job of colonial governor overwhelming. Governors had an extremely difficult task, far from their connections at home, transplanted to an alien land of which they were often ignorant, and where they were perched between four vocal sources of power and influence. The most powerful was the British government's Colonial Office. It wanted its colonies to add to Britain's prestige, operate without any trouble and cost as little as possible. Despite often having little understanding of colonial situations, it micromanaged its colonies, and governors had to obey orders. These could be trivial: one authorised Franklin to appoint three extra constables. Paradoxically, governors were both colonial autocrats and London's puppets.[2]

In the colonies, governors' independence was limited by the second power group, senior public servants sitting on councils of advice. Franklin's colonial secretary (the top job), treasurer, attorney-general and chief police magistrate formed his Executive Council, with whom he worked on a day-to-day basis. The larger Legislative Council of appointed members passed legislation. An authoritarian governor and natural politician like Franklin's predecessor George Arthur kept these men in line, and also worked easily with the Colonial Office. A milder man like Franklin had difficulties.

Colonists formed the third group. They wanted improvements, development and privileges for themselves, which often ran counter to the government's plans. Friction was inevitable. Colonists had no official power, but they, and disgruntled public servants, could complain to London, or even go themselves and lobby the Colonial Office. Malcontents could all too easily gain a hearing in the local press, the fourth power group. Newspapers ranged from responsible organs to scurrilous rags, which titillated readers with vicious personal attacks. Occasionally such articles were reprinted in London, to Jane Franklin's horror. At least in Van Diemen's Land 'every body knows the malignant foundation of it, but in England, in my own home, where things are necessarily judged of as they appear, & not as they are' it was terrible. 'Is there no refuge?' However, most such articles were positive, *The Times* printing one that admired her intellectual character.[3]

Sir John, an optimistic man—'I always look on the bright side of the question'—tried to ignore the press. His wife averred stoutly that 'I shall never die of the newspapers', but she took a keen interest. 'They cause in me the purest disgust, the most unmitigated contempt & just sufficient indignation to keep me alive & excited—for indignation is a most vivifying sensation.' Once, 'it was a newspaper evening … As they did not appear, I asked for them.' She read everything, even the worst articles, reading them aloud to their subjects to keep that indignation alive.[4]

When the Franklins arrived in 1837, there were six newspapers in Hobart and two in Launceston, half supporting Governor Arthur and half opposing him. At first all supported Franklin, but soon, seeing him working with Arthur's officials, the anti-Arthur papers opposed Franklin also. There was generally one newspaper that supported Franklin strongly, and others supported or criticised him to varying degrees. But newspaper influence is debatable. As Jane Franklin said, the public allowed for editors' biases, and the more scurrilous papers had tiny circulations, as few as 150 copies, not many among 50 000 people.[5] All colonial governors faced such criticism, which cannot be taken at face value.

Nothing in John Franklin's career prepared him for his job as governor. In the strictly disciplined British navy no one dared question orders, and Franklin could control his men in the kindly way he preferred. He had little experience or ability in administration and politics, and no particular political philosophy, reacting to events instead of ordering them. 'Rectitude of conduct & principle should be our support as it has I trust been our guide', he wrote—but that was not enough. He did not have so much as a political drop of blood in his body.[6]

Much as they liked, even loved, him, none of his contemporaries claimed Franklin was an able governor. Even his devoted wife thought him 'of too tender hearted a nature for his work'. 'A very excellent & kind hearted man—striving to effect all the good he can; but … the sort of responsibility vested in a governor is quite out of his way,' wrote George Frankland, the surveyor-general. Robert Crooke could not praise Sir John enough—he was kind to a fault, hospitable, liberal, 'and in any other position would have been universally beloved and respected ... unfortunately he was a weak man, of little or no capacity for business ... He was at heart a sailor', continued Crooke, 'cheerful and happy in temperament. He wanted to see others happy too, and looked upon business as wearisome and fatiguing.' And these were comments by people who liked Sir John. Roderic O'Connor, who did not, claimed London could not have found any man in Great Britain more incapable of governing the colony.[7]

To some, Franklin's end was clear from the start. In October 1837 an anonymous contributor to the *Sydney Monitor* prophesied that, as 'a man of sincerity even to simplicity', he would become the tool of men compared with whom he was a mere child in intrigue and politics. 'After a tedious and thorny reign of six years, he will be ousted by some low faction; and his latter days of retirement will be clouded by the recollection of the painful struggles, mortifications, and cheatery, he endured.'[8] This is exactly what happened.

However, Franklin was not a bad governor. The astute historian John West, who lived in the colony during most of this period, commented that Franklin's former pursuits had not prepared him for his role. But his administration was honest and open. Unlike Arthur, he had no private financial speculations or secret agents, and no hint of corruption. He was charitable and pious. For West—and, he implied, most colonists—these positive attributes did much to outweigh the negatives.[9] West was right. Franklin could point to few great achievements, and suffered in comparison with his outstandingly efficient predecessor, Arthur. But he oversaw no disasters, and his government functioned smoothly.

He felt himself satisfactory. 'You know well that I am no Theorist and am not apt to be visionary and can lay no claim to brilliancy of mind or genius', he wrote to his friend Richardson, 'but I do think my mind fitted for patient enquiry and calm investigation of matters though they may be somewhat difficult[,] and prompt as well as firm in action when I am convinced the course is right.'[10] His letters show that he was no imbecile, as his enemies claimed, but a sensible, straightforward man—though one who, realising his mediocrity, relied on advice from others, in particular from one trustworthy person who would be his confidante and guide. Richardson had filled this role, but he was now far away. Franklin needed a new chief adviser.

The person who would have expected to fill this role in Van Diemen's Land was John Montagu, the leading civil servant. He could look down on the Franklins, for he was socially superior (related to a duke) and better educated, though not wealthy. An army captain, he married a niece of George Arthur, and accompanied Arthur to the colony to make a career. Competent, intelligent and zealous, he became colonial secretary. Shrewd, reserved and cunning, wrote Jane Franklin after meeting him.[11]

Montagu's ally was Matthew Forster, another army captain who married an Arthur niece and sought his fortune in Van Diemen's Land. Also efficient and intelligent, though more forthright than Montagu (in letters to Arthur, Montagu toadied shamelessly while Forster did not), he was appointed chief police magistrate. Montagu and Forster, best friends, performed well, and were impossible to remove unless they made some major error. These two men led the Arthur faction, dedicated not so much to maintaining Arthur's policies as to keeping power. They were tough, Forster telling Jane Franklin, 'When once I stick my harpoon into a man, I don't take it out again'.[12]

However, as his first chief adviser Franklin chose his own private secretary, Alexander Maconochie. An ambitious, self-confident theorist, Maconochie had caused problems as secretary of the Royal Geographical Society in London, and Franklin was asked to take him away to Van Diemen's Land. The Society for the Improvement of Prison Discipline asked Maconochie to report on convict management in the colony.[13] On the voyage out the Franklins became friendly with the Maconochies, and he gave lectures, explaining his theory that white races probably had black ancestors, the black secretion which coloured the skin flying off as the intellect grew. Jane Franklin thought him interesting and lively, though annoyingly bumptious.[14] She invited the family to live in Government House.

Montagu detested Maconochie as an impractical theorist full of fancies, a challenge to his influence. The challenge did not last long. Maconochie despised his job—'a Household drudge'—and despised Sir John as puzzled and bewildered, won over by flattery. Attempting to show him reality (or what Maconochie considered reality) was 'like trying to force a piece of Barley-Sugar out of a child's mouth', melting away on impact. Maconochie started encroaching on the governor's responsibilities, telling Jane Franklin that he aimed to become governor himself. Mary Maconochie believed Montagu turned Franklin against her husband; at all events, Franklin reined him in. Sulkily, Maconochie worked to rule.[15]

Mary Maconochie described an attempt to oust the family from Government House, by forces unnamed. Only Jane Franklin stood their friend:

> there was a grand fracas, Lady Franklin became agitated & distressed beyond all measure … Lady F. is all kindness & he a mere cipher, alas! alas! It has been a most unfortunate appointment for him … Poor dear Lady F most sincerely do I feel for her; few <u>can</u> know what her trials are. For my own part I am certain in her place I should have gone crazy.[16]

As his chief adviser John Franklin now turned to Montagu, his leading civil servant—competent, experienced and very willing to assist since this meant he gained power. By May 1837 he was in control. The anti-Arthur press, a loose alliance of editors and a few leading colonists, hated this and depicted Franklin as the Arthur faction's tool.[17]

On his arrival, Franklin promised the colonists that he would 'see with his own eyes, hear with his own ears, and judge with his own judgement'. The press applauded, but after a while asked when this analysis would result in action. Lack of achievement became the main local criticism of Franklin's government—something which did not hurt ordinary people much, or dent his popularity. Action would have impressed London, but it was not Montagu's job to initiate it, and Franklin did not know how. Franklin was a good man who wished to do right, wrote Montagu, but more than wishes were necessary: 'the fairness,—vigor of mind and those other higher qualities which were so conspicuous in Sir John at the North Pole have not accompanied him to the South'.[18]

Even with Montagu's help, Sir John found his position difficult, and by the end of the year there were reports that he wished to return to England. The easy position he had expected turned out to involve hard and complex work for which he was unsuited. But there was no chance of resigning: surely his wife would have opposed such an idea most strenuously. In London, John Richardson heard rumours of Franklin's problems, and wrote to his wife (Sir John's niece) that 'your Uncle is too mild for Van Diemen's Land and that he will not take a bull by the horns but succumb to the spirit of party ... You see Lady F has plunged her husband into difficulty that he would otherwise have avoided.' And later: 'Poor fellow—before he undertook the management of a colony he should have asserted his right of governing his own family'.[19]

Richardson would not have been surprised at Jane Franklin's growing political role. She probably did not intend this when she came to Van Diemen's Land; after all, Sir John had performed satisfactorily in Greece without her doing more than a little prodding. However, gradually she became more involved. Her political activity had four phases. In 1837–38 Montagu was chief adviser, and she merely helped her husband at home. From 1839–1841 Montagu was in England, and she stepped into the vacant role. Montagu returned in early 1841 to find himself ousted. He challenged her, lost, and in early 1842 returned to England to complain to the Colonial Office. For the rest of the Franklins' period in Van Diemen's Land, 1842–43, Jane Franklin reigned supreme.

She was always interested in politics anywhere she went, but at first in Van Diemen's Land she kept to the sidelines. She and John Montagu were friendly, he providing the facts and gossip she loved: 'When I suggested that [the surveyor-general] was more accomplished than efficient, M^r. M. laughed, & s[ai]d never was any one less fitted for his office'. To her sister, Jane admitted that 'There was a time Mary when I was caressed & flattered by M^r. M'. He showed her his official correspondence and asked her opinion about political measures, and in 1870, long after the event, a newspaper accused them of undue interest in each other. No contemporary source supports the story, but clearly the pair were friendly enough to cause some speculation, while Jane herself mentioned being caressed—surely only metaphorically. (In 1870 the Hobart *Mercury* was outraged at the rumour: Lady Franklin, far from being beautiful, was distinguished by a highly gifted mind and a love of power; Montagu was highly honourable, an excellent husband and kind father; while our 'good old governor' was a hero who loved children.) However, any close friendship between John Montagu and Jane Franklin did not last. By early 1838 he was describing her as 'a lump of vanity', and she was writing doubtfully, 'As M^r. Montagu & I were such good friends to day'—hardly the words of lovers.[20]

Montagu's dislike of Jane Franklin developed as he realised she was advising her husband, usurping what Montagu saw as his own role. But she could hardly help becoming involved. With Maconochie defeated as adviser, Sir John needed a sounding-board at home and naturally turned to his wife, the one person he knew would be utterly loyal to him. More intelligent and widely read than her husband, much more politically astute, she had always tried not only to advance his career but to support, even protect, him, since that far-off day in 1828 at the Russian reception. She continued in Van Diemen's Land—naturally. As she said, 'every woman whose husband is in public life helps him if she can & if he gives her the opportunity which he will not fail to do if he can trust in her ability & discretion', and hers not only gave her the opportunity but asked for her help. 'Come back as soon as you can for I much want your good advice', he wrote, and as early as September 1837 he sent her his ideas on government matters. 'I am most anxious to have your opinions and mine embodied ... Pray therefore do use your best efforts to get your ideas completed.'[21] By December 1838 Jane had become more proactive, noting that 'I wrote [Sir John] a long letter of suggestions & recommendations', and she often discussed politics with guests at dinner, and advised Sir John accordingly.[22]

Montagu realised what was happening, and in December 1837 told Arthur that one cause of the colony's weak government was 'the Petticoat influence which Rules', for Sir John did nothing without consulting his wife. He was, wrote Montagu,

> *the tool of every rogue who will flatter his wife for she in fact governs. Her influence on him is wonderful and he never does a single thing without consulting her ... he is the weakest minded man I ever had to do business with ...*[23]

However, Jane Franklin did nothing overtly, and during 1837–38 relations remained courteous between Montagu and the Franklins. This was partly due to Jane's policy. Sir John wrote that she saw through Montagu and his ally Forster before he did, but wanted 'to make the best of them, and if possible to keep them as friends in check, seeing how dangerous they would be as enemies'[24]—a sensible plan.

Meanwhile, Maconochie, still private secretary, sent home his report on prison discipline, which strongly criticised the system Franklin was operating—in Franklin's diplomatic bag, without telling him fully about the contents. Maconochie admitted that he deceived Franklin, but 'my great defence for everything is my Cause'. Franklin forced him to resign and leave Government House, to Jane Franklin's anguish.[25] London penal reformers loved Maconochie's report, which advocated a new system of treating convicts with systematic reform built in, and Maconochie was sent to Norfolk Island to put it into effect. Partly due to his report, in 1840 transportation to New South Wales ceased, and all convicts were sent to Van Diemen's Land to be organised under a new probation system. Franklin had to start this, without sufficient finance, staff or instructions. He was not particularly successful, but he left before the system's huge problems became apparent.

In 1838 Montagu grew dissatisfied, feeling there was no credit or stimulus in working with such a weak governor as Franklin. He applied for leave in England, ostensibly for his health, really to seek a new job. The Montagus sailed in February 1839. 'I hope we shall at last escape from the trying scene of incessant conflict & excitement', wrote Jane Franklin, an example of her over-reaction to events, for to outward appearances recent months had been quiet enough.[26]

Montagu suggested that his ally Forster become acting colonial secretary and Franklin agreed, but straightforward Forster did not like Jane Franklin, and did not bother trying to cultivate her. This is apparent in his description to Montagu of 'My Lady's intrigue' to have a Mr Jackson appointed Sir John's private secretary. Forster said he could not work with Jackson, a member of the anti-Arthur faction. Sir John 'in his usual timid manner' said he was puzzled about whom to appoint. Jane Franklin saw Forster privately, and said that since the secretary would live with the family she had a right to a voice. 'After a good deal of <u>simpering</u> and <u>bush</u> beating, out it came, that Mr Jackson was the man ... She tried for two hours to convince me ... words escaped me in the heat of annoyance, for I observed that an Intrigue was carrying on'. He won, and Jane Franklin's second choice was appointed. Forster told Arthur he never felt safe owing to 'the intrigues of the court'.[27] Less wily than Montagu, he was more defensive and less influential.

For their part, the Franklins did not like Forster. Jane thought him bold and cunning, leading Sir John astray. So the role of chief adviser was vacant, and Jane naturally stepped into it, the one capable person Sir John could trust. When she was in Sydney in 1839 he sent her reports to read, and begged her 'not to delay your return'—she would be so much help when the Legislative Council was sitting.[28] Once back home she became closely involved, throwing herself heart and soul into politics: this dominates her diary, taking up 75 or 80 per cent of the daily entries. Her other interests such as her Huon settlers— let alone family matters—receive scant mention compared with the thrilling minutiae of day-to-day politics.

'I am now consulted in all the most important matters', Jane told Mary:

The proposed despatch on the new Constitution for the colony was decided on in the Library that my suggestions or approval might be obtained—the draft despatches are often submitted to me, for correction & alteration—the present important despatch upon Transportation adopts several ideas which I suggested ... This has grown gradually & imperceptibly ...[29]

Her strong influence can be seen in her letters to Sir John. One ran:

I hope your measures for wheat will answer. Have you really tendered for 5,000 bushels at 18 shillings? I am anxious to hear what your answer will be to the Launceston and other addresses. You will of course insist on the probationary gangs ... Your answer to Captain Maconochie is not satisfactory to me ...

And it continued. 'I hope you will <u>not</u> yield the Paving and Lighting Act, whoever may oppose it.' 'I trust you will press this measure [tolls on roads].'[30]

She did not press only Sir John. 'I was employed all the morning in writing down my ideas on the school Gazette notice & on the education of the poorer classes in this colony—I intended this for M[r]. Forster'; and when the Legislative Council rejected a long, waffly memorandum about Christ College, 'a simple, more succinct & somewhat dry document [was] substituted—I managed the alterations of this chiefly myself'.[31] She cultivated several senior civil servants, such as George Boyes. But it was not always easy, and her frustration at having no official power is clear:

I am in a position the most unfavorable for my anxious & ardent feelings—hearing every thing sooner or later, but often not till it is too late, entertaining often opinions widely opposed to those of

Sir John's advisers & while scarcely ever having found reason to
doubt the soundness of any opposing judgments I have formed,
yet unable to make them available & dreading above all things
to be supposed to exert any influence ... my mind is always
on the stretch & that sometimes it seems to threaten to fail me
altogether.[32]

Perhaps she tried to exert influence in another area. Montagu accused
her of involvement in the press: leaking information, writing articles
and buying a newspaper, the *Hobart Town Advertiser*. Edward Abbott
started the *Advertiser* in early 1839, and it became the government
newspaper. Montagu was skilled at twisting facts and this accusation
has never been taken seriously, but in December 1839 Jane Franklin
noted in her diary: 'M[r]. E. Abbott sent proof col[umn]s of newspapers
& request to correct—declined it—ab[ou]t Regatta'.[33] This shows at
least some involvement with the press—in which Jane became heavily
involved back in England.

Another important task was lobbying the Colonial Office in
London. Jane's letters ring with orders: Mary was to tell this person
this fact, show that person that letter. 'Do you think there could be
any harm in your touching on such a subject to M[r]. Gairdner [of the
Colonial Office]?'; 'Try & make a friend of Mrs Gairdner'; 'It is in your
power to make some of these facts better understood in England'.
The Colonial Office once complained of her unofficial communica-
tions. Jane realised that this occurred when dear Mary sent them the
'abstract of my plans' (on her orders), but argued her way out of the
accusation, at least locally.[34] Lobbying in London grew more important as more disgruntled colonial officials complained about Sir John,
who, unable to manage them, dismissed or suspended them.

The hardest of all Jane Franklin's self-imposed tasks was supporting her husband, as Mary Maconochie had noticed. 'Dearest Mary you
hardly know what I have to bear', Jane wrote to her sister. 'I have to
support myself my husband too ... his health & spirits which give me
the bitterest suffering.'[35] She was not always successful in heartening

and influencing Sir John, but he mostly followed her advice. She knew how to manage him: 'the best way is to humour him & to assure him that I care nothing at all about any thing that may happen ... I do not feel all this, but nothing agrees with him half so well as this method.' Her husband was 'trusting to me for everything':

> I work like a slave I cannot tell you what I do not do—& then I have to try and conceal that I do anything. Sir John's sensitiveness is beyond conception & it is in fact a country where people sh[oul]d have hearts of stones & frames of iron. Nevertheless this must not be told.

Mary must give the impression that all was well in Van Diemen's Land. 'Do not give to any one any thing but a cheerful view of things.'[36]

So, from her own admissions, Jane Franklin was heavily involved in politics. She read widely on every topic, consulted and cultivated sympathetic people, made up her mind what was to be done, then tried to implement her decisions through her husband, or other pliant politicians. She was involved in decision-making, and drafted or assisted in writing official documents. She possibly influenced the local press; she certainly lobbied London to boost Sir John's reputation.

Jane insisted to her sister Mary that her only motive was supporting her husband. 'There is no other gratification in my position than that I am enabled to be of some use to Sir John. It is exceeding disagreeable to me to be thought to meddle with affairs of state.' A constant refrain through Jane's letters to Mary was that her political actions must be kept hidden: 'Dearest Mary this is the profoundest of secrets ... You must not say I had any hand in it.' Her efforts were hampered by her husband, who was 'extremely incautious in making use of my name, in public'. When Montagu asked Sir John who was to replace him as colonial secretary, Sir John replied that he would consult Lady Franklin before he decided. 'Sir John is now cured of this habit'—too late. Montagu had proof from Franklin's own mouth of his wife's interference.[37]

In any case, it seemed well known in the colony that Lady Franklin assisted her husband. Hostile newspapers occasionally accused her of petticoat government, as part of their attacks on her husband. In December 1837 came the first mention: 'Now that we have a queen on the throne, we presume we are offering a compliment to Sir John Franklin when we most unequivocally and unhesitatingly assert that the island and dependencies of Van Diemen's Land are ruled by a Governor *under petticoat government*.' Occasional attacks followed. In 1838 a newspaper announced that Her Ladyship, 'a female of great ability', was Sir John's principal adviser. In 1839 another claimed she dominated her husband, 'it being very common for ladies to rule their husbands when their husbands are not able to rule them'. One newspaper was moved to verse:

QUEEN STREET.
The Council met to consider the Bill,
But the Governor paus'd in declaring his will,
"My Queen's absent," said he, "and 'twould not be meet
To go on without her—I live in Queen-street."

Then up arose Forster, and striking the table,
Vow'd that petticoat rule was quite discreditable . . .

But the others—Judge Pedder, Colonel Elliott—agreed:

Law, Army, and Fleet
We all fare alike—we all live in Queen-street.'[38]

So John Franklin was not the only one, and petticoat rule was a subject for joking. Less amusing was a comment that an eccentric woman like Lady Franklin 'is not the model after which parents in this Colony ought to wish to see their daughters formed, far less, that, by which the young men, the future fathers of our Isle, ought to wish to see their future wives, and the future mothers of the Colony trained'.[39]

How much did such accusations hurt Jane Franklin's reputation? Immensely, has always been the assumption, but was this really the case? Criticism of her appeared only in a few hostile newspapers. No one else complained. There are no critical comments in contemporary diaries or letters, and after she left Van Diemen's Land she was remembered admiringly, not for interfering in politics, but for her 'deep interest in all that could possibly promote the advancement of the colony'. While she was in the colony, the pro-Franklin press often praised her as gifted, intellectual, adventurous and indefatigable: 'Our best wish for the ladies of the colony is that the example of Lady Franklin may exert its proper influence over their tastes and engagements'. Jane reported home in 1839 that all was going well, with 'both Sir John & myself universally beloved & respected'.[40]

Besides, many people expected, even desired, that Lady Franklin play at least a quasi-political role. New Zealand colonists asked her to take a political message to her husband; South Australians hoped her visit would do away with jealousies between their colony and Van Diemen's Land; several people requested her to ask her husband for jobs. For example, Mrs Jeanneret sent Jane Franklin a book of seaweeds she had collected, with a flattering letter; Jane suspected she was being bribed to suggest that Sir John promote Dr Jeanneret.[41]

Robert Crooke wrote in his memoir-cum-novel that Lady Franklin had a natural talent for politics and intrigue, and should have been the governor instead of her husband. 'The real business of the country' was done in her study: appointments given, men dismissed, decisions made. But even Crooke, who did not like her, did not object. Some people preferred her to the Arthur faction. Van Diemen's Land's solicitor-general wrote to the secretary of state in London bemoaning 'the temporary absence in S. Australia of Lady Franklin, whose judgement, it is believed, affords the main counterbalance to the reckless policy of the acting Col. Sec^ry [Forster]'. (Far from being grateful for this praise, Jane thought it an 'unblushing piece of impertinence', bringing her actions to London's notice.)[42]

Although in theory women were meant to confine themselves to domestic affairs, in practice, as Jane Franklin herself commented, many did help their husbands. This occurred quite widely in Britain, but was especially the case in new frontier societies like America and Australia, where people lacked the networks of family and friends they had in Britain, and employees were scarcer and less well trained. Men often relied on their wives to assist them, and in the Australian colonies it was taken for granted that enterprises—farms, shops, pubs, businesses—involved the whole family, all doing what they could. Other women besides Lady Franklin extended this assistance to politics. In America, Abigail Adams (1797–1801) and Sarah Polk (1845–49) assisted their presidential husbands much as Jane Franklin did. Both were criticised, but fairly mildly, and it stopped neither— Abigail, nicknamed 'Mrs President', knew she should follow the example of non-political Martha Washington, but told her husband she would rather be 'bound and gagged and shot like a turkey'.[43] In Hobart, it was usual for wives of high officials—including Mrs Arthur and Mrs Montagu—to copy confidential documents, so essential a task in the days before copying machines, and this led easily to discussing the contents. With so many women assisting their husbands in so many areas, the attitude in the colony seemed to be: if clever Lady Franklin was helping that nice husband of hers with his work, why not? As far as the colony was concerned, she succeeded in treading the fine line between public and private, between innocent and culpable interference. Unfortunately for Jane Franklin, the bureaucrats at the Colonial Office in London had a more restricted view of women's role.

13

JANE FRANKLIN v.
JOHN MONTAGU

In 1841 the third phase of Jane Franklin's political activity started, after John Montagu returned from England to Van Diemen's Land. In many ways the two were alike: intelligent, shrewd, ambitious, good at scheming and intrigue, ignoring the truth when it suited them, believing the ends justified the means. Montagu told blatant lies in his letters, but so did Jane Franklin, claiming she took no part in politics when her diary shows she was taking part as hard as she could. They were also alike in competence: no matter who was advising Franklin, the colony's administration ran smoothly enough.

While Montagu was away on leave, from 1839 to 1841, Jane Franklin cemented her position as Sir John's chief adviser. In early 1841 she left for New Zealand. Shortly afterwards Montagu arrived back, having been unable to find a better position. Franklin welcomed him, '[requesting] me to conduct the public business precisely as before'. Franklin's diary shows him working well with Montagu and Forster, and perfectly capable of day-to-day administrative decisions, such as sending assistance to a brig that lost its top masts. He was firm where he believed he was morally right. The Presbyterian minister John Lillie was hurt by one of Franklin's decisions, and warned that the Legislative Council would sympathise with him. 'I never will be intimidated by a threat to sanction any thing of which my conscience disapproves', Franklin told him. 'We shall both have to answer for our actions & conduct before a higher than human tribunal.' Threatened with God, Lillie backed down.[1]

Montagu had enough time, three months, to settle back into his role of chief adviser—and then, in June, Jane Franklin returned. She had been fretting in New Zealand: 'I am extremely anxious to get back, and desirous of being at home again. My thoughts are constantly fixed on what may be going on while I am away.'[2] Once she was back, Montagu found himself supplanted. He had just been able to bear working with Franklin when he himself was, and was known to be, the real ruler. When this place was taken by Franklin's wife, he found it unbearable.

The Franklins also hardened against Montagu. Jane found him supercilious and unfriendly, and feared that in London he had heard criticism she had written to Mary, which meant he returned 'with a spirit of malice & vengeance against me & a determination to injure me'. It seems more likely that he developed this hostility when he realised she was his rival in dominating Sir John. He hated it. Yes, he wrote to George Arthur, some of Sir John's correspondence did lack calmness, because Lady Franklin wrote the drafts and introduced an angry, discourteous tone. Sir John's 'inability for his Office becomes daily more and more apparent, while she, on the contrary, becomes daily more anxious for authority, to gratify her voracity and eccentricities'.[3]

John Montagu and Jane Franklin particularly disagreed over Christ College, her pet project that Montagu thought a waste of money. The Legislative Council passed £5000 for the building, which needed £15 000. Jane Franklin invited Montagu to dinner:

> She knew from experience that I always avoid her questions about Public Business ... but upon this occasion she was not to be beaten—She not only told me what my advice was in the

*Ex[ecutive] Council respecting the college [which her husband
must have passed on to her], but she even said to me, why not
advise the Go^{vt} to accept the tender and build to the extent of the
money voted by the Leg[islative] Council, for surely, she added,
that body will never permit such a building to remain unfinished
from want of funds after £5000 of the Public Money has been
expended upon it? I, of course, gave her to understand that I
would do nothing of the kind …*

(but this is only Montagu's side of the discussion). She gave him up
as unpersuadable, he wrote, but he had no doubt 'that she would take
the earliest opportunity of making a difference between Sir John and
me'.[4] They were both convinced the other was the enemy. Montagu
attacked her because she threatened his power (as Maconochie had
done), not specifically because she moved out of woman's accepted
role. However, her 'unwomanly' actions were useful to him as ammu-
nition for criticism.

Well aware of this danger, Jane Franklin was displeased on hearing
that Gairdner of the Colonial Office told Montagu he hoped there were
no Mrs Austens in Van Diemen's Land—Mrs Austen being, reput-
edly, a governor's wife who sent home despatches in her own name,
for which her husband was dismissed or reprimanded. Jane Franklin
instructed Mary to find out what Gairdner meant. She herself thought
the story mythical; and if Gairdner referred to her, he was wrong, she
wrote. Her handwriting never entered Sir John's office, unlike Arthur's,
whose womenfolk copied despatches for him:

*But then they were stupid or silly, & I have the reputation (and a
woeful reputation it is in the estimation of weak-minded & malicious & jealous men) to be very clever—And then if a Governor's
wife is 'very clever' & is known to sit much in her own room, &
does not exhibit her fancy works, & has travelled on 3 continents
& is suspected of writing a book, why if she does not overturn the
state, or keep it going, it is not because she has not the means, or*

that she has not the <u>inclination</u> is of no avail—Woe to that poor
woman if the <u>man who wishes to rule her husband</u> suspects she
thwarts him in his design—he intends her for his <u>victim</u>.[5]

She tried to hide evidence of her political activity, writing to Mary that
'my habits are so retiring & my knowledge of what is going on so small
& my caution so great, that [the Arthur faction] have nothing tangible
to lay hold of'. Then Montagu saw his chance. In October 1841 Dr
Coverdale at Richmond was called to attend a convict patient but did
not go. The patient died. At the inquest the jury accused Coverdale
of culpable negligence. Montagu recommended his dismissal and
Sir John agreed. Jane Franklin happened to be staying in Richmond,
and her host told her Coverdale was highly esteemed and had been
badly treated. She told Sir John. A petition from Richmond begged for
Coverdale's reinstatement, and Sir John agreed.

Montagu was furious, accusing Lady Franklin of improper interference in politics. She was behind the petition, she caused Sir John
to overturn the decision, against Montagu's advice. Jane denied
everything—but admitted to Mary that she had influenced Sir John.[6]
Montagu knew it. 'I am very thankful that his period of service will
expire next January, when I hope a Gov' will succeed him who will
have mind enough to govern for himself', he told Arthur. 'A more
troublesome, interfering woman I never saw—puffed up with the love
of Fame and the desire of acquiring a name by doing what no one else
does.' Montagu's next move was to tell Franklin he would work to rule,
giving him no extra assistance. He was trying to break him, assumed
Franklin; unable to cope, the governor would beg for mercy. He
claimed he put his shoulder to the wheel and coped, but Boyes thought
Franklin found the work too much, and Montagu's version was that
'She has now got the reins—and a pretty mess they are making of the
public business between them'.[7]

Franklin showed no signs of breaking, so in December Montagu
apparently upped the pressure. The *Van Diemen's Land Chronicle*,
whose editor was a friend of Montagu, printed a libellous article about

Franklin, claiming that his incapacity, feebleness and unfitness for his position had long since outlived respect. Similar articles followed: 'the imbecile reign of the Polar Hero', deplorable weakness, misrule, notoriously plastic memory, and a wife who ordered the government gardener to stop supplying cabbages to the Montagus. She indignantly denied it, but she did order that vegetables be sent only to Government House.[8]

The Franklins blamed Montagu for the articles, but he denied involvement and implied that Sir John's memory was faulty. Boyes thought Montagu was guilty. 'Sir John has a fine game in his hand if he knew how to play his cards', wrote Boyes,

> *but notwithstanding the abetting & encouragings received from Lady F. Henslow [his private secretary], and young [Dr] Bedford I suspect he will forego all his advantages and make an inglorious peace with the offended power by admitting he was wrong and soliciting oblivion for the past.*[9]

Boyes was wrong. On 25 January 1842 Franklin suspended Montagu for refusing to cooperate with him, using disrespectful language and refusing to uphold in the press the governor's position. The real reason, Jane Franklin wrote, was that he made himself a greater man than the governor.[10]

Montagu had not expected Franklin to suspend him, and desperately tried to regain his position. He apologised for the disrespectful language, to no effect, then sent Dr Turnbull, a mutual friend, to ask Jane Franklin to mediate between him and Sir John. Jane was torn between conflicting feelings for her husband and Montagu, 'poor man'. Amazingly, she felt 'acute sympathies of which I cannot divest myself when I think of M'. M.'—whatever had happened between them? Sir John refused her mediation but did, unwisely, write Montagu a glowing reference.[11]

Vowing vengeance, Montagu went to London to lay his case before the Colonial Office. He claimed he was innocent. Nothing would have happened if he had not mentioned Lady Franklin's interference in the Coverdale case. Franklin himself wrote that his wife 'cannot help being clever but that is what [Montagu's] party cannot bear—They think they could have got on with a simple unsuspicious & obstinate old fool like myself, but that her discernment has unveiled them'.[12] He was probably right.

Some colonists sympathised with Montagu, others with Franklin, glad that he had triumphed at last after 'being almost trampled on'. Boyes and historian John West thought both sides at fault. 'No one who reads the dispute will deem it necessary to weigh nicely the reproaches which were current on either side', wrote West. 'To destroy or be destroyed is the usual choice of official war; and Montagu had not been bred in a school where more generous maxims prevail': Franklin was naive, Montagu was brutal.[13]

Boyes took no part in this. He did not trust Franklin, whose government, he wrote in his diary, was deservedly falling into ruin and contempt. Then Franklin asked him to become acting colonial secretary, and he accepted—he had his career and family to think of. He stopped criticising Franklin, except for odd mentions that he was 'duller than usual' or talked 'twaddle for an hour'. His diary depicts Franklin as a ditherer, forever asking advice about every issue that cropped up, but Boyes worked competently enough in his new role. He admired Jane Franklin's input. For example, one day Sir John read a draft official letter to her and Boyes, and she suggested a sensible, conciliatory addition. She was one of the few people Boyes admired, enjoying talking to her, even arguing with her at dinner. One evening she was so upset at the thought that convicts sent to rescue her party on the west coast might themselves have perished that Boyes too was moved: 'This generous kind hearted woman … certainly is a noble creature.'[14]

With Montagu gone, Jane Franklin was supreme as 'Sir John's best friend & adviser', as she wrote. Forster was subdued, Boyes admired her, and politics ran reasonably smoothly through the rest of 1842. Her only challenge came from Francis Henslowe, Sir John's new private secretary, who wrote her a letter of 'bitter strictures', accusing her of interfering—specifically (her summary ran) of usurping a chair in his office, asking for less work for her nephew and his subordinate Tom Cracroft, and recommending that Tom use narrower margins and smaller writing. 'These things seem to me very petty ... by what right it is that you have assumed the privilege of making yourself the censor of my conduct', she asked:

I find myself guilty of being devoted to my husband, of trying to be of use to him of yielding to his belief that I can be so, of exerting over him whatever influence I possess not to magnify myself & to gratify a love of power or distinction, but in furtherance, according to the best of my belief of his interests, reputation & character.

'Dear Mr Henslowe', she concluded, 'do not write to me nor speak to me again till you can do so in a spirit of kindness'. This masterly letter, putting Henslowe entirely in the wrong from a morally superior position, resulted in his complete submission.[15] Because she denied political activity Jane Franklin could not usually defend herself, but here she states her defence: everything I do is to assist my husband, and therefore permissible, even laudable, in a devoted wife.

There were still two flies in the Franklins' ointment. One was a continual drip of newspaper criticism, now from the pro-Arthur press. Sir John was unfit for office, a perfect nightmare, blamed for everything, even delayed mail. Fancy rewarding convicts for the west coast trip! A pardon just for helping Lady Franklin through the floods! The Arthur faction sent this accusation to London, and the Colonial Office made Sir John justify these perfectly legitimate pardons. Not only would she never die of the newspapers, Jane told Mary, 'neither I trust shall I die of the Colonial Office'.[16]

Hostile newspapers also criticised Lady Franklin: she used public funds to make a road to Ancanthe, she was eccentric and condescending, and her protégé, Joseph Milligan, was appointed to a position beyond his powers (as her supporters agreed, privately). 'Every one knows the evil influence which leads Sir John astray': she was the Lady Governor, unlike her predecessor:

> Lady Arthur was a gentlewoman; she did not go on a gipsey expedition, traversing the wilds of New South Wales in a dray in the company of men! She had no sawing establishment at the Huon—no botanical garden; she undertook no expedition to Macquarie Harbour, in company with a lot of prisoners of the very worst description ... These are a few of the monstrosities of the most despicable dynasty who now rule us.[17]

A horrible article to read, to know other people were reading, though Sir John wrote stoutly that 'We have learnt thank God to look upon these attacks with the proper spirit'.[18]

One newspaper called Jane Franklin the She-Governor, and replied to criticism for dragging a lady into the public arena by saying that if people obtruded themselves into public life 'by exercising an unauthorized and unacknowledged influence for good or evil in matters which seriously affect public weal', they lost their right to privacy— even more so, because an unauthorised person was irresponsible, and the press was the only check on them. When a female

> steps beyond the circle which is the proper sphere of her sex, when, from conviction of superior abilities, to direct the public affairs of the community in which she lives, from a restless intermeddling spirit, from a desire for notoriety, or even a wish and a conscious ability to do good, she begins to intermeddle with public affairs, much more when she exercises a paramount influence in those affairs,—her every act having reference to those affairs, [she] becomes the legitimate subject of notice and comment.[19]

However, a few hostile newspapers did not represent popular opinion. Other newspapers supported the Franklins, and hardly anyone else criticised them: contemporary diaries either sympathise with them or do not mention them. Louisa Anne Meredith, who published an account of her experiences in the colony, thought attacks on Lady Franklin disgraceful and unmanly; the lady's kindness and ability should have met with gratitude and respect. The insults were the acts of a few, said West: 'The frank and humane temper of Sir John Franklin won the affections of the settlers'. The pro-Franklin *Hobart Town Advertiser* commented that the colonists had a high personal regard for Sir John; a people's devotion shielded him from his enemies—and Sir John Franklin had enemies any honest man should be proud of.[20] Still, coping with those hostile articles must have been hard going.

The other problem for the Franklins was fear of the future. Suave, urbane, well-connected Montagu was in England, putting his case to the Colonial Office. Would he be reinstated, or worse, made governor? Would the Franklins be vindicated or humbled? Jane Franklin worried— about the future, Montagu, the significance of news from England. Late in 1842 she became ill. She recovered, but decided to visit her elderly father in England, crossing the Andes on the way. Why would Jane, the devoted wife, leave her husband at this difficult time? Eleanor thought it was because she could bear the colony no longer. This plan fell through because the captain of the only possible ship refused to take her.[21]

In early January the despatch about Montagu's suspension arrived from Lord Stanley, the secretary of state for colonies. It was disastrous, hostile to the point of cruelty. The Franklins did not realise that James Stephen, the administrative head of the Colonial Office who believed in upholding colonial governors where possible, already had a low opinion of Franklin—mainly created by Franklin's own despatches and actions. He did not send relevant information; his reports were too voluminous; he was at times 'too kind, too forbearing and too patient', but dismissed or suspended too many officers, sometimes injudiciously. After Franklin dismissed an officer for addressing him rudely, 'There prevails in Van Diemen's Land an opinion that Sir John Franklin is a person who may be safely addressed in language which few other Governors would tolerate'. Stephen concluded that he 'is deficient in the authority and self-reliance required in such an Office'.[22]

By 1842 Franklin could do little right, as indicated by the Colonial Office's severity over the convict pardons. Montagu's evidence was the nail in his coffin. Franklin was unable to control his subordinates, Stephen told Stanley. He (Stephen) believed Montagu really governed the colony, because Franklin was incapable, weak and indolent. Montagu's evidence convinced Stephen that Lady Franklin, 'a vindictive intermeddling woman' with a weak man under her control, was 'a great and discreditable incubus' on the government of Van Diemen's Land. He was convinced she did write the despatches, because Sir John, 'a plain Sailor and a man of sense', would never use their feminine phrases and over-excited style—would never have written that he was 'inexpressibly shocked', for example (and it is not the sort of wording he did use). 'It is indeed to be lamented that Lady Franklin's name should be mixed up with these matters, but if it be true that she had forfeited the immunities of her sex by meddling in Public Affairs I think Mr. Montagu is hardly to blame for refusing them to her.'[23]

Despite his irritation with Franklin, Stephen had not previously mentioned Jane Franklin's name. His information about her came from Montagu. Stanley repudiated Franklin's accusation that Montagu influenced Colonial Office staff,[24] but Stephen does seem to have believed and confided in Montagu. Stephen's confidential comments about Lady Franklin 'intermeddling'—an unusual word—and losing protection by moving out of the feminine sphere were repeated in a Hobart newspaper, presumably via Montagu.

But John (and Jane?) Franklin made matters worse by sending Stephen long, waffling despatches justifying their actions, while Montagu's defence was short and to the point. Years of frustration boiled over, and Stephen, in Stanley's name, wrote a harsh despatch, which arrived in January 1843. It stated that Franklin's proceedings were not well judged. He should not have suspended Montagu, who was exonerated from all but one of Franklin's charges against him. Yes, he had gained too much authority—because Franklin lacked energy and decision. Montagu had not used Lady Franklin's name improperly. He was given a superior position at Cape Town. However, though the Colonial Office thought Franklin weak, they also thought him a 'man of sense', and decided to let him serve out the usual term of six years (due to end soon, in January 1843), then replace him without criticism—though without making this decision public.[25]

The Franklins found the despatch devastating. 'My whole mind is overturned on the means of reparation for the injuries I have received', wrote Sir John, and Jane urged her English friends to see Stanley and put him right. Boyes thought the despatch insulting, 'becoming a Lord possibly but beneath a Gentleman', fatal to Franklin's character and government. However, added Boyes, Franklin was an imbecile, weak and mean. He suspected everyone of trickery, forgot his promises and shrank from activity and decision. Exaggerated perhaps, but possibly indicating the depths of Franklin's distress in this terrible situation. His wife was just as upset. One evening at dinner a guest's mention of recent events brought tears to her eyes. She wept immoderately, she wrote, because the tears melted some soap round her eyes and they smarted[26]—well, that was her story.

In April the new colonial secretary arrived: James Bicheno. Roughly Sir John's age, temperament and stout shape—Jane Franklin thought they made a droll-looking pair—he worked well with him, reporting that when he read Stanley's despatch in the Colonial Office, he exclaimed, 'Holloa, is this the way you snub the Governor? how do you expect him to take it? What has a Col. Secretary to expect if you treat a Governor so?' Jane Franklin discussed politics with him (she worried that he did not realise how dreadful Forster was), and asked him if Sir John had been recalled—the term generally used, though it was not official. Yes, was the answer, so at least they knew. In July they read in an English newspaper that Sir John Eardley-Wilmot had been appointed. 'It is the triumph of villainy I find so hard to bear!' exclaimed Jane.[27] Now, as always, the Franklins averred that both were entirely innocent of any charge. Whether Jane Franklin willingly ceded her position as adviser to Bicheno is not clear. Little of her writing remains for this period, which is perhaps telling, but there was no reported friction.

Worst of all, Stephen showed Montagu Stanley's despatch. Montagu sent a copy to his Hobart friends, with his letters to and from Stanley and supporting letters from friends. They formed what was known as 'The Book', which Hobart people could read—a terrible situation for the governor. In it, Montagu blamed Lady Franklin for his downfall. Her interference in public matters 'is so great and her mode of proceeding so extraordinary that there is scarcely any subject she is not so prominently conspicuous in'. Montagu was more vicious about her than Sir John, whom he depicted as merely incapable. The eighteen supporting letters mostly only regretted Montagu's departure, but one claimed he had 'fallen a victim to a system of mean and deceitful intrigue, carried on by Lady Franklin and an unprincipled coterie of flatterers ... to see him and the Colony sacrificed to female artifice excites universal indignation.'[28] Montagu's defence is a mixture of truth, exaggeration and omission—much the same mixture that Jane herself was writing.

In July the Bishop of Tasmania, Francis Nixon, arrived with his family. They became close to the Franklins, accepting their version of events, as Mrs Nixon wrote:

> *Lady Franklin is a very superior woman, but retiring and shy in her manner, and too unworldly to be popular in the very second-rate society there is here. Her whole mind seems bent on doing good to the Colony, and future generations will bless her memory. But oh, she has been fearfully traduced ...*
>
> *I remember your hearing in Downing Street that Lady Franklin was governor here. Now, this is one among the many falsehoods disseminated by the Montague party. Though a very superior woman, she has taken no part in public measures.*[29]

(But gossip that she ruled had penetrated to Downing Street.) Sir John, said Mrs Nixon, was honest, straightforward and right-minded, too single-hearted for the double-dealing of the Montagu party. The bishop said that Jane Franklin 'is the most amiable, simple unassuming person he ever met with, and that if her stockings are blue, her petticoats are so long that he has never found it out'.[30] This must have pleased her—though she must have been a good actor to convince him she was simple.

By now it was known that the new governor was arriving, and the hostile press had a field day. Hurtful placards announced, 'Glorious News! Sir John Franklin's Recall!' There were snobbish sneers: Wilmot was the representative of an ancient family, not a 'parvenu of yesterday'—did readers realise that Sir John's brother-in-law was the landlord of a London hotel, very low on the social scale? Lady Franklin was 'the influence behind the throne, greater than the throne itself'.[31]

In August the Franklins took the bishop on a trip to the Huon district. At 2.30 one morning the remaining inmates of Government House were woken by a thunderous banging on the door. The new governor would arrive next morning; they must leave as soon as possible. It was just another in the long list of insults that Sir John had no prior notice of his successor's arrival (the ship bearing the despatch was delayed, but still …).[32]

The Franklins held a clearing sale of their goods, among them 'nic nacs, collected from every quarter of the globe'. A sad end for Jane Franklin's collection, but freight was expensive. Their last weeks in Van Diemen's Land were marred by Wilmot's discourteous behaviour, killing the Christ College plan and usurping the Tasmanian Society with his own Royal Society, but the Franklins were thrilled by 'the universal respect I might almost say homage which we every where receive'. Sir John was presented with congratulatory addresses, praising his character more than his administration—the governor 'whose judgment might err, but whose kindliness of heart and unwavering integrity of purpose might be unhesitatingly confided in'. Hobart citizens commended 'the benevolent and philanthropic exertions of your amiable and excellent Lady', and the Tasmanian Society delivered a eulogy. Sir John and Lady Franklin had tried to introduce 'something better than a mere money-getting spirit', to see the colony as more than a penal settlement. Had the amiable and highly gifted Lady Franklin remained longer she would have been better appreciated, her virtues and charities realised, and she could have raised the minds of colonists nearer the standard of her own.[33] Sir John's reply—surely only penned after consultation with her—summed up the way she wished to be seen: limited and inadequate in her womanly way, but devoted and altruistic:

> however limited her sphere of action, or however inadequate her means and her ability, her heart has been disinterestedly and fervently devoted to the fulfilment of her duties, in which she has ever regarded the promotion of every object tending to the moral and intellectual improvement of the Colony as an essential part.[34]

On 3 November the Franklins sailed from Hobart. Sir John walked to the wharves, where thousands of people, Hobart's largest crowd so far, cheered him to the skies, 'a loyal & generous people paying a heartfelt tribute of affection to a truly good man … Thus departed from among us as true and upright a ruler as ever the interests of a British colony were entrusted to.'[35]

As on their arrival, Jane Franklin was not there. The ladies joined Sir John in the evening. They played no public role.

The Franklins inspected the Huon settlement, then sailed back towards Hobart, dropping off John Gell, who had just become engaged to Eleanor. Jane had had enough of emotional partings:

> I left the dinner table & retired into the back cabin whither Eleanor joined me—M^r. Gell soon came in—I clasped him in my arms whilst he sobbed with intense emotion—Leaving him with Eleanor, I then stood upon the ladder to avoid the rain upon deck & the company of any one else.[36]

It was easier to write down one's feelings, and her farewell letter to her old friend Dr Turnbull was emotional, with the slightly flirtatious undertones she often employed:

I suffered much in parting from you ... but perhaps my over-charged heart too readily betrayed my emotions ... Nevertheless, Sir John tells me I acted precisely as he should have expected & as I "ought" to have done, & moreover, he proved to me by some examples I had not myself been witness to on that day how strong a personal interest he had in approving of his wife's mode of bidding an old friend farewell ...

*I felt indeed, & still feel that in all human probability we met for the last time ... Dear D*ʳ*. Turnbull, if we meet not again in this world, may we be found worthy, tho' I dare not believe it in my own case, to enter that holy presence in which you, I firmly believe, will be an accepted & a sainted worshipper.*[37]

What had been happening? Nothing, probably, just another of her enjoyable platonic friendships with an intelligent, responsive man. In the years to come Jane Franklin had an astonishing influence with statesmen and other leaders in Britain and America, which no rational explanation based on existing evidence can really make comprehensible. Perhaps this flattering, intimate, flirtatious-but-innocent, you-are-so-special style helps explain it.

After a visit to Melbourne, the Franklin party left Australia on 12 January 1844. Despite her later travels round the world, Jane Franklin never returned.

Did Jane Franklin interfere in politics? Clearly she did. Did she interfere improperly? Officially she did nothing, and her actions can be seen as within (just) the spectrum of acceptable wifely assistance to a husband. No one in Van Diemen's Land except the small Arthur faction accused her of impropriety; in John West's measured judgment, though her 'masculine intellect' and adventurous spirit led some to ascribe to her more than the usual feminine authority, this was acceptable because 'her influence was exercised on the side of religion, science, and humanity'.[38] However, if she did all she claimed, drafting despatches and government policy, her actions can be construed as improper interference by a person with no official role.

Four factors diminish any impropriety. Firstly, there were no bad effects. No disasters occurred because of Jane Franklin's advice. Like her husband, she had no overriding political principle, no aim to change the direction of government; her advice was based on ad hoc reaction to events, and usually seems sensible. Her one major impractical plan, for Christ College, did not happen. Secondly, there would have been little reaction if Montagu had not raised her activities with the Colonial Office, for his own ends. Thirdly, in the context of colonial politics any impropriety was minor—John West saw Governor Arthur's land speculations as more improper. And lastly, neither John nor Jane Franklin had much option. Being John Franklin he needed an adviser, and naturally turned to the person who had advised him since 1828; and being Jane Franklin, when her husband asked for help she gave it.

The difficult episode taught Jane Franklin valuable lessons, which helped her greatly in the years to come. One: use the press to your advantage, have articles printed that give your point of view—and need not be accurate. Attack is more effective than defence; a dynamic, interesting article grabs attention, a reactive defence does not. Two: develop a network of influential friends and supporters, who must be continually cultivated to keep them onside. Three: above all, remain in the approved feminine role. Step outside it, and she became open to attack; remain within it, and she was protected by the code of chivalry, which said that a gentleman must not criticise a lady, should not even mention her name in public.

What do Jane Franklin's experiences say about Van Diemen's Land, about all Australia? She was by anyone's standards unusual, even eccentric, yet apart from the small Arthur faction people admired and esteemed her. Perhaps woman's expected role was not as circumscribed in practice as has sometimes been assumed.

14

JOHN FRANKLIN
DISAPPEARS

Jane Franklin arrived back in England in 1844 as an obscure private person. Ten years later she was internationally famous, her fame gained by using skills she had developed in Van Diemen's Land.

The Franklin party landed in June 1844 to a warm welcome from their friends and relations—though when someone was tactless enough to mention Van Diemen's Land troubles, Jane had such a violent attack of hysterics that her sobs could be heard all over the house. Sir John was intent on gaining redress from Lord Stanley. After months of lobbying by Sir John and his friends, Stanley did write a grudging, partial apology. Not enough: Sir John wanted to print his defence. Jane opposed this 'horrible publication', but John insisted. So she supported him, and she, Eleanor and Sophy were busy copying documents and organising material.[1]

The situation changed dramatically in December 1844. James Ross told Sir John that the Admiralty was planning an expedition in the ships *Erebus* and *Terror* to solve, finally, the question of the Northwest Passage. It was seen as straightforward, merely passing through the short section still unknown. Ross himself, the obvious leader, would decline the command. 'I shall certainly offer myself', replied Sir John.

He went straight to London and started lobbying. Many people had reservations: he was 58, with limited Arctic experience gained twenty years before, and had never commanded a ship there. Beaufort, Sabine, Back and the Admiralty pressed Ross to reconsider, offering a baronetcy, a pension and postponement. However Ross, Parry and Richardson strongly supported Franklin, Parry telling Lord Haddington of the Admiralty that Franklin would die of disappointment if he were not appointed. Jane Franklin was ambivalent, she wrote to Ross. She was worried about John going but would like him to be asked, and surely he would accept only if he felt fit. The appointment would heal the hurt from his recent treatment; 'I dread exceedingly the effect on his mind of being without honorable & immediate employment'. There is no evidence that she pushed Sir John into the post, or lobbied for him; it was not necessary, for he was desperate to go, lobbying hard himself. No alternative leader appeared, for Ross refused all pleas, the Admiralty thought Barrow's protégé James Fitzjames (appointed captain of *Erebus*) inexperienced, while Francis Crozier heard the news too late to volunteer. In any case, he told Ross, he felt unfit to lead, though he wanted to serve as second-in-command.[2]

In February 1845, Haddington interviewed Franklin. In a last-ditch effort, he implied that Franklin was too old to take command. 'I know your age: you are 59.' 'Not quite', said Franklin: there were two months to go. Haddington made more objections, but Franklin claimed absolute fitness. Haddington felt he had to give in, so appointed Franklin and, at the urging of Ross and Franklin, Crozier as second-in-command. The expedition was to undertake scientific observations, but its instructions stated that completing the Northwest Passage was its main aim. Taken up with organising his glorious expedition, John Franklin handed preparation of his defence pamphlet to Jane, with 'the most perfect reliance on your own judgment'. The 157-page pamphlet (or rather, short book) was privately printed later that year, but such old news did not gain much attention.[3]

What with Stanley, the pamphlet and the expedition, it was an anxious time for Jane Franklin. As well, the family had no settled home, and often moved; Uncle Guillemard was ill, and she helped care for him until he died; her elderly father was also ill; and John had a cold, and was irritated with Fanny. The Franklins were presented at court, which was good, of course, but something else to organise. Despite hating sewing, Jane made John a Union Jack to be flown when he achieved his aim, as his first wife had done. When he was dozing one evening, she threw it over him. 'Oh Jane! what have you done?' he exclaimed, alluding to the superstition that this was bad luck, since the flag was used as a shroud at sea.[4]

Sophy was a problem. Family dynamics had changed. John's adored daughter Eleanor, now released from the schoolroom, had taken Sophy's place as the central young woman of the household, the Franklins assuming Sophy would return to her mother. Sophy assumed she would remain with the Franklins in her previous role as quasi-daughter. She was hurt, and wrote her aunt Franklin a bitter, slightly hysterical letter. Despite her living with them for eight years as a daughter, 'both Eleanor & my Uncle prefer that I sh[oul]d not be in the family … [they] feel this visibly'. All she wanted was to help her aunt and uncle, for no one could feel more affection for him than she did (despite his not wanting her in the family?). Jane's reply has not survived, but from now on Sophy was seldom with the Franklins. She refused marriage proposals from Francis Crozier and Owen Stanley, making both deeply unhappy. 'I am not well and out of spirits', she told Mary Price, but continued, staunchly, 'I am not married or engaged & as I do not care for the people who wanted to marry me, I am much better as I am'. Meanwhile, Eleanor eagerly helped her father, and Jane's letters to her show the two women on friendly terms. Jane wrote as one ally to another, albeit a junior one, asking Eleanor to keep an eye on Papa's letters and encourage him to be kind about Fanny.[5]

Finally all was ready with Franklin's ships, described as the best-equipped ever to leave Britain, with modern steam engines, modern heating and provisions for three years, including the latest tinned food. Dr Richard King, an eccentric explorer disliked by many but with the awkward talent of often being right, warned that the ships

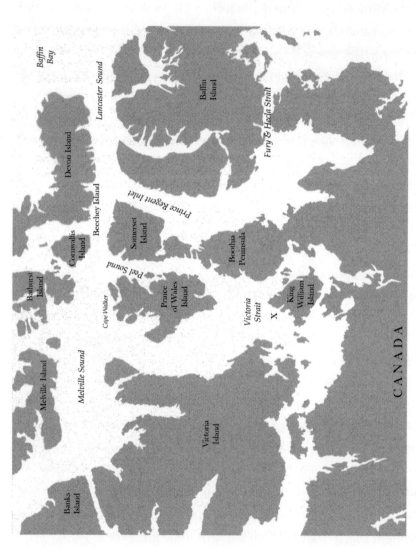

The Northwest Passage—area of exploration
X = *Erebus* and *Terror* beset here

were too large, there were too many men, and Franklin would end up the nucleus of an iceberg. Everyone ignored him. Dear Papa was in excellent spirits, reported Eleanor. His wife was less robust, worry and work taking their toll, but she provided the expedition with all the comforts she could, including a monkey and a cockatoo. On 19 May 1845, Jane, Eleanor and Sophy were on the wharf to wave goodbye. Last letters came that summer from the ships in Baffin Bay, reporting everyone cheerful except poor rejected Crozier.[6] Then they disappeared into the Arctic.

Now it was a question of waiting for news. Sophy went home to her mother. Jane and Eleanor spent the next couple of years mostly travelling. Only extreme optimists hoped for news in 1845, but there was reasonable hope of hearing something in 1846. Nothing. In 1847 Richard King announced that the expedition might be in danger, and relief should be sent at once to save it from starvation or cannibalism. The public started to worry, and when autumn brought no news the Admiralty announced rescue expeditions. In 1848 James Ross was to sail along Franklin's supposed route; John Richardson and a Hudson's Bay Company employee, Dr John Rae (an expert in solo travelling in the Arctic, living off the land Inuit-style), were to travel west along the coast from the Coppermine River; and a relief ship was sent to Bering Strait in case Franklin appeared there.[7]

So began the Franklin Search, which lasted twelve years, was extremely expensive, and involved twenty search expeditions, three aborted expeditions, eleven supply expeditions, one relief expedition and four bi-purpose expeditions, 39 in all, sent by the British Admiralty and private interests in Britain and America. The largest search of all time? It was certainly the greatest mystery of its age, capturing the imagination of the western world; mass-circulation newspapers were relatively new, and this was the first rescue to be reported in newspapers round the globe, from the London *Times* to the New Zealand *Taranaki Herald*. The Search (as the family called it, with a capital S) had everything a drama needed. 'No hunt was ever so exciting', claimed a British journal: missing men and theories about where they were, continuing action of one sort of another—reports that Franklin was alive, mysterious bottles in Siberia, tinned food found putrid, clairvoyant predictions and so on—and a personification of tragedy in Lady Franklin, the devoted wife giving her all to find her lost husband.[8]

All but the last expedition failed. Why? The Search covered a huge, remote, inhospitable, largely unknown area, navigable for four months a year at most, with problems even then of freezing temperatures and seaways blocked by ice. Franklin's instructions were clear—to sail southwest from Cape Walker on North Somerset towards Bering Strait or, failing that, north up Wellington Channel—but there was much debate, as people remembered what he had said to them and followed their own pet theories: he could be anywhere. Planners were hindered by hoaxes, rumours, vague information from Canadians, misunderstandings and premature conclusions—an utter lack of information and a glut of speculation. Their knowledge was limited, even so-called authorities sometimes having little. Incompetence and doubling-up of effort were also factors. And it all looked so easy on the map, in comfortable London.[9]

Basically, the searchers looked in the wrong places. The route Franklin actually took, south down Peel Sound or perhaps McClintock Channel, was usually blocked with impenetrable ice, so it was assumed he had not gone there. The Search focused on the west, towards Melville Island, and north, up Wellington Channel. Possibly some people had other motives, and some commanders seemed more interested in finding the Northwest Passage themselves and claiming the £10 000 reward than in finding Franklin.[10] In the terrible climate, mere survival was hard enough, and some accounts barely mention actually looking for Franklin. Some sent sledging parties to search further, but they too looked in the wrong places. Expedition after expedition returned with no news.

In early 1847 Jane Franklin claimed she was not too anxious about her husband, a letter sounding happy and carefree in a way her later letters never did. Then King published his dire warning, and she became consumed with worry. By November she was in despair, wanting action—'Everything should be done at <u>once</u>'. She had nearly given up the ships: apart from the most painful explanation of their absence, what alternative was there? Ross and Richardson tried to calm her, as Franklin had asked them; Richardson and Strzelecki suggested that she leave everything to the Admiralty; the Admiralty sent soothing letters. However, her fears were too intense for her to be the passive wife these men wanted. They did manage to dissuade her, at 56, from trekking through Arctic Canada with Richardson, but once the relief expeditions were announced she urged action on the leaders—do not scruple to ask for two ships, she told Ross, the Admiralty 'require to be very plainly spoken to'; and make sure you look at the north coast of Baffin Bay.[11]

Sophy Cracroft told a story which, though it might be apocryphal, shows her opinion of Jane Franklin's determination, plain speaking and success. When Lord Auckland of the Admiralty politely visited Lady Franklin to report progress, she told him James Ross needed steam launches. 'Why Lady Franklin, you will be asking next for Balloons', exclaimed Auckland, and received the reply, 'and if Balloons were thought necessary, you would add them of course'. Auckland supplied the launches.[12]

However, in 1848 Jane Franklin was only moderately involved in the Search. She (and sometimes Eleanor) interviewed officials at the Admiralty and the Hudson's Bay Company—the latter 'useless', said Jane—and she offered a reward to induce whalers to search for her husband. Other interests obtruded occasionally. Feared Chartist riots came to nothing; Eleanor tried to save someone from the Catholic church; Sophy came to Jane for advice when she was threatened with legal proceedings for having implied that a woman in Van Diemen's Land was an ex-convict (the case fizzled out); and Jane herself was often unwell. But the Search overrode everything. By the end of 1848, when the expedition's three years of supplies would have run out, Jane was deeply despondent. She was not alone; relatives and friends of all

129 missing men worried. 'How long did we hope, even against hope, for tidings of him!' wrote a Franklin niece. 'How often have I dreamt that he was again among us in England!'—and then to wake and realise it was only a dream.[13]

Jane became much more actively involved in the Search in 1849, and for the next decade it dominated her life. She felt even more urgently that it was now or never, if anyone were to be found alive; that no one else was doing enough; that success rested on her efforts. In January, with three expeditions in hand (Ross, Richardson and the Bering Strait relief ship), an informal Arctic committee of explorers came into being, which gained semi-official status as the only such body the Admiralty could consult. Jane Franklin was not a member but had influence, discussing ideas with members before meetings, holding some of these at her house. Strongly urged by her, the government offered huge rewards: £20 000 to anyone rescuing Franklin and, later, £10 000 for finding his ships, and £10 000 for completing the Northwest Passage.[14]

'Mama has been very active in stirring up people to consider the necessity of searching every where at once', Eleanor wrote to her father in early 1849, sending her letter with a relief expedition just in case. For a start, Jane went to ports to ask whalers to look for Sir John. They agreed, but with no result. However, press descriptions gained her magnificent publicity: 'this most estimable lady, with all the fervour of a devoted wife ... ', her 'pious pilgrimage ... her most touching cause ...' More publicity came in May when she wrote to the American President asking for his help. Her magnificently crafted letter appealed to sentiment, Christianity, national pride, financial gain and competitive spirit, as she asked a 'great and kindred nation ... to take up the cause of humanity' and wrest the glory from Britain of saving adventurous navigators from a terrible fate, relieving 'the intense anxieties of a wife and daughter' (the last time she allowed Eleanor a role). The President replied positively though did nothing; but Jane's letter, praised in Parliament as one of the most eloquent ever written, was widely published, presumably provided by Jane herself. John Gell, now ordained a clergyman, returned and assisted her, helping organise prayers in churches.[15]

Finally, with so many areas in the Arctic unsearched and time running out, Jane Franklin decided to send out her own expedition, and accompany it. Family and friends were appalled; but, undaunted, she engaged a broker, ordered her investments to be sold out, and asked the Admiralty for £5000 or the loan of two ships. They refused. So she planned to buy a whaling ship, using her own funds, donations from supporters and an Arctic Bazaar, at which she sold her travel mementoes. The plan fell through and she became hysterical, blaming obstructive family and friends, feeling everyone was against her. She had to be content with paying £500 to a whaler to search north Baffin Bay. 'Poor dear Woman', wrote Isabella Cracroft, 'she has worked herself up to such a state of excitement she cannot command her feelings'. The press described her 'restless energy ... soliciting aid in all directions'. A letter in a London newspaper praised Lady Franklin as an Englishwoman with strength of will, determination and fire of soul, like Elizabeth I.[16]

This letter, like other articles ('this most estimable lady ...'), is very much in Sophy Cracroft's style, and 1849 was the year she came to live with Jane Franklin. In June Eleanor married John Gell. She had been her stepmother's live-in companion and assistant, and Jane needed a replacement. A plan that she would live with the Gells fell through, and the obvious person came to live with her: Sophy Cracroft, who had experience in Van Diemen's Land.

Sophy had spent a boring four years, living with her mother in straitened circumstances in a country town. Her suitors were married or absent, no new ones appeared, and she had little money. She was in her thirties and life offered only more of the same, until the summons came to join her aunt. This was her chance, and she took it. Jane Franklin was fortunate. Instead of Eleanor, who tried to restrain her, for the rest of her life she had Sophy at her side, encouraging, sympathising, working hard (all night before a ship sailed, to complete the paperwork, for example[17]), happy to obey Jane's every wish, the ideal companion. Her subordinate role was not always easy, for Jane could be demanding and exhausting, but memories of those four tedious years would help. Sophy had her reward in a home in London, feeling needed, and sharing Lady Franklin's fame—not to mention some of her own, with her name placed on maps. 'Captn Inglefield has put me down upon a cape in Jones Sound', she told her mother in 1852. 'I was laughed at last night in a complimentary way, for my headlands in various parts.'[18] So enjoyable!

In 1849 Sophy was the only one to encourage Jane Franklin to buy a ship, and by summer the two women were inseparable. Sophy was vital to Jane's success. She admitted that inspiration came from Lady Franklin, but she provided the back-up: writing letters and interviewing people when Jane could not, writing glowing accounts of Jane's activities for the press, accompanying her almost everywhere, taking over when she was ill, opening letters when Jane quailed in fear of their contents, probably doing the household organising Jane detested, and seeing her through the frequent devastating times when bad news arrived. Returning with no news, one captain was afraid to meet Lady Franklin, but found her less upset than he expected, for Miss Cracroft 'seems to keep up her spirits'. 'Poor thing, she seems to cling to me more than ever', was Sophy's version. 'Sophy has been almost consistently with me & has been to me as a daughter since E's marriage—without her aid I shd not have been able to get thro' this work', Jane wrote to her husband.[19]

Sophy had another role, as Jane's 'personal Rottweiler'. Jane's letters (those that missed the cull) were tolerant, temperate, sometimes charming: Sophy's were often abrasive. She was the one who rebuked people, for example remonstrating with one man after he had the temerity to put a proposal to the Admiralty without clearing it with Jane. Historian Ian Stone concludes that Sophy treated this man 'despicably'. She gave orders, telling a ship's captain how to run his ship ('You must not permit your men to go ashore at Valparaiso ...'). Sophy the disciplinarian was indispensable to Jane Franklin, making it possible for her to remain within her womanly role. Occasionally

Sophy's feelings ran away with her, and her letters could be hysterical (she loved underlining, an ominous sign). Then Jane had to correct her, but on the whole Sophy was a wonderful asset, her one unfailing supporter. Sophy herself was thrilled to be Jane Franklin's companion. 'I cannot express to you how entirely I honor and love her', she wrote to Sir John, 'and to be permitted to endeavour to comfort her and share her sorrow is a privilege which I value above any other.'[20]

In the summer of 1849 Jane and Sophy went to the Orkneys, ostensibly to gather news from whalers, though they did more sightseeing than news-gathering—'I am enjoying myself most thoroughly', Sophy wrote home.[21] Huge relief came in October 1849 with the arrival of an Inuit map showing Franklin was safe, his expedition merely beset by ice with James Ross. Jane and many others believed this. Her hired whaling ship returned having done no searching. Then came catastrophic news. Both Richardson and Ross were back, with nothing except proof that the Inuit map was false—and Ross had only reached the top of Prince Regent Inlet. Jane Franklin had relied on him, and felt this was 'an almost fatal extinguisher' to her hopes. Even worse, there was public speculation that after four years the expedition must have perished, and further searching would be useless. Parry and Barrow wrote consoling letters, Parry saying feebly he could not think what more could be done.[22] Needless to say, Jane Franklin could.

15

JANE FRANKLIN'S
SEARCH

With every detail of the Search at her fingertips, Jane Franklin believed she alone now knew where to look and what to do. To be on the spot, she and Sophy moved to lodgings near the Admiralty. 'If the great folks at the Adm[iralt]ʸ think I am here for interfering purposes, they do my insignificance too much honor', she told James Ross, in one of her statements which meant the opposite, for she was interfering all she could.[1]

The first activity was to challenge ideas that searching was useless, by re-evaluating the Inuit map to show that hope remained. Jane Franklin's network wrote to newspapers and the Admiralty urging their case. They hit a national nerve, and by the end of 1849 had turned around the despair that Ross's return had brought.[2] As 1850 dawned Jane was frantically busy, urging the Hudson's Bay Company and 'dear Dr. Rae' to search the north American coast; organising Captain Penny, a whaler, to submit plans to the Admiralty for an expedition (and rewriting them for him); flattering Henry Grinnell, a wealthy American, into financing an expedition; pressuring the Admiralty ('They understand very little of the details of the search', 'the Admʸ have done <u>nothing</u> of their own accord, but only by pressure'). 'She is closetted from morning to night with her niece her only and most faithful companion ... day after day, and week after week, doing all she can to promote the object nearest and dearest to her heart', wrote an admirer. Two passionate letters in *The Times* by 'An Observer' sound like Sophy. Were we to forget our gallant countrymen, looking vainly for succour? The Admiralty was dozing, rescue attempts had been futile. Richardson, too old for the expedition, was satisfied with finding nothing; Ross came home early; another party searching from the east was needed. 'Let 1850 be the year to redeem our tottering honour'; we must not hold back merely because other lives would be risked.[3]

Jane Franklin also sent out her own expeditions. Between 1850 and 1853 these numbered four. In 1850, Captain Forsyth took *Prince Albert* to the top of Prince Regent Inlet; in 1851–52, Captain Kennedy took *Prince Albert* further down the Inlet; in 1852, Captain Inglefield explored north Baffin Bay in *Isabel*; and in 1853 Kennedy took *Isabel* as far as Valparaiso. For the first expedition in 1850, Jane Franklin bought a pilot boat and astutely named it *Prince Albert* after Queen Victoria's husband. As leader she chose Captain Charles Forsyth R.N., and as unofficial second-in-command ebullient William Parker Snow, a merchant seaman. Neither had any Arctic experience. Jane and Sophy were extremely busy organising everything to do with the expedition. It was a busy year for the Search in general, with six expeditions. The Admiralty sent *Enterprise* and *Investigator* to the Arctic via Bering Strait, then, after intense lobbying by Jane Franklin and her supporters, a four-ship expedition under Captain Austin via the east. Also from the east came Penny's two ships, *Lady Franklin* and *Sophia*; John Ross in two ships, assisted by the Hudson's Bay Company and public subscriptions; Grinnell's two ships; and *Prince Albert*, with provisions for two years. But support was waning, the influential *Times* warning that the expeditions must be 'a LAST effort', since it was impossible that they would have any result.[4]

Just before *Prince Albert* sailed, Jane Franklin offered urgent information from an unusual source. In trying every possible avenue to help
her husband, she consulted clairvoyants. This fad was sweeping Britain,
the theory being that clairvoyants could report events in distant places,
a sort of mental telegraph. Many, even in distant Hobart, were asked
about Franklin's whereabouts, and at least ten offered answers—all
different, all wrong. All said Franklin was still alive.[5]

Jane Franklin and Sophy Cracroft visited two clairvoyants, and
Sophy described one, Ellen Dawson. In May 1849 Ellen 'saw' two ships
in the ice and an old gentleman, looking well and happy, giving orders
to others. On a second visit, she said the ships could not pass through
a wall of ice and needed relief, which must come from the west. Sophy
asked about the captain of the second ship. He was always thinking
of the lady he loved, who would not marry him, reported Ellen. He
wanted to marry her when he returned to England with more money.
'Has money anything to do with it?' asked Sophy. No, said Ellen, the
lady would marry him because he had been away. But the ship was
lost. The lady would be sorry, and never marry. (So Sophy's romance
with Francis Crozier was common enough knowledge for a clairvoyant to have heard of it, and Sophy, keenly questioning, did have some
regrets.) Jane and Sophy seemed to take some clairvoyants seriously,
but did not act on their information.[6]

In early 1850 Jane received the supernatural advice that most impressed
her, as coming 'from a higher source than those which are founded on
mere reasonings'. A Captain Coppin told her that his three-year-old
daughter Louisa, 'Weasey', who had recently died, appeared to family
members. Her sister asked her where Franklin was, and letters appeared
on the wall. Versions differ, but all include 'P.R.I.' and the words 'Victory'
and 'Victoria'. Coppin urged Lady Franklin to search Prince Regent
Inlet, Victory Point and Victoria Land. She hurried to instruct Forsyth
and Snow. 'Poor, revered Lady!' wrote Snow. 'She was always strongly
impressed and influenced by what she told me of the "revelation".' Forsyth
was already going near this area, chosen because no one else was looking
there; the new instructions only emphasised searching further west.

Even though Weasey happened to be correct, rational people were not meant to be influenced by the supernatural (Eleanor was afraid of shocking her father when she wrote to him that she and Jane were cheered by clairvoyants). Jane Franklin's papers were culled of every mention of the Coppin incident, but other papers make it clear that it occurred. Coppin, a shipbuilder, became a major supporter, though he and Jane agreed not to mention the supernatural in appeals to businessmen. She and others did not follow this rule with the Admiralty, where reports offering supernatural guidance were not well received. 'Has proved wholly incorrect', 'I know what *I* think', and 'Humbug!' noted officers in the margins.[7] This did nothing for Lady Franklin's standing at the Admiralty.

The Franklin publicity machine did not mention clairvoyants. It preferred to paint charming pictures of ships leaving for the Search, while on the wharf 'the figures of Lady Franklin and her devoted companion, with hands extended, pointed them on their way with the smile of hope'. One article, in Sophy's style, praised Miss Cracroft for her unceasing attention and ardent participation in all Her Ladyship's labours, making her the subject of universal praise.[8]

Once the 1850 ships left there was a quiet period, for none was expected home until 1851. However, October brought dreadful news: *Prince Albert* returned, having found nothing. The failure was mainly due to unsuitable and inexperienced personnel. Captain Forsyth found Snow difficult to work with; too many officers were useless, argumentative or both; and the crew, though capable, were not used to naval discipline. Forsyth visited Prince Regent Inlet, found the ice impenetrable and came home.[9]

Devastated, Jane Franklin became severely ill. She (reproachfully) and Sophy (bitterly) blamed Forsyth, and planned to send *Prince Albert* out again in 1851 with the same instructions (down Prince Regent Inlet and southwest). As captain, Jane chose William Kennedy, a Canadian Metis (of Indian-Scottish heritage) who volunteered in gratitude for the help Franklin had given him as a boy. Jane and Sophy praised him, patronisingly, as a rough diamond of the purest water, with courage, energy, modesty—but he had no navigational experience. He took lessons in using nautical instruments, and visited the Coppins to obtain Weasey's instructions. Jane Franklin enlisted John Hepburn, Franklin's old attendant, and as second-in-command selected Joseph Bellot, an enthusiastic Frenchman, the latest of her charming young protégés. She called him 'my French son', and he greatly admired her: 'That noble sorrow, so courageously supported, that indefatigable ardour in the prosecution of projects which many regard as desperate ...'[10]

It was another busy few months getting *Prince Albert* ready, complicated by financial problems—subscriptions had not been enough, and work estimates were exceeded. The ship sailed in June 1851. Back in London, Jane and Sophy lived quietly, 'in a way which would grieve her friends', wrote Sophy. 'She is quite unfit to be left alone, to her own painful imaginings ... nothing is plainer than my duty to her & my dearest Uncle ... it is not a blessing to be lightly relinquished—that of being of use & comfort'. All who understood Arctic affairs were hopeful of her uncle's return, Sophy wrote valiantly.[11]

Yet 1851 brought only bad news. In July a report of Franklin's safety was announced in two London theatres, but proved false. The 1850 expeditions returned, having found only that Franklin wintered in 1845–46 at Beechey Island. Contrary to standard practice, he left no information about his plans. Three graves of members of his expedition were found, with biblical quotations: 'Choose ye this day whom ye will serve', and 'Thus said the Lord of Hosts, consider your ways'. Had there been trouble, disobedience, even mutiny? There was speculation that the expedition perished on the way home, and a large stack of empty tins led to fears that the provisions had been unsatisfactory, as others from the same supplier had proved. Jane Franklin was extremely busy, seeing visitors, writing and receiving letters—and at the end of the year she turned sixty. Not everyone supported her: she received a 'very unfeeling and painful note' from Parry, who thought it useless spending more money on searching Prince Regent Inlet. But Beaufort admired the ladies for standing firm against the petty feelings, paltry irresolution and cold calculation shown by so many, hints of discord about which there is no more information.[12]

Nothing daunted Jane Franklin. In the autumn of 1851 she and Sophy tried a new venture. Through sympathetic friends they orchestrated a petition campaign, urging the government to send a steamer north from Beechey Island up Wellington Channel under their new protégé Captain Penny. The Admiralty received 89 petitions from across the country, with thousands of signatures. They refused: but it was all good publicity for the Search.[13]

Then Jane Franklin obtained a steam yacht, *Isabel*, and offered it to any captain who would continue the Search. Donald Beatson volunteered to go to the Arctic via South America, but this fell through—he could have been the man who 'misled & deceived me', as she wrote to her husband. In 1852 Captain Inglefield in *Isabel* competently explored the west coast of Baffin Bay after a cairn was reported there, but found nothing. Jane also offered Lieutenant Pim £500 to look for Franklin via Russia.[14] Kennedy returned in October, having taken *Prince Albert* down Prince Regent Inlet. Sledge parties explored northwest, but found no trace of Franklin. By now, conventional wisdom was sure he had gone north, and optimists claimed that (after seven years) the expedition was still sailing round an open Polar Sea, eating birds and fish, unable to find an outlet through the ice.[15]

In 1852 the Admiralty despatched a five-ship expedition under Edward Belcher to search the north Arctic. Meanwhile, in Van Diemen's Land Henry Kay opened a subscription to help Lady Franklin. 'As the utmost sympathy is felt in this colony in any particular which bears upon the fate of our late respected Lieutenant-Governor', he raised the huge sum of £1872. Jane used this to fund her 1853 *Isabel* expedition. Kennedy planned to sail round South America to the Arctic, but only reached Valparaiso, where the expedition disintegrated. Also in 1853, Grinnell sent a second American expedition to the Arctic under Elisha Kane, and the Admiralty sent Inglefield with Bellot to supply Belcher.

No one found anything but Bellot drowned, more sad news. Jane Franklin became ill; she was often ill during these years, not surprisingly with so many disastrous disappointments.[16]

A bizarre story also ended badly. William Parker Snow was still trying to help, believing Sir John was alive in the open Polar Sea. Using money he made in the Australian gold rush, he set out from Melbourne for the Arctic in a tiny ship. Violent gales forced him to put into the Clarence River in New South Wales, where his men deserted.[17]

Bad followed worse. In 1854 the Admiralty removed the men of the Franklin expedition from the Navy List, assuming them dead since they had been missing for eight and a half years. Most of Sir John's relations and friends accepted this as inevitable, but Jane Franklin was appalled. Parts of the Arctic had not been searched, Belcher was not back and there was no evidence of the deaths, she told the Admiralty.[18] This year, for the first time since 1850, she sent out no expedition. Perhaps even her energy and determination were faltering, after no result from four expeditions.

Belcher returned in October 1854, having abandoned four of his five ships. He did rescue McClure in *Investigator*, which had been beset for three winters. McClure claimed to have discovered the Northwest Passage, having sailed or walked right through from Bering Strait. Now, said George Simpson of the Hudson's Bay Company, 'nobody will trouble themselves about this useless passage ... The public seem at length to have given up Sir John Franklin's case too, as hopeless'. Even previous supporters agreed, and Jane and Sophy had to sit through a sermon that used polar expeditions as an example of the vanity of searching for temporal knowledge. It made them 'tingle from head to foot'.[19]

Then came another bombshell. Jane and Sophy were visiting friends in the country, when at 2 a.m. a carriage drove furiously up to the door and a man demanded to see Sophy, with a letter from the Admiralty. It was devastating. All these years John Rae had been surveying the coast of north America for the Hudson's Bay Company, looking for Franklin as well. In 1854 Netsilingmiut Inuit showed him articles from the Franklin expedition, such as engraved cutlery, and told of other Inuit who some years earlier saw a group of about forty thin white men travelling down the coast of King William Island, dragging a boat on a sledge. Later that season, Inuit found thirty corpses on the coast and five on an island. 'From the mutilated state of many of the bodies and the contents of the kettles, it is evident that our wretched Countrymen had been driven to the last dread alternative, as a means of sustaining life', Rae reported.[20]

Sophy broke the news to Jane. 'No words can describe the horror of that night.' Despite the lapse of time they had still hoped for survivors, and the possibility of cannibalism was appalling. So was the realisation that all their efforts had been in vain, in the wrong place. Jane Franklin claimed she asked her ships to search this area—but she suggested many other places as well.[21]

Although some people belittled Rae's report as Inuit hearsay, the relics were all too convincing, and it became generally accepted that all members of the Franklin expedition had perished. Jane now believed her husband had died, but rejected 'details of horrors, the very existence of which is more than doubtful, and which ought never to have been published or even recorded'. She was not alone. Rae's mention of cannibalism horrified people. (It horrified Rae too—he had not intended it to be published, merely reported it to the Admiralty.) Few could believe that British gentlemen would descend to such a level, and many people, including Charles Dickens, unleashed a storm of extremely hostile criticism at Rae for even suggesting such a thing.[22]

Why did Jane Franklin become involved in the tough, masculine world of the Franklin Search? No other friend or relation of a missing expedition member did. Various reasons have been suggested. Guilt at forcing Sir John to go: there is no evidence that she forced him, and nowhere in all her voluminous papers could I find any hint that she ever felt guilty about anything. Revenge on the British establishment for the way she and Sir John had been treated:[23] possible, but there is no evidence. She loved Sir John so much that she would do anything to find him: this was tacitly accepted at the time, and in a letter to Sir John in 1853—heart-rendingly emotional—it is the reason she herself gives (as one would):

> *My dearest love*
> *… You must always have felt sure that I cd never rest till we had more tidings of you. It is my mission upon earth, it keeps me alive, it is my heart's sole thought, the one only object & occupation of all my faculties & energies, my own d[ea]r husband it is for you I live … the work which God has assigned me which my heart has accepted as its own …*[24]

I believe that her actions were in keeping with her attitude ever since she became engaged to John Franklin. She was his protector, of his person and his reputation, and come what may she would show him as successful (and herself the wife of a successful man).

Claiming supreme authority because of her position as the devoted wife of the expedition's leader—'public sufferer-in-chief', as a cynical relation wrote[25]—she was indefatigable. She sent off four expeditions herself, was responsible for at least three more, and encouraged, even forced, others to act. To this task she brought her outstanding abilities: determination, even obsession; perseverance; practicality; skill at reading widely and quickly understanding the gist; skill at public relations; the self-assurance that went with the lack of guilt. Anyone with a different view was wrong, and she would not compromise. She never doubted: she knew what she wanted and she was going to achieve it. All these talents enabled her to continue fighting for years, despite disappointment after disappointment.

Jane Franklin had superb political skills. Her journals describe how she wrote, received and copied endless letters, sent copies to some people (but not others), kept up with every last detail of what was happening, asked advice, accepted or rejected it, planned how to overcome obstacles, invited visitors to discuss events, wangled introductions to new people involved in the Search, and plotted her next moves, working with friendly officials who could not write openly, so there was an enjoyable element of scheming. She sent out so many letters, particularly to the Admiralty, that her friends called the lodging she took nearby 'The Battery'.[26]

After her Van Diemen's Land experience, this indomitable woman knew that to be effective she had to appear womanly. Fortunately she was slightly built with a soft voice, no physical amazon; people found her gracious, kind, affable—just what a woman should be, 'charming, so clever yet so gentle & such a lady', according to Alfred Tennyson, who married Sir John's niece. She presented herself as a weak woman struggling to find her husband, only her grief giving her courage to act: so suitably wifely. In skilful letters she often described herself as humble, a mere woman doing her best (purposeful echoes of Elizabeth I's famous speech?). She never challenged the patriarchy and was no radical, holding conventional views about politics, religion, woman's place, in fact everything except the Search. As she had done in Van Diemen's Land, she worked behind the scenes and tried to keep her role hidden, using men such as parliamentarians to forward her aims in public, and telling her supporter Benjamin Disraeli (a family friend since the 1820s) that she 'would rather be kept out of sight as much as possible'.[27] She was entirely successful, never criticised publicly for being unwomanly, instead praised as the epitome of womanliness—what more womanly task than devoting oneself to looking for one's husband? As she had used society's expectation that a woman have a man in charge of her when going up the Nile with Johann Lieder, so convention protected her now. Whatever she did, however manipulative she was, no one could criticise her publicly because a gentleman did not criticise a lady, as long as she remained within the accepted role for women.

Important people were a major weapon. Lady Franklin wrote to Queen Victoria, the President of the United States and the Emperors of Russia and France, and though they did little actively helpful, their sympathy—how could one not sympathise with this tragic figure— was excellent publicity. Prince Albert, perhaps flattered by having a ship named after him, even influenced the Admiralty on her behalf.[28]

Arctic explorers were the authorities on the Search, and Jane Franklin cultivated them, for it was important for her credibility to have their backing. Her husband's friends, like Richardson, Beaufort and Parry, supported her—with some reservations—and she flattered and encouraged them to continue the fight, forming a circle of loyal supporters who could be asked to write letters and do other tasks. Some realised their subordinate role. 'I have obeyed your aunt's orders', wrote Francis Beaufort to Sophy, signing his letters, 'Yours to command', but he maintained a little independence, asking Lady Franklin to tell him the points she wanted made so he could write them in his own language, 'to satisfy my own scruples'. Jane continually tried to add to the circle, befriending newcomers such as Leopold McClintock with charming letters. A typical letter, written at Jane's instruction by Sophy in 1854, informed McClintock that strong pressure was necessary on the House of Commons to continue the Search. 'We are told my Aunt ought to procure the written opinions of Arctic officers … My Aunt naturally turns at once to you, whom her hopes & ardent wishes point to': could he write, within a fortnight? She suggested wording for the letter.[29]

It was vital to have Parliament onside, but this was a challenge since some hard-headed members thought Arctic exploration a waste of money, that Franklin's men were dead so it was useless to look for them. Fortunately the Search was outside party politics, and most parliamentarians were sympathetic. Jane Franklin cultivated several with fawning letters, dinners and meetings, and in reply they moved motions, made announcements and kept her cause moving. Her letters to Disraeli, the Conservative leader, show her skill. She did not ask him to move motions: he was too important. Instead, she asked him for support ('a few eloquent words from your lips would be deeply appreciated') and to have a word with influential people. She sent information to back up her requests and thanked him for his help ('the most beautiful & kind things you said last night'). As a result, the House of Commons heard of 'the rare intelligence, the indomitable perseverance, the womanly, the high and enduring spirit, with which

Lady Franklin urged on the prosecution of the search for her brave husband'.[30]

Jane Franklin made sure she had friends at the Admiralty, and went there when she could see them rather than someone unsympathetic. She cultivated friends in the Admiralty dockyard, where her ships were outfitted.[31] Other influential people must be courted. Jane found Roderick Murchison unpleasant, full of himself and showing 'wonderful ignorance'; but he was President of the Royal Geographical Society, so she worked on him, turning him into a devoted ally. So successful was she at lobbying that she became a byword. Over a century later, when British explorer Wally Herbert was running out of money and support in Greenland, he wrote to his wife and manager, back in England, 'You could try the technique (if you can bear it) of doing a Lady Franklin'— meaning, 'getting in touch with the big shots'.[32]

Another of her political talents was using information to best advantage: Jane Franklin had always believed that the means justified the ends. She interpreted facts liberally. The Franklin expedition was in a 'prosperous condition' in spring 1846, she told the Admiralty in 1854, though there was actually no evidence, and three deaths, higher than usual, implied problems. When asking Disraeli's help she told him that every expedition had been in preparation by the end of January, but in 1845 Sir John himself had not been appointed until February. And so on: many of her statements were just not quite accurate. One historian comments that she might have been capable of deliberate falsehood: 'the extent to which she was honest, scrupulous, or principled affords considerable scope for conjecture.'[33] But no one did conjecture about her honesty, at least publicly.

A huge help was Jane Franklin's wonderful, almost saintly, public image. In 1849 Jane and Sophy were looking for lodgings in a small Scottish town. Jane thought one landlady's charges were excessive, but after she gave her name the woman's face lit up. 'Oh Ma'am if you are Lady Franklin I'll jist let you have it', she exclaimed, and called her daughter down to hear the exciting news. 'Another proof of the extraordinary enthusiasm manifested by *all* classes', wrote Sophy complacently.[34]

How had an obscure landlady heard of Lady Franklin? Through newspapers, now with mass circulations. With few reporters, they would print unsolicited articles, so it was easy to get published. Newspapers often reprinted articles from other papers, so an article about the Search might move from a London newspaper round the world. Jane Franklin, Sophy Cracroft and their circle cultivated editors and wrote many articles, anonymous letters and replies to occasional criticism, and one series in particular, obviously written by the same person, appeared in two London newspapers, the *Standard* and the *Morning Chronicle*. In 1852 Sophy often noted that she had written letters for the *Chronicle* (all anonymous), and the articles too are in her style, gushing, emotional, slightly hysterical—just what the public loved. Everything about the Search is wonderful: Lady Franklin the devoted wife, Sophy the devoted companion, every action successful. For example, the writer described Lady Franklin's first expedition, which achieved virtually nothing, as an 'extraordinary and unexampled exploit' unequalled in the whole history of Arctic navigation. *Prince Albert* boldly steamed the waves, went very far, very fast, and returned to bring vital news (actually minor). Reading this article, whose almost every claim is wrong, takes the breath away, but someone, almost certainly Sophy, had the gall to write it.[35] The number of articles decreased over the years, but they had their effect: Lady Franklin was accepted as a heroine, Sophy her ardent companion. If those two were not entirely responsible for Lady Franklin becoming a national heroine, they had a great deal to do with it.

Jane Franklin tried to control everything published about the Search, editing her captains' books so that everything appeared rosy, with negative events such as infighting omitted. She was furious when Elisha Kane's book described graphically the appalling Arctic winter: this might harm subscriptions to her expeditions. Her attitude to her own fame was mixed. She said she shrank from publicity, and when a letter of hers was published without her knowledge, described herself as 'thrilled & vexed',[36] which shows her ambivalence: thrilled to gain the publicity, but vexed to be given prominence—or was it that someone dared to act without her consent?

And so Lady Franklin became a national, even international, heroine. As a writer (not Sophy) put it in 1852:

> *The heroic woman, whose devotion to her gallant husband has made her name a household word in two continents [Europe and America], whose appeals in his behalf have touched all hearts, and filled all eyes with tears, whose conduct has added another illustration of conjugal affection, of indomitable perseverance and courage, to the long list of examples of woman's faith and woman's fortitude, the wife of the lost Franklin still hopes ... While such a hope is strong in the soul of this noble woman, it will live in the hearts of all Christendom.*[37]

A more prosaic skill than guiding the world's press was raising money. Here Jane Franklin excelled, mainly. Results were disappointing for the subscription lists she launched for each expedition, perhaps because people thought the Admiralty would do it better, or because they were discouraged by Lady Franklin's lack of actual results. In particular, lists of donors included few relatives of Franklin or any other member of his expedition. However, Jane was never short of money, and was skilled in raising it in other ways. A friend recalled travelling in a London cab with her, when she suddenly ordered the driver to stop outside Franklin's optician. She went in and returned, eyes gleaming, with a large donation. As she became well known, public sympathy meant many people either gave money or, more often, supported her in kind. For example, hotel proprietors presented her with a blank sheet for the bill, 'saying they could not think of taking a farthing from me, knowing I had spent a fortune already in my husband's cause'. She saved expenses by persuading the Admiralty to, at least partly, equip and provision her expeditions, and by accepting volunteer officers. She spent her own money, talking of sacrificing her fortune, but she never seemed short herself, and equipped her ships liberally ('I wish you to have every thing that can contribute to your comfort').[38] Somehow she managed her finances successfully despite the huge outlays, and though minor money worries were endemic, they were never over-whelming, and never affected her expeditions.

Like everyone, Jane Franklin had her weaknesses. The sentiment she used to argue her case, and her assumption that the holiness of her cause justified anything, could alienate people. Some, convinced Franklin was dead, she could never win over. The Admiralty grew tired of her numerous demands and manipulations, and after 1854 her requests were often refused or ignored. A hint that some people disliked her appeared when, despite her lobbying, 'Arctic officers' would not allow her to sign a retirement testimonial to John Barrow, saying they had complaints from 'other relations'.[39]

Jane Franklin wanted to stay in control, and micromanaged her expeditions, appointing officers, arranging provisions and equipment (her agents needed permission for any expenditure, even for vital things like rigging), telling captains where to search—no detail was too large or too small (a list of equipment descends to breadbaskets). However, her knowledge of ships was limited, and she tended to appoint men impulsively because she liked them, not because they had the necessary qualifications. Historian Ian Stone concludes that her expeditions were successful 'in inverse ratio to the amount of direct involvement she had in them'.[40] But the Admiralty's expeditions found little more than hers did.

Another weakness was her tendency to overreact to criticism. Anyone who agreed with her was good, and anyone who opposed her bad, for she could never compromise, never admit that an opponent had valid grounds. But the occasional setback only made Jane Franklin fight harder, and overall her achievement was amazing. No other woman in the nineteenth century, perhaps no other woman ever, sent out five (eventually) expeditions, influenced the Admiralty, Parliament and private citizens to send others, and became (made herself?) a world-famous heroine, the epitome of the devoted wife. Johann Lieder, training Protestant ministers in Cairo, must have enjoyed a quiet smile.

16

FAMILY UPSETS

Jane Franklin's activities in the Search were achieved at a cost: family relationships. This is hardly surprising. She was so obsessed with the Search that she had little time for anything else, and the overwhelming stress of worrying about Sir John made everything harder. Other family members were just as distressed, but thought Jane crazy to send out her own expeditions, especially when the first four failed to find anything. In her obsession, she saw even the slightest opposition as betrayal. Relationships might not have been as bad had they been close in the first place but, apart from her father, husband, sister Mary, Sophy Cracroft and possibly sister Fanny, none of the family loved Jane Franklin, or even liked her much. She had never been interested in the her husband's siblings with their quiet, provincial lives, and Mary's children, the young Simpkinsons, resented her. Add to this disputed wills, an overcrowded home and quarrels over money, and problems are not surprising. This is the area with the greatest contrast between the Franklin archive—which gives a picture of Jane and Sophy, the heroines in their successful quest to find Sir John, bravely battling selfish, grasping, horrible relations— and other documents, which tell a quite different story.

Jane's most difficult relationship was with her stepdaughter Eleanor. John Franklin took it for granted that the two people he loved best would love each other. 'I can give but little hope of Eleanor's being disposed to leave her mother in my absence or of Mama's liking to part from her', he wrote fondly on his departure in 1845. But both women wanted to come first with him, and there was duty, and possibly mild affection, but no love between them.[1]

Sir John left his two ladies to care for each other in his absence, the plan being that after he returned victorious in a couple of years, Eleanor would marry John Gell. After Sir John's departure, the two women spent the next three years together, travelling—Madeira, the West Indies, the United States, Italy, at a breakneck speed which Eleanor found exhausting—or living quietly in London. Not for Eleanor the bright social life of Jane's young womanhood, but she sounds happy, living for letters from her dear fiancé John. Letters between her and Jane sound amicable, even fond, but Eleanor was learning to stand up for herself. Once when she and Jane were riding, their shadows were thrown on an opposite ridge. 'I was undoubtedly the centre of the picture, but Eleanor disputed it—she was very obstinate, & yet she thought me so', wrote Jane. A Simpkinson daughter sympathised with Eleanor for being lonely 'with only Aunt F & no one else who can talk or sympathise with you … but you know dear E that you are going in the path of duty & not of pleasure'.[2]

This fragile relationship broke apart in 1849, when both women were desperately anxious about Sir John. In late 1848 John Gell, now a clergyman, returned from Van Diemen's Land. He and Eleanor wanted to marry but Jane opposed them: the marriage would acknowledge that John Franklin was not returning immediately, and tensions had erupted over her plan to send a ship in search of him. Eleanor, who believed that searching was best left to Admiralty experts, tried to restrain Jane. Jane was furious. John Gell claimed that, in search of funds, she tried to open her husband's will, but he (Gell) dissuaded her from this highly unorthodox action. Seeing this as a refusal of support, she became hysterical, Eleanor fearing she was 'slightly deranged'.

No wonder that the wedding, in June 1849, was difficult, with Jane's ill-feeling obvious. Many friends and relations sympathised with Eleanor: 'your position is a very painful one'; 'you have indeed much to try your faith & patience dear Eleanor'. All urged her to be kind and patient with her stepmother though, as Marianne Simpkinson wrote sympathetically, Eleanor had great provocation and the fault was all on Aunt Franklin's side.[3]

Eleanor's attitude can be seen in a letter to her father, written in May 1849. She barely mentioned her stepmother, but urged her father on his return to 'settle in the peaceful home of your son and daughter'.[4] Of course he would not, since he would live with his wife; but the suggestion shows that Eleanor too was under stress—'slightly deranged', Jane might have thought.

The last few months had been a perplexing trial, wrote Eleanor after the wedding, 'but now I feel that all is peace'. No chance: she was feeling resentful, Jane was feeling betrayed, and now she had Sophy Cracroft with her. Sophy was determined to become Lady Franklin's indispensable companion. Not only was she submissive to Jane—no claims of larger shadows here—but she wanted to crush opposition. The main challenger was Eleanor, and though it would seem she was out of the running, living happily with her husband in his London parish, Sophy was taking no chances. Even in 1845 she showed jealousy of Eleanor, and now Eleanor could do nothing right. In January 1849 Sophy accused her of not sympathising enough with her stepmother, and the next surviving information has Eleanor in trouble for not writing to her stepmother until five days after her wedding.[5]

Money matters made things worse. Mr Porden had left his daughter (John Franklin's first wife) a considerable sum. After her death, her husband had life interest, and on his death, the money would go to their child, Eleanor. The Porden money was John Franklin's main income. While he was away, his second wife Jane had power of attorney: but did this include control of the Porden income? Jane claimed it did, but John Gell argued that Eleanor had a moral right to it (he, only a curate or assistant priest, had a small salary). On his urging, Jane made them an allowance, £200, from the annual Porden income of £600.[6] They wanted more, thinking Eleanor Porden's money should support her daughter and grandchildren, not be wasted on unsuccessful expeditions; but Jane wanted every penny for the Search.

In the summer of 1849 Sophy's letters to her mother contained diatribe after diatribe about Eleanor. She did not pay enough attention to her stepmother; she did not write; when she did, her letter was insolent; she only ended 'your affectionate Eleanor', without any warmth; her dress was too gay for a clergyman's wife.[7] Presumably these were also Jane's opinions.

Meanwhile, Eleanor and John settled down into happy married life. None of her letters to him survive, but his to his darling Eleanor sound devoted.[8] Their first baby was born in 1850, and more followed regularly, seven in ten years. Eleanor assisted her husband in the parish and was busy with her children and their illnesses—a baby nearly died and her oldest son, John Franklin, suffered from some serious disease. She was just as concerned about Sir John's safety as Jane, just as buoyed up with hope and cast down by despair, with her own network of friends exchanging even the smallest piece of news or speculation; but all her anxieties remained private.

Because of the Gells' claims for money and their disagreement over Jane's expeditions, and because upright John Gell was appalled by her behaviour, their relationship with her was never good, and sometimes it was disastrous. Both sides thought themselves right, and grew more and more entrenched. Eleanor thought Sophy made things worse: 'I think [Mama] could be influenced for good again, were Sophy not with her—but she keeps her up to her determination instead of encouraging finer feelings'. Sophy was what a relation called 'a good hater'. She continued her barrage of criticism: Eleanor was scornful, disrespectful; she refused to send the baby round; when she did it was crying—and this to all and sundry. 'Eleanor absolutely <u>hates</u> my Aunt', Sophy wrote to the wife of the Tasmanian bishop. Visitors too were informed: 'Louisa called heard all abt Gells.' Fanny and her husband egged Jane on: on being told how dreadful the Gells were, 'Fanny stamped on floor with indignation', and her husband 'intreated I wd not shrink, but wd carry war to extremity'.[9] This hardly helped. Sophy's writing about the Gells is venomous. Jane's has been culled of mentions of them, so cannot be assessed—but she allowed Sophy's venom. Eleanor's letters are merely sad.

Franklin relations mostly sympathised with Eleanor, though urging her to attempt reconciliation—very trying, but her duty as the younger person ('we are not to have unalloyed joy in this world'). Other letters were more comforting. Mary Price said she did not believe all she heard and could not judge, 'but from what I know of you I can not blame you'. She refused to answer Sophy's breathtakingly nasty letters. John Franklin's sister Aunt Wright wondered if Jane and Sophy, on their summer trip to the highlands, were waiting purposely to stumble upon Queen Victoria as if by accident. Just my little joke, she added.[10]

Eleanor did try—Sophy reported that the Gells claimed to have done all they could towards reconciliation—but Jane and Sophy did not make things easy. Shortly after the wedding, the quarrel over money became so bad that John Gell told Jane to remember she was answerable to a higher tribunal, which upset her so much that Frank Simpkinson forbade the Gells the house. John wrote an apology, but refused to admit he was in the wrong and, according to Sophy, said affection could not be compelled. There was a brief reconciliation when the Gells asked Jane and Sophy to dine—Sophy made them understand the Arctic question, Jane reported—but then more trouble erupted over Sir John's will.[11] Desperate for money for the Search, Jane had it opened in the presence of her lawyer but not the Gells—which angered them. To her fury, she found that Eleanor was residuary legatee, with only a lump sum for herself. She felt she was now in the Gells' power. John Gell took steps to prevent her getting hold of the will, explaining she was not to be trusted with it. That brought another explosion, but it all calmed down, and in 1851 they had Christmas dinner together. Then things went downhill again. 'Has Lady F had any communication with you? or does she still determine to have nothing to do with you?' Marianne Simpkinson asked Eleanor. The Gells pressed for more of Eleanor's mother's money and put an injunction on the bank to stop Lady Franklin withdrawing cheques: but they could not inherit until John Franklin's death was proved, and Eleanor did not want her beloved father's death assumed.[12] Jane continued to spend all available money on the Search, which was bringing no result.

Everything came to a head in October 1853, in an appalling public fight in *The Times*. It began when two anonymous letters drew attention to Sir John Franklin's 'nearest and dearest' connection. Surely his deserving son-in-law, an excellent curate, should be given a parish of his own. The authors were unknown to the Gells (not even Sophy accused them of organising the letters).

In reply came a letter from 'One of the Public'. It was almost certainly by Sophy, written in her slightly hysterical style, and showing knowledge, motive and malice not shared by anyone else. 'I cannot admit the justice of the appeal made to us on behalf of Mr. Gell', the letter started. 'The heroism of Lady Franklin, to whose untiring exertions and sacrifices your correspondents appear to be indifferent or blind' commanded everyone's respect. Gell had discouraged the Search, the letter continued. He menaced Lady Franklin with legal proceedings to compel her to produce and prove Franklin's will, to admit his death and end the Search. He paraded his impecunity, but to support the Search Lady Franklin had reduced her income to less than half the income the Gells found insufficient.

This letter, which 'from its style I much fear proceeds from Sophy's pen', could not be left unanswered, Eleanor wrote to an aunt. One of the Beauforts asked her why Lady Franklin grudged Mr Gell a living: was she 'jealous lest any but herself should share the public sympathy? I fear this is too true'. John Gell replied to *The Times* letter under his own name. He listed six Arctic explorers as witnesses to his support for the Search, but they worked with the Admiralty. Lady Franklin had never admitted him into her plans, and he was not in a position to give a substantial subscription to her. It was untrue that he, Gell, had menaced her with legal proceedings, but he did show 'extreme displeasure' when she opened Sir John's will. 'I feel it was treating him as if he were dead before his time, and that, too, against the known wishes of his daughter.' The comparison of incomes was also untrue, Gell claimed, but he was glad to know that his 'impecuniosity'

> was no disparagement in Sir John Franklin's eyes, when I solicited from him the hand of his only child. My wife and children are his child and grandchildren, and I trust his wife will learn some day that they are hers also, when the fever of excitement is past, and she sees that our counsel and advice would have been more valuable to her than the wild schemes of needy and sometimes unprincipled adventurers who have made their account in practising upon her passions and feelings.[13]

'One of the Public' could not keep silent. Gell's letter was false. He had tried to get money from Lady Franklin and threatened proceedings in Chancery. Lady Franklin's captains were all very upright. Jane Franklin sent *The Times* a statement from her lawyer, but it was not published.[14]

These letters inflamed the quarrel. Both sides insisted relations and friends sympathise, acutely embarrassing most of them. Jane Franklin and Sophy Cracroft claimed the high moral ground, accusing John Gell of slandering Lady Franklin by saying she opened the will; he was in the wrong and must apologise. They would never acknowledge that he was right (she *had* opened the will), that anonymous attacks were unfair, or that Sophy had anything to do with them. Others disagreed, one writing to Eleanor that 'the time will come when [Jane Franklin] will be sorry for all the mischief she has done, that is if her conscience is not quite gone. You and dear Gell have done all you can to promote a good feeling'. Most family members and others like John Richardson sympathised with the Gells, especially over the 'malicious' anonymous attacks and the 'nasty excitement' they caused.[15]

The Admiralty announced that in March 1854 Franklin expedition members were to be taken off the active service list—that is, presumed dead. This was a terrible blow to Jane Franklin: if her husband were dead, why support a search for him? 'I fear for poor Jane's mind', wrote a sister-in-law. Eleanor asked people to put on mourning for Sir John, but Jane, wrote Eleanor, 'changed the deep mourning she has been wearing for years for bright colours of green and pink'. A truce came only in 1854 after Rae's disastrous news that everyone on the expedition had died. Eleanor invited her stepmother to visit: 'If you cannot forgive us as we heartily forgive you, we must after all be disappointed'. Jane replied that John Gell alone could remove the barrier to their union. 'He has done me grievous wrong', and if he made a public retraction, she would visit. 'It would indeed be the greatest of consolations to me if, while my heart is bleeding with the overthrow of all my dearest hopes, I were to find in room of the devoted husband I have lost, the children he has bequeathed to me ... This is not of course with a view of imposing any conditions ...' A letter in her most skilfully manipulative style: but John Gell was never going to retract publicly what he believed to be true. The Gells came to Jane's door but were not admitted—a private apology would not do. However, she finally accepted a private written retraction (which Gell later withdrew), and visits were made.[16]

There were still disputes over the will, now proved. What did residuary legatee mean? Eleanor claimed everything except Jane's lump sum: Jane said it referred only to money, not to Sir John's portraits, journals and manuscripts. Both women were collecting material for a biography of him: both wanted to be keeper of the flame. Jane found she was on shaky ground. A lawyer told her 'I shd have everything to prove myself as they [the Gells] had nothing to do but be quiet'— but she defeated them, of course, using as weapons her position as the older person, sentiment, a money offer, and relations instructed to pressure Eleanor, who yielded on the understanding that Jane would leave everything to the Gells (she did not). An agreement was signed in 1855—a shaky peace, but it held, more or less.[17]

Meanwhile, there was terrible trouble at Bedford Place, the home of old Mr Griffin (Jane's father) and the Simpkinson family: Mary, Frank and three of their five children, Frank junior (a naval officer on half pay), Marianne and Emma, all around twenty. The older son John, a clergyman, lived elsewhere, and Louisa was about to marry. The Simpkinsons looked on Bedford Place as home, but so did Jane Franklin—and the house was not large.

The Simpkinson children did not like their aunt. 'In spite of Aunt F's zeal & ability & ingenuity, common sense will make itself heard', wrote John of some issue, and the daughters resented Aunt Franklin's domination of their mother: 'Mama is always in such subjection to her sister, such fear of offending her'; 'I dread her being with us this winter, but I am afraid she will, for Mamma says she would do anything, that is, she does not care if I sleep on the ground, these are her words, rather than not gratify every wish of Aunt F's'. They were sceptical about their aunt: 'How delighted Lady F must be at all this noise & parade!'; 'she and Sophy are making great fools of themselves'.[18]

Aunt Franklin's visits were bearable when Eleanor was her companion, but the Simpkinsons thought Sophy Cracroft encroaching. On Jane and Sophy's return to London in 1849, the Simpkinson daughters did not want them at Bedford Place, where Sophy was a nuisance, and doubtless both women's obsession with the Search was wearying. Jane and Sophy moved to lodgings, but soon moved back.[19] In 1850 Mary became seriously ill. Her husband also ailed, and died the next year. Frank junior, Mr Griffin's favourite grandson, was now effectively in charge, and he did not like Aunt Franklin. He told her there was no room in the house for her, charged her board and objected to her many callers. When Jane returned from a visit, 'Not one member of family took slightest notice of my comm[unicatio]n'. Then, after she had Franklin's will opened, Frank told the Gells about it. Their reaction horrified him. He returned home and abused his aunt, calling her dishonourable, and when she asked Sophy to be a witness, Frank said Sophy was an utter stranger and no relation of his. Sophy and Marianne quarrelled violently; Jane refused to dine with the others; the Gells tried to end the quarrel. It did calm down—temporarily.[20]

In May 1852 Mr Griffin died, at the great age of 94. Opening the will was dramatic. In a codicil made the year before, he disinherited Jane for Frank: 'Frank has got <u>every</u> <u>thing</u>', Sophy told Mary Price. Jane was devastated. She claimed that she had married without a proper settlement and relied on her father's promise to leave her money in his will, but family members had convinced him that she, Jane, was ruining herself sending out fruitless expeditions and would waste any more money in the same way. Now the Simpkinsons were in charge, and Jane and Sophy moved to lodgings. In 1853 a deed was found which did provide Jane with some money from her father's estate, and eventually she was reconciled with the Simpkinsons.[21]

Mary died in 1854, aged 61. Jane's three main supporters—her father, husband and younger sister—were gone, but Sophy was proving a good substitute.

There were other upsets. John Franklin's sisters were hurt to be excluded from any acknowledged role in mourning their brother, but they were deep in the country and did not matter. Jane's relationship with her sister Fanny had its ups and downs. Emma Simpkinson reported that Fanny's husband Ashurst Majendie was on friendly terms with Jane 'again', and that Jane was 'reconciled with her sister on condition of never speaking of family matters'—'but I am afraid family matters will be disputed as much as ever', wrote Marianne on hearing this. Once Jane, Sophy and Fanny went to view a panorama, and to Sophy's extreme annoyance, she heard Fanny pointed out as herself—Fanny, who was 'as usual' making herself conspicuous. Then in 1855 there was a dreadful argument with John Simpkinson about a will, presumably Mary's. Jane and Sophy wrote about him as vitriolically as they had about the Gells, and Ashurst Majendie, in his inflammatory way, said John (a clergyman) wanted exorcising. However, by the late 1850s everything had calmed down.[22]

Until 1849 and after 1859, Jane Franklin's family relationships were harmonious. It was only in the 1850s, the period of the Search, that harmony broke down. Obviously the stress over the expedition's fate was a major cause—Jane was in a heightened emotional state, as were many other people—but the way she quarrelled with nearly everyone and repulsed efforts at reconciliation makes one wonder whether she really wanted peace. She gained advantages from disharmony, advantages which helped her prosecute the Search, her overriding objective in these years.

Routine bored Jane Franklin, and she enjoyed, almost needed, indignation. She certainly gained it from her quarrels. Did they provide her with energy to promote the Search? A second advantage was that Jane and Sophy could project themselves as victims of malicious, underhand, rapacious relatives, so supporters would pity them, and open their wallets more. They made no effort to keep these quarrels private, even publicising them.

Perhaps the main advantage was that quarrelling with relatives—who were also relatives of Sir John—gave Jane Franklin an excuse to keep them at arm's length, and leave them out of anything to do with the Search. She and Sophy were its heroines. No one else was ever mentioned as mourning Sir John, let alone the other 128 missing men. It was all about Jane and her satellite Sophy. The main challenger would have been Sir John's daughter Eleanor, and it was with her that Jane had the most sustained argument.

So family quarrels actually helped Jane prosecute the Search on her own terms. Surely she did not force quarrels with this aim, surely they all happened fortuitously; but she did turn them to her advantage. The Gells, Simpkinsons and Franklins, without her political skills or her tough but strengthening experience in Van Diemen's Land, did not have a chance of standing up to her.

17

VICTORY

When 1855 opened, Jane Franklin was at a low ebb. She was shattered by Rae's report. It made Sir John seem a failure, losing
all his men, finding nothing, a possible cannibal. She herself was
acclaimed as a devoted wife, but Rae's discoveries made it clear that all
her efforts had been useless. Infuriatingly, she had become 'poor Lady
Franklin'—when people thought of her at all. The community (and the
Admiralty and Parliament) believed the Search was over, and interest
focused on the Crimean War.

Jane Franklin was not going to give in. She was determined to
make her husband's memory shine, as a hero and the discoverer of the
Northwest Passage. This depended on what 'discovery' meant, Beaufort
told her. Jane claimed Sir John's expedition had penetrated far enough
south to link up with previous discoveries along the coast of America.
But other people were also using flexible meanings of 'discovery', and
eleven others could claim the title.[1] Jane faced an uphill battle—but
she had never been one to shirk hard work. Again she brought her
formidable skills into play, and by 1860 she was totally victorious.

At first things went badly. She urged the Admiralty to send an expedition to check Rae's claims but, busy with the war, the Admiralty refused. Parliament awarded McClure £10 000 for finding the North-west Passage and Rae £10 000 for ascertaining Franklin's fate. Jane Franklin protested vehemently: Franklin's men had discovered a north-west passage six months before McClure, and their fate was by no means ascertained. Parliament took no notice. Jane Franklin's influence was definitely waning. More pleasantly, she edited (firmly) Richardson's biography of Franklin for the *Encyclopedia Britannica*. In describing the discovery of the Northwest Passage, Richardson wrote a sentence Jane Franklin loved: 'They forged the last link with their lives'—typical of the sentiment with which she and her supporters surrounded the expedi-tion. It was also satisfying that her old Tasmanian enemies were dying off, Forster and several editors in the 1840s, Montagu in 1853.[2]

Meanwhile an American whaler found *Resolute*, one of Belcher's abandoned ships, which the American government renovated and presented to the British. Jane organised a Christmas dinner for the officers, which was disastrous. The weather was terrible, the American captain was ill, the other officers could not find transport, and the guests comprised mainly her own family—and then she forgot to present Fanny to Lady Murchison. A Christmas party was more successful, with a magnificent Christmas tree which Sophy cleverly organised so the best presents went to the Americans.[3]

With the Admiralty uncooperative, refusing not only to send an expedition but to lend Jane Franklin *Resolute* or any other ship, she planned her own expedition, her fifth. The American hero Elisha Kane agreed to lead it, coming to London in 1856. By then he was seriously ill, but Jane clung to the idea of him as leader, visiting him every day, offering remedies, desperate for his recovery. 'The woman would use me, if she could, even now', Kane wrote home. He died shortly afterwards.[4]

To raise money, Jane Franklin launched a national appeal. Subscriptions were disappointing, but she sold land in Australia and in 1857 bought a small ship, *Fox*. As leader she selected Captain Leopold McClintock, an experienced Arctic explorer and sledger, who was 'likely to carry out his work at any cost without regard to the suffering of those under him': it was high time an expedition of hers succeeded, come what may. After Rae's discoveries McClintock knew where to search, and Jane Franklin gave him the vaguest of instructions: to look for documents, relics, information and survivors.[5]

At Beechey Island McClintock erected a tablet she provided in memory of the dead. Sailing south, at her request he named the Tasmania Islands, to thank colonists for their support. (They are a particularly uninspiring group, but doubtless McClintock did his best.) In summer, sledge parties combed the King William Island area. Inuit provided more relics, and told of white men walking south dragging boats, dropping dead as they went. McClintock found skeletons, including one which had fallen on his face, clearly having dropped as described—an important point, showing the party never gave up. Inuit testimony also indicated that the men were still under naval discipline, with no breakdown in authority. Best of all was a cairn with a note: the expedition had wintered at Beechey Island, circumnavigated Cornwallis Island, sailed south, and been beset by ice off King William Island. This note, written in May 1847, ended 'All well'. An addition written the next year stated that John Franklin died in June 1847, the expedition had been beset for another winter, and in April 1848 the surviving 105 men abandoned the ships to walk south. McClintock also discovered a boat containing two skeletons and many objects.

McClintock's explanation of the expedition's fate was that the men starved, weakened by inevitable scurvy (one of his own men died of scurvy after only two winters). Walking south, dragging heavy sledges loaded with inessentials, they could not transport enough food and were in a barren area where 'nothing can exceed the gloom and desolation'. McClintock said nothing about cannibalism, although later Inuit reports claimed he was told about it. However, only he and the interpreter, his friend, talked to Inuit. In his book he noted that skeletons' bones were disarranged, 'dissevered' and gnawed, but attributed this to animals.[6] If the men saw cut marks on the bones or other ominous signs, everything encouraged them to keep silent: their employer's opinion, public opinion in Britain, and their careers, after the brutal

criticism Rae suffered after mentioning cannibalism. Nor did McClintock query the death rate by April 1848—24 out of 129, a fifth, much
higher than any other expedition except Franklin's first. (McClintock
was a sensible man. He went on to a knighthood and a stellar career.
Rae was never knighted.)

A biography of Jane Franklin cannot attempt to discuss the
fascinating question of what happened to the Franklin expedition,
especially the unprecedented 24 early deaths. Ian Stone, an authority
on the topic, considers that 'It is simple ... no one knows. Theories are
legion'. Lead poisoning from tinned food seems to him the most plau-
sible explanation, but botulism is also a possibility.[7]

While *Fox* was away, Jane Franklin took Sophy Cracroft travelling.
In 1858 they toured the Mediterranean, Lady Franklin's fame bringing
them courteous treatment wherever they went. Sophy loved it. 'Excited
by such foreignness', she ate 'a peculiar dish called bouilliabaisse', saw
people dressed 'somewhat wide of the mark of decency' and climbed
Mount Pelion in Greece. Then their excellent maid died, and Fanny
'has been making one of her odious observations to my Aunt—"I
hear you tire out all your companions" ... nothing is safe with her
from being disagreeably interpreted & repeated'. They returned home,
Sophy exhausted by being the maid. There was no shortage of money,
for they stayed in the best hotels, Sophy wrote. In 1859 they were in the
Pyrenees when they heard that McClintock was back.[8]

The discovery of Franklin's fate made headlines round the world, and
McClintock's gripping book about the expedition became a runaway
bestseller. Jane Franklin gave away copies liberally. Not surprisingly:
McClintock presented her as a heroine. 'Deep sympathy with Lady
Franklin in her distress, her self-devotion and sacrifice of fortune ...
seemed the natural promptings of every honest English heart.' She organised the expedition, appointed him, asked him to discover her husband's
fate, then with womanly modesty stepped back. He felt commanding
the expedition was 'a *great national duty*'. In the Cinderella-like story,
little *Fox* succeeds where so many larger ships failed, and Franklin
is a hero, brave, noble and gallant, and 'the *first real discoverer of the*

North-West Passage'. It was tragic that all the men died, but they went bravely, having succeeded in their quest, never giving in, in the true British spirit—much as Robert Falcon Scott was later admired.[9]

The book cemented Lady Franklin's place as an international heroine. She had been well known before, but now her perseverance in finding her husband's fate, her triumph where so many others failed, 'elicited the admiration and sympathy of the world'. Her friend Captain Sherard Osborn wrote a book reconstructing Franklin's voyage. The crews bravely suffered privation, but it was all worthwhile, for a sledge party returned to the ships triumphant, having discovered the North-west Passage—just in time. Franklin lay on his deathbed, but the news 'lit up that kind eye with its last gleam of triumph', and he died happy.[10] All imaginary, but this sort of publicity made Franklin one of the most acclaimed British heroes of the day. No one ever mentioned problems in Van Diemen's Land—Lady Franklin had buried them in the past.

Lady Franklin was celebrated in ways which reached virtually everyone: from an example of indefatigable wifely fidelity in an instructive book for young ladies, to just as faithful a wife in widely circulated ballads for the working class:

Lady Franklin's Lament
My Franklin dear long has been gone,
To explore the northern seas,
I wonder if my faithful John,
Is still battling with the breeze;
Or if e'er he will return again,
To these fond arms once more
To heal the wounds of dearest Jane,
Whose heart is griev'd full sore.
Chorus
My Franklyn dear, though long thy stay,
Yet still my prayer shall be
That Providence may choose a way,
To guide thee safe to me.[11]

Jane Franklin became the first woman presented with the Royal Geographical Society's Founder's Gold Medal. Her supporter Roderick Murchison proposed it to the Society, and who having read this far can doubt who gave him the idea. To commemorate the discovery of the Northwest Passage by Franklin, the Society announced, it presented Lady Franklin with the medal in token of its admiration of her noble and self-sacrificing perseverance in sending out expeditions until at last her husband's fate was ascertained; and McClintock was awarded the Patron's Gold Medal for his skill and fortitude in ascertaining it.[12]

Her wifely duty done, Jane took Sophy off on an extended world tour. They were in America when they heard that Jane's final opponent had died. Eleanor Gell had never enjoyed good health since she arrived back in England in 1845, and bearing seven children in ten years, as well as the family disputes, cannot have helped. In 1860 the Gell family was on holiday in Wales when one of the children caught scarlet fever. Nursing him, Eleanor caught it herself and died, aged only 36.[13] Jane's reaction is unknown, but she was now the undisputed keeper of John Franklin's memory. She had won on all counts.

Having succeeded totally in one overriding ambition—making her husband a hero and herself his revered wife—Jane Franklin returned to her other major ambition, which she had been pursuing when possible since she left school: living life to the full, seeking travel and adventure. She had the freedom, the lack of responsibility and the money (apparently from property inherited from Uncle Guillemard) to do what she pleased, and here too she gained total success. 'Lady Franklin had an ardent desire to see all parts of the habitable globe, and she was afraid of no fatigue or heat or rough accommodation in her determination to miss nothing which was worth seeing', wrote her nephew.[14] It was still unusual for women to travel as much as she did—the great women travellers appeared later in the century—and in her day, Jane Franklin was probably the most travelled woman in the world.

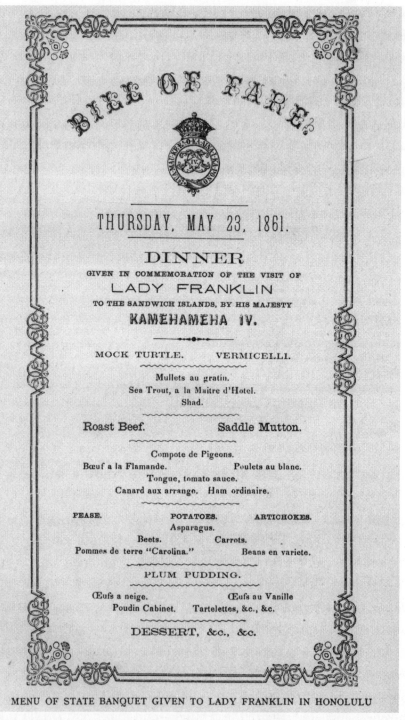

BILL OF FARE.

THURSDAY, MAY 23, 1861.

DINNER

GIVEN IN COMMEMORATION OF THE VISIT OF

LADY FRANKLIN

TO THE SANDWICH ISLANDS, BY HIS MAJESTY

KAMEHAMEHA IV.

MOCK TURTLE.   VERMICELLI.

Mullets au gratin.
Sea Trout, a la Maitre d'Hotel.
Shad.

Roast Beef.   Saddle Mutton.

Compote de Pigeons.
Bœuf a la Flamande.   Poulets au blanc.
Tongue, tomato sauce.
Canard aux arrange. Ham ordinaire.

PEASE.   POTATOES.   ARTICHOKES.
Asparagus.
Beets.   Carrots.
Pommes de terre "Carolina."   Beans en variete.

PLUM PUDDING.

Œufs a neige.   Œufs au Vanille
Poudin Cabinet.   Tartelettes, &c., &c.

DESSERT, &c., &c.

MENU OF STATE BANQUET GIVEN TO LADY FRANKLIN IN HONOLULU

Lady Franklin became a Personage on her world tour, as seen in this state banquet given by the King of the Sandwich Islands (Hawaii) in her honour, 1861. (Scott Polar Research Institute)

In 1860–62 Jane and Sophy went to south and north America, and enjoyed a trip like Sir John's, up a river in a canoe paddled by Indians through exciting eddies and currents. Lady Franklin Rock in Yosemite commemorates her visit, a modern guidebook commenting that as she was very feeble, guides carried her to the rock on a chair to view a waterfall. She might have been carried, but she certainly does not look feeble in the photograph taken of her that day, triumphant at the top of the walk—the only photograph known of her. Then it was on to Hawaii, where Jane and Sophy became friendly with the royal family and, wearing bloomers, climbed into the crater of a volcano (not bad for a seventy-year-old). To Japan, rarely visited by Europeans at the time, and home. After this, they voyaged south each winter and had some longer trips, to India and to Alaska, this in 1870 when Jane was nearly eighty. She was still indefatigable (though Sophy sometimes felt the strain), and in their month in Sitka in Alaska they took long daily walks, visited every local building, and made boat trips to beauty spots. They did get tired of Americans, 'so odd!' with their dreadful twang, hot rooms and interest in women's rights, all irritating; but the local paper welcomed this world-famous heroine and noted 'every citizen vying with the others to make her stay pleasant and agreeable'.[15] Although she had become such a notable woman, one of the few to make her name in a man's world, Jane Franklin had no sympathy with proponents of women's rights. Her contribution to the feminist cause came from her example to other women, not from any espousal of feminism.

In London in the 1860s, for the first time in her life Jane established her own home, where she lived with Sophy, still her inseparable companion. Jane leased a house in Kensington Gore, off Hyde Park. It no longer exists, but a later house of Jane's, also in Kensington, is an imposing four-storeyed detached home with an extensive garden—a home which today has separate buzzers for 'house' and 'trade'. Jane obviously lived in some style. She enjoyed renovating the Kensington Gore house, building a Japan Room, hanging portraits of Arctic explorers and her Tasmanian pictures framed in Huon pine. Visitors praised everything, though, as ever, 'Fanny did not admire the library carpet'. With this charming base, Lady Franklin became famous for her dinners. As a celebrity she could ask whom she pleased, and it was said that one could meet almost anybody there, from a black bishop to a daring admiral. Eleanor and John Gell's son Philip, who often acted as host, recalled that when Henry Stanley landed at Liverpool with news of Livingstone, Jane Franklin telegraphed him an invitation to dinner that evening. On receiving his acceptance, she rapidly gathered a table of geographical celebrities. Dramatically, Stanley narrated for the first time the story of his successful search, 'culminating in his Yankee salutation, "Dr Livingstone I presume" '.[16]

John Gell, shattered by his wife's death, only slowly recovered. However, he had previously been a favourite with Lady Franklin, and in the mid-1860s they resumed their friendship, discussing topics of mutual interest like church controversies and imperial federation, while he was useful as host at her dinners. Jane was never interested in young children, wrote Philip, but as the Gell boys grew older she encouraged them to 'work' in her garden or act as aides-de-camp at garden parties, paying them a shilling each time. She brought the children presents from her journeys, and often joined them on their summer holidays; Philip remembered a relationship 'brimming over with kindliness', so Jane Franklin mellowed in old age. But she still preferred males: when the Gell boys' sister visited, aged sixteen, Jane described her as wearing a ridiculous bonnet which 'left her very fat cheeks and her ears uncovered'.

A nephew recalled Jane and Sophy as short and stout, with kind expressions (a less flattering description of Sophy was 'very fat and red'). Aunt Franklin often had a stream of fun bubbling up, despite her endless anxieties—for example, both women had poor eyesight, Jane since the 1850s. Both 'good churchwomen', they supported missionary work enthusiastically.[17]

The most dramatic event was a visit by Queen Emma of the Sandwich Islands (Hawaii). Philip Gell and a Franklin nephew found her attractive, and her visit to England was a great success; but, as often happens, guest and hosts clashed. It was an honour to host a monarch, of course, but Jane and Sophy found Queen Emma difficult. She did not understand etiquette, keeping them waiting at dinner, signing a note just 'Emma', far too informal; she received a visitor in the library, from which peals of laughter were heard; she vanished to her room after or even during dinner; she refused to go shopping with Sophy. Queen Emma herself felt that '<u>My Aunt</u>' and '<u>My Niece</u>', as she called them, were trying to organise her, reading her letters, angling for invitations. When someone else took her sightseeing, 'the very fact of loosing sight of <u>My Aunt</u> & <u>My Niece</u> & going from them was a very great pleasure—one felt as if a load had quite been taken from our back—there was no restraint, but instantly felt merry'. 'We can only release her by writ of Habeas Corpus from the state of durance in which it seems she is held by Lady Franklin', wrote a Foreign Office official. Eventually Queen Emma moved to a hotel, but she and Jane Franklin remained on civil terms.[18]

Overriding everything else, Jane was John Franklin's devoted widow. She collected materials for a memoir, over two thousand documents from his boyhood French exercises onwards, but never actually wrote it. Why not? For someone of her organising ability, managing the huge mass of material would not be difficult; she had the time and the energy; and the topic—heroic Arctic explorer—ensured a wide readership. Perhaps her deteriorating eyesight deterred her; perhaps she feared that her writing style would not do her sacred subject justice, and that she would face criticism—and she had had enough of that. Perhaps she still feared comparisons with her husband's gifted first wife. Nevertheless, she read everything published about her husband, and often corrected it. (Her comments on a Porden niece's biography of Franklin are not known: after presenting a glowing picture of Eleanor and John Franklin's marriage, it merely stated that as Lady Franklin was still alive, the author would not praise her, though her name 'even now awakens a thrill of sympathy in every English breast'.) In 1869 the American explorer Charles Hall reported more relics and bones of the Franklin expedition, which supported Rae's findings, including cannibalism. Jane Franklin downplayed his importance, but went all the way to Cincinnati to visit him, and persuaded him to return to the area to find more.[19] Hall was murdered by his subordinates before he could fulfil his promise.

Then there were memorials, so important as visual remembrances. In 1861 the residents of Spilsby, Franklin's home town, erected a handsome statue with great fanfare. Parliament unanimously voted £2000 for a statue of Franklin in London, and his widow supervised the sculptor, casting, inscription and site—Waterloo Place. When she heard people in Hobart were suggesting a memorial to Sir John to show respect for his memory (and associate themselves with a hero, rather than their shameful convict past) she swung into action. A supporter moved a motion in the Tasmanian Parliament, which voted £1000 to erect a statue on the site of old Government House, to be known as Franklin Square. Jane organised a duplicate of the Waterloo Place statue, possibly paying for it herself. In 1865 an admiring crowd watched its installation—although the plaque announced that Sir John 'lost his life trying to find out the North West Passage', which would have infuriated his wife (he did not just *try*, he *succeeded*).[20] Franklin still looks down from his square over central Hobart.

Waterloo Place was all very well, but Jane Franklin wanted to have her husband commemorated at the best place, Westminster Abbey. For the last time, her indomitable perseverance won the day. In her eighties, she organised the sculptor and the bust, sending Sophy to the studio to instruct on details—no flag at half-mast, no extra ropes. For the inscription she turned to Franklin's nephew-by-marriage Ally—Alfred Tennyson, the Poet Laureate:

> *Not here: the white north has thy bones; and thou,*
> *Heroic sailor-soul,*
> *Art passing on thine happier voyage now*
> *Toward no earthly pole.*

The unveiling of the bust was Jane Franklin's final triumph, depicting both her and John as she would have wished: the faithful widow celebrating the heroic discoverer whom she loved with such unselfish devotion.

Pedants might argue that Franklin had not been aiming for an earthly pole, but the inscription was widely quoted. Some Hobartians thought they should inscribe it on their statue. There were objections: the poem referred to Westminster Abbey, of course the bones were not in Hobart; should they write 'Not here too! the white North ...'[21] Eventually Tennyson's inscription was added as he wrote it.

Always absorbed in Arctic exploration, Jane Franklin became something of an icon among explorers, and on the British Arctic Expedition of 1876 a young officer carried a locket containing the romantic painting of her as a young woman. She never gave up urging more searches for Franklin documents, and when Allen Young, a volunteer on *Fox*, suggested a voyage, Jane planned to sell her belongings and charter a ship for him. 'Was there ever such madness!' wrote a Franklin niece. 'Poor Sophy Cracroft will be worn and worried to death!' Jane was not forced to this extremity; the money was found, and *Pandora* sailed in June 1875. Perhaps it was just as well Jane did not see its return, for it was the same old story: route blocked by ice, back early, found nothing.[22]

Finally, at 83, Jane Franklin's health was failing, but she retained her spirit to the last. She never had much faith in medicine, and still refused it. After everyone else offered it in vain, they gave the glass to her manservant, who could often persuade her when no one else could—to the end she preferred men to women—but with a flick of her wrist, the glass lay shattered on the floor. However, not even Jane Franklin's iron will was immortal, and she died on 18 July 1875.[23]

Newspapers printed obituaries, which ranged from measured ('one of the most remarkable women of her times') to gushing (her name is a household word which will never be forgotten—Sophy Cracroft's final effort?). They praised her as an exemplary wife, an indefatigable promoter of Arctic exploration, the finder of her husband's fate and the most travelled woman in the world. Not just this world, for:

all who honour devotion, fidelity, and high motive will regret her departure to that bourne whence no traveller returns, though our regrets will be softened by the reflection that death may reveal to her what remains of that Arctic mystery which was the problem and the purpose of her life.[24]

If there was any chance of this, we can be sure Jane Franklin took it.

A team of Arctic pallbearers—not family—carried her coffin, and she shares a vault with her sister Mary at Kensal Green Cemetery. 'Daughters of John Griffin Esq / Lovely in their lives / In death they were not divided', runs the inscription. Still no place for Fanny, dead for seven years. A fortnight later George Back unveiled the Westminster Abbey memorial to Sir John, with the added words: 'This monument was erected by Jane, his widow, who, after long waiting, and sending many in search of him, herself departed, to seek and to find him in the realms of light.'[25]

In the mid-nineteenth century, Jane Franklin was one of the best-known women in the western world. Even then, there were some sceptics. 'Is Franklin the only man who is lost, that his wife should be so earnest to find him?' asked Henry Thoreau in 1854. A Franklin biographer suggests that this was not the point. Jane Franklin gained her fame because in searching for her husband so indomitably, she became the incarnation of an idea, the embodiment of wifely fidelity, bringing comfort to all men who left home to seek their fortunes. 'Somebody cared; that was what it came down to in the end.'[26]

Nothing could please the Victorian era more. At a time when women were beginning to rebel against society's restrictions, a woman who was active, who organised her own searches, who succeeded— but in the most conventional, praiseworthy of causes, without being a virago and without challenging male dominance—pleased everyone. But such fame does not last, and she was quickly eclipsed by Florence Nightingale, a similar woman (iron will, intelligent, excellent organiser, managing to retain an appearance of charming femininity) but with a much greater achievement in establishing the nursing profession.

The odd revisionist criticised Jane Franklin (in about the 1920s Harold Nicolson is reputed to have called her a conceited prig with a 'horrible restless arrogance', though no one can now find the reference) but few others took any notice of her. When in 1941 a Cracroft descendant gave her papers to the Scott Polar Research Institute, she instructed, 'take out whatever is of polar interest, and burn the rest'—it was private, unimportant (fortunately her advice was not followed).[27] Biographies presenting Jane Franklin as a saintly heroine, by a Franklin relation in 1923 and Frances Woodward in 1951, did little for her lasting fame; exploration fell out of fashion and children stopped learning about Sir John at school; and even Ken McGoogan's popular biography of Jane Franklin (2006) did little to revive interest outside his native Canada. Mention Jane Franklin today in Britain and you are met with blank looks. Her husband has fared little better, eclipsed by Scott, Shackleton and the romance of the Antarctic. The London memorials remain, little remarked, and only in remote Spilsby are the Franklins remembered, with the statue, a plaque on the house where Franklin was born, the Franklin Centre Unisex Hair Salon and Nail Studio and the Franklin Hall, where a Franklin display stands forlorn behind piles of gym equipment. Lady Jane Franklin Drive on the outskirts of Spilsby is possibly Jane's only memorial in Britain.

It is a different story in Tasmania, where Franklin is a familiar name. As soon as John Franklin was appointed to the Northwest Passage expedition, any criticism stopped, and the colony revelled in its connection with such a hero, 'the great and good Sir John Franklin', 'the best man who had ever set foot in this colony'. Citizens strongly supported the Search, and Mrs Dawson often sang the ballad 'Franklin's Fate' at Hobart's Theatre Royal, to 'a silence indicative of the sympathy cherished in Tasmania for the fate of "that gallant band"'. To change the mood, her next song was, 'I've eaten my friend'.[28] (This was before Rae's revelations of cannibalism.)

'Everything connected with the intrepid explorer and former Governor of our colony Sir John Franklin is dear to the hearts of Tasmanians', commented the Hobart *Mercury*, and enormous interest was shown in Franklin relics. A few arrived from the 1845 expedition, such as 'bones remaining from meals taken at the last camping-place of the ill fated expedition'. Less grisly items came from the Franklins' clearing sale. Periodic exhibitions were popular, one with a guidebook: *Sir John Franklin: a pilgrimage to the relics*. When Jane Franklin died, obituaries mourned her. News of the death of 'that best of all women, Lady Franklin' would 'cause a pang of regret in many a Tasmanian breast'. One devotee put the Bock portrait of her on public display, so that 'those who choose may silently gaze at the beautiful, and think of the past'.[29]

People vaunted their links with the Franklins, and many an obituary mentioned meeting them, travelling with them, working for them or being spoken to by them. In the Huon Valley the Thorpes prized a whale vertebra on which Sir John used to sit when he visited for a pipe and a yarn. Once, they recalled, he invited himself to dinner. Mrs Thorpe was flustered as she only had potatoes, but Sir John replied, 'Good potatoes, like old boots, need no apology', and dined heartily. Recollections often mentioned food. A man who worked on a Hobart newspaper described Sir John looking at ink rollers, which were made of treacle and glue, and commenting, 'Many a man would be glad to eat those rollers'. The narrator remembered this when 'the gallant explorer was lost in the Arctic regions'.[30]

Personal memories continued well into the twentieth century. In 1903 death silenced the last of Jane's chair-carriers, 'an amusing romancer' who loved telling people what he said to Lady Franklin as he carried her through the horizontal scrub. In 1926 the family of George Davis of Bruny Island heard for the last time how Lady Franklin held him on her knee when bad weather forced her party to land near his home. The final reminiscence appeared in 1940, when a centenarian recalled the Franklins coming to her father's school, and giving the boys a holiday. She could have been no more than three at the time, but still claimed to remember the celebrated visit.[31]

Jane Franklin was praised for her adventurousness. John Geeves of Geeveston described her as 'a great woman to travel for the bush'. She would not trouble to go round a fallen tree, but would simply say, 'Kindly let me put my foot in your hand', and would spring to the top of the tree trunk as easily as if she were mounting a staircase (at fifty?). In 1902 an audience heard she walked in the bush in men's trousers, but sadly both these stories are unreliable, claimed so long after the event with no provenance.[32]

The Hobart regatta and the Royal Society of Tasmania, as it became, lauded their founder, and the name Franklin was given to a Hobart wharf, the main town in Jane Franklin's Huon settlement and its electorate, the Lady Franklin Parlour Coach, many hotels (alas!), the Lady Franklin branch of the Labor Party (even worse) and the 'exceedingly well-built' Lady Franklin corset (only marginally better). Farmers grew Lady Franklin wheat, greyhounds raced in the Sir John Franklin handicap, axemen competed in the Sir John Franklin teams chop. Especially in the Huon, babies were called after the illustrious couple. Last baptised was John Franklin Burton in 1953.[33]

With so many fond recollections, the Franklins were mythologised in popular memory. Their period became the good old days, when the noble governor and his excellent lady reigned (sic) in the island: a time of prosperity, intellectual ferment, scientific research and farsighted initiatives such as advances in education. In 1873 a visitor to Tasmania reported that the colonists looked back to Sir John's days as 'the golden days of Tasmania ... both he and Lady Franklin are spoken of with the greatest veneration'. Their former servant drove carriages round Hobart, naming them 'Sir John Franklin' and 'Lady Franklin'—though sadly, said the visitor, they were very jolty and uncomfortable.[34] Well, it was something.

The height of John Franklin worship appeared in 1936 when Ethel Nairn Butler published *V.D.L. a hundred years ago*. She mentioned Jane Franklin only in passing, but praised Sir John to the skies: 'their beloved Governor', kind-hearted, honest, charitable, brave, the man who hated taking life.[35] By this time, Jane was mildly admired as the founder of the Huon settlement, and a devoted wife.

Serious Tasmanian historians varied in their assessment of her role. In 1852 John West depicted her as a public benefactor, if with more authority than was usual for a woman. In his lesser 1884 history, James Fenton emphasised her 'wild exploits' like climbing mountains. In 1983 Lloyd Robson claimed she played with fire in a man's world, her interference in politics giving her husband's opponents a chance to attack him, doing more harm than good to his career. Henry Reynolds in his shorter 2012 history of Tasmania ignored Lady Franklin.[36] Clearly this is possible; but any history which includes social and cultural trends must mention the Tasmanian Society and the Huon settlement, one of the most successful in Australia, while Jane Franklin is one of the most interesting individuals in Australian history.

In 1949 Kathleen Fitzpatrick published her study of the Franklins in Tasmania, depicting them extremely positively as champions of liberty, culture and general improvement. Jane Franklin she showed as clever, appealingly unconventional and innocent of any improper activity. Among the enormous mass of Franklin papers, Fitzpatrick ignored any negative evidence, but she did not convince everyone about Sir John. Though many Tasmanians remained fond of him, his fame faded as the assumptions of the past were challenged, the British Empire lost its prestige, and some historians depicted him not as a hero but as an inept explorer who lost far more men than anyone else. Even a Tasmanian claimed that everything the Franklins did failed: the regatta became a riot, Mathinna died of drink, the museum was forlorn, and then Sir John died: 'to fail nobly was the Franklins' lot'.[37] In later years they have been seen, in Australia and Canada, as prime examples of British imperialism, forcing their ideas on locals, and the accusations of cannibalism have been virtually proved. Jane Franklin's treatment of Mathinna is seen as particularly problematical.

However, in Tasmania at least, Fitzpatrick's praise and Woodward's biography started a wave of admiration for this dauntless woman, especially as interest in women's history developed. In 1950 students at the new women's college of the University of Tasmania named it Jane Franklin Hall, since its patron 'would undoubtedly have been in complete sympathy with this whole venture'.[38] In the 1970s Jane Franklin was depicted as a prototype feminist, a woman before her time, climbing mountains, helping female convicts and encouraging girls' education (neither of which she actually did), achieving mightily despite patriarchal shackles. Penny Russell, the major recent Australian historian of Jane Franklin, was influenced by this view, in her chapter in *For richer, for poorer* (1994) and many articles. She saw Jane as an active and unconventional woman devoted to her husband's career, and the Franklins as trying to bring culture to Van Diemen's Land, though strongly criticised by colonists and the Arthur faction. Russell depicted Jane Franklin as largely innocent politically but a focus of criticism, not just for her unwomanly exploits, but for challenging male supremacy.[39] Since then the reputations of both Jane and John Franklin have varied. Recent books by English and Canadian authors have depicted both as wonderful heroes, or a bumbling fool (John) and ghastly virago (Jane). It is not everyone who can evoke such different views two centuries after being born.

Jane Franklin is certainly not forgotten in Tasmania today, especially by women. No blank looks here: the most common response to her name is, 'I do admire her!', 'What a wonderful woman she was!' In the Huon, the Geeves family remember how fairly she treated them, the Clarks treasure a teaset she drank from.[40] In Hobart, her museum is a golden sandstone gem standing in an attractive park, used by the Art Society of Tasmania for its exhibitions. When in 2011 a subdivision threatened to overshadow it, residents packed the local hall at a protest meeting. Speaker after speaker praised Jane Franklin's vision, urging that the Franklins' dream of developing the mind must be kept alive. Ronald Gunn's great-great-grandson made an impassioned plea for a renewal of Jane Franklin's botanic garden. The land should be bought for the people, another speaker urged, in honour of 'Tasmania's premier female in two hundred years of history'.[41] Ironically, the only place to honour Jane Franklin is the island she despised.

ACKNOWLEDGEMENTS

M any people assisted me with this book. Grateful thanks to Arts Tasmania, which funded my research trip to England. Thanks also to the helpful staff of the following institutions. Overseas: Scott Polar Research Institute (Naomi Boneham Archivist, Shirley Sawtell Librarian); Derbyshire County Archives (Paul Beattie Archivist, Mark Smith); Lincolnshire County Archives; the Goldsmiths' Company (David Beasley Librarian, Eleni Bide); National Maritime Museum, Greenwich; Westminster Abbey (Christine Reynolds); Auckland War Memorial Museum (Rose Young); George Eastman House (Barbara Galasso). In Australia, thanks to Runnymede historic house (Gemma Webberley); Queen Victoria Museum and Art Gallery (Yvonne Adkins), Tasmanian Archive and Heritage Office, Tasmanian Museum and Art Gallery (Jacqui Ward), University of Tasmania Archives. At Allen & Unwin, enormous thanks to publisher Elizabeth Weiss and in-house project editor Karen Ward, as well as copyeditor Janice Bird.

Others too have been marvellous. Two of Jane Franklin's relatives, Edward Simpkinson and Marion Sargent, kindly provided photographs and a family tree. Jenny Parrott, who in the 1990s inspired the project to transcribe Jane Franklin's Van Diemen's Land writings, generously allowed me access to the transcripts. Susanna Hoe and Derek Roebuck took James and me to lunch at the Athenaeum Club in London, the Franklins' home-from-home, and Derek provided legal expertise. Thanks also to Richard Barber, Rhiannon Evans, Naomie Clark-Hansen, Norrey Drummond, Dick Geeves and the Huon Valley Family History Society, Richard and Sara Himsworth, Russell Mann, Jo Pillinger, Brian Rieusset, Julie Hawkins and Kim Eidjenberg, doctors Claire Smith and Hilary and Alan Wallace, Frances Underwood for discussing the position of the governor's wife, Chris Goodacre and Jean Elder who recreated Jane Franklin's climb up Mount Wellington, Patrick Hiller and Stuart Whitney for being chair-carriers, and Kit Hiller who painted fabulous pictures of Jane Franklin. Enormous thanks to fellow historians Graeme Broxam, Trudy Cowley, Lucy Frost, Alison Inglis, Craig Joel, Christine Leppard, Colette MacAlpine, Gill Morris, Robert Nash, Roslyn Russell, Dianne Snowden, Rod Thomson, Elisabeth Wilson; and Russell Potter, Penny Russell and Ken McGoogan, fellow historians of Jane Franklin. Particular thanks to Trudy Cowley, for her expertise with the maps.

Thanks to people who commented on the text: Jude, Catherine and Ted Alexander, Peter Boyce, Graeme Broxam, Pam Galloway, Wendy Rimon and Christine Wilson. The following read the whole text: James Alexander, Patsy Hollis, Annaliese Jacobs, Sue Johnson, Michael Roe and Leone Scrivener. Special thanks to Ian Stone, editor of *Polar Record*, who read the whole text and rescued me from Arctic errors and Australian solecisms. However, any mistakes remain my responsibility.

Annaliese Jacobs generously shared with me her own work for her forthcoming PhD. My Hobart U3A classes of 2010 and 2012 were wonderful. Family members Annabel, David and Jonathan Fowler in England made excellent suggestions, and my children Jude, Cathy and Ted have been fantastic, as usual.

Most of all, thanks to my husband James, always willing to discuss any aspect of Jane Franklin's life, and an expert photographer. He particularly wants to be acknowledged for cooking many roast dinners while I was working.

NOTES

Abbreviations

AAR	*Austral-Asiatic Review*
CC	*Cornwall Chronicle*
CT	*Colonial Times*
HTA	*Hobart Town Advertiser*
HTC	*Hobart Town Courier*
JF	Jane Franklin
TAAR	*Tasmanian and Austral-Asiatic Review*
TC	*True Colonist*

Introduction

1 Heard, p. 208.
2 MS248/156, 21.3.1837; MM4/1/3, JF to Eleanor [March 1837].

Chapter 1 A girl who did not fit in

1 MS248/266/1, 2; Rawnsley, p. 9.
2 Goldsmiths' Company Apprentice Book 8, p. 207, Book 7, p. 34; Freedom Book 2, p. 163.
3 Woodward, p. 15; information from Marion Sargent, Edward Simpkinson; Rawnsley, pp. 9–10; MS248/266/2.
4 MS248/411/1.
5 MS248/266/2; information from Robert Nash; William Butler, *Chronological, Biographical, and Miscellaneous Exercises*, Couchman, Couchman, 1807 (in possession of Brian Rieusset).

6 MS248/266/2; MS248/169; MS248/2, p. 1.

7 MS248/266/1, 2.

8 MS248/411/1; Woodward, p. 27.

9 Woodward, pp. 24–7.

10 MS248/168; MS248/11; Russell, *For richer, for poorer*, p. 53.

11 MS248/266/2.

12 MS248/229, p. 139; Woodward, p. 97; Russell, 'The allure of the Nile', p. 225.

13 Woodward, pp. 15–16, 27, 31, 66–7, 73; MS248/28, 30.6.1817, 10.7.1817; MS248/229, pp. 26–7; MS248/266/2; LA447/1, p. 230.

14 MS248/12, pp. 2–15; Woodward, p. 31.

15 MS248/50, 2.3.1824.

16 http://search.ancestry.com/iexec?htx=view&r=an&dbid=8978&iid=MD XHO107_671_672-0468&fn=John&ln=Griffin&st=r&ssrc=&pid=7159363: John Griffin, 1841 census [29 October 2012]; http://search.ancestry.com/iexec? htx=view&r=an&dbid=8860&iid=MDXHO107_1507_1507-0526&fn=Janes&l n=Franklin&st=r&ssrc=&pid=2620611: John Griffin, 1851 census. [29 October 2012]; MS248/28, 10.7.1817.

17 The Goldsmiths' Company, Court Book 23, pp. 4, 145, 197, 270, 328, windowpane; translation, Rhiannon Evans; MS248/28, 15.7.1817; LA447/1, p. 244.

18 MS248/39, p. 158; MS248/35, 25.5.1819.

19 MS248/43, p. 121; Woodward, p. 59.

20 Woodward, p. 33.

21 Woodward, pp. 46–57; MS248/171/4.

22 MS248/28, 11.7.1817; MS248/229, p. 154.

23 Woodward, pp. 91, 95; thanks to Elisabeth Wilson.

24 MS248/28, 11.7.1817; Woodward, pp. 97, 115.

25 MS580/2.

26 MS248/173/14.

27 MS248/39, 4.12.1819, 25.12.1819; MS248/45, 3.12.1821.

28 MS248/50, p. 21.

29 MS248/229, p. 139; Woodward, p. 134.

30 Woodward, p. 146; MS248/56, 15.5.1826.

31 MS248/2, p. 82; MS248/50, 18.7.1823.

32 MS248/229, p. 28; MS248/43, p. 14; MS248/44, p. 125.

Chapter 2 The Franklin connection

1 MM4/1/3, 25.10.1800; Traill, p. 14.

2 LA477/1, p. 282; MS248/167; [Anon], pp. 4–7.

3 MS248/296/1–5; [Anon], p. 8.

4 MS248/229, March–April 1818; MS248/298/7.

5 Gell, pp. viii–xii, 1, 21; [Anon], pp. 15–17.

6 [Anon], p. 16; MS248/35, p. 99, 2.6.1819; MS248/45, p. 166; Woodward, p. 99.

7   What to call the people Franklin called 'Indians' is a contested question with many possible answers, different in Canada and the United States. Since Franklin used the term 'Indians' and it is a major contender for usage today—mainly among Indians themselves—I have used it in this text. Thanks to Annaliese Jacobs and Norrey Drummond for advice. See http://en.wikipedia.org/wiki/Native_ American_name_controversy for a summary of the situation. Franklin, *Narrative of a journey to the shores of the Polar Sea*, vol. II, pp. 93, 36, 21.

8   Franklin, *Narrative of a journey to the shores of the Polar Sea*, vol. II, pp. 260, 336, 399; Rich, *Journal of Occurrences*, pp. 206–12, 224–7, 241–3, 254–61, 313; Davis, *Sir John Franklin's Journals and Correspondence,* pp. xliii–cvii; Markham, p. 142; Gell, p. 111; MM4/1/4, 24.10.1822; Bellot, p. 252; Davis, 'Fact and fancy in history and biography', pp. 5–12; Owen, p. 96.

9   Gell, pp. 89–90, 103–13, 142–4.

10 Gell, pp. 147–8, 185–6, 198–9, 278.

11 Gell, pp. 97, 148; MS248/50, 24.4.1823; Owen, p. 101.

12 Traill, p. 113; Gell, pp. 239–42; MM4/1/4, 4.11.1824; MS248/388/1.

13 MS248/50, 10–11.5.1824, 1.6.1824; MS248/388/2.

14 Gell, pp. 240, 296–9; Woodward, pp. 154–6; Lamb, p. 133.

15 Woodward, p. 148; Gell, pp. 270, 293, 300; MM4/1/4, 26.9.1824.

16 Gell, pp. 271, 284, 289, 302–06; Woodward, p. 156; MS248/56, 5.2.1825; Traill, pp. 117–18; [Anon], p. 21.

17 MS248/56, 1.3.1825; Woodward, p. 157.

18 MS248/298/15.

19 MS248/150, 29–31.10.1827, 10.11.1827; Woodward, p. 151; Owen, p. 142.

20 Traill, pp. 145–6.

21 Owen, p. 141; Traill, p. 152; [Anon], pp. 10–12, 43.

22 MS248/172/59; [Anon], p. 43.

23 Woodward, pp. 159–60; MS248/66, 28.7.1828.

24 MS248/151, 17.9.1828.

Chapter 3 An occasional marriage

1   Woodward, pp. 160–1; MM4/1/4, 11.12.1828; Owen, pp. 144–5.

2   MS248/303/1; MM4/1/4, 31.3.1829.

3   MM4/1/4, 6.4.1829, 18.5.1829.

4   MS248/172/1; MS248/172/10; Woodward, pp. 160–2.

5   MM4/1/4, 15.12.1829, 9.2.1830; thanks to Dr Claire Smith, Drs Hilary and Alan Wallace.

6   MS248/172/1–2, 4; MS248/303/3; MM4/1/4, 19.4.1830, 21.7.1830.

7   MS248/303/5–6; Woodward, p. 164.

8   MS580/1.

9   MS248/152, especially 19.12.1831.

10 MS248/303/10; Woodward, p. 166; Rawnsley, pp. 14–15; MS248/152, especially 14.12.1830, 21.1.1831.

11 MS248/172/4–5; D3311/109/2, [1830].

12 MS248/172/4, 10.

13 MS248/172/8–10, 12–13.

14 Owen, p. 154.

15 MM4/1/4, 24.2.1832, 1.8.1832.

16 MS248/172/47, 54.

17 MS248/173/4–5, 7; Woodward, p. 172.

18 MS248/170, 26.10.1831; MS248/72; MS248/172/17–18.

19 MS248/73, 24.4.1832; MS248/172/19; MS248/190; MS248/72, 15.4.1832.

20 MS248/172/20–21; MS248/173/10; MS248/73.

21 MS248/75, 23.7.1832.

22 MS248/172/30; *Era*, 13.1.1839.

23 MS248/172/31–32; MS248/76, December 1832.

24 MS248/173/12; MS248/172/59.

25 MS248/172/36; MS248/303/35, 41, 61.

26 MS248/172/36, 55; MM4/1/4, 21.6.1833.

27 MS248/78, 2.9.1833.

28 MS248/172/57, 61.

29 MS248/172/55, 57.

30 MS248/79; MS248/172/57, 65.

31 MS248/154, 19.1.1834–20.2.1834; MS248/172/70; MS248/173/22; Woodward, p. 189.

32 MS248/173/22; MS248/154, 18–21.2.1835.

33 MS248/154, 24.2.34–28.4.1834.

34 MS248/173/23; MS248/172/67–68; MS248/311, 2.11.1834.

35 MS248/303/6.

36 Stock, p. 46.

37 MS248/172/69; MS1503/11/5; Woodward, p. 183.

Chapter 4 To Van Diemen's Land

1 MS248/303/59; MS1503/11/5.

2 MS248/174/4; MS248/311; MS248/172/65; MS248/80, p. 13, 27.2.1835.

3 MS248/80, p. 81, 21.3.1835.

4 MS248/81; Woodward, p. 195.

5 McIlraith, *passim*; Parry, *passim*; Courtney, pp. 290–1.

6 MS248/80, 21.6.1835.

7 MS1503/18/1, 22.2.1838; MS248/303/66–67; MM4/1/3, 26.3.1836.

8 MS248/303/68–69; MS248/173/12; MS248/472/5.

9 D3311/123; D3311/28/5; MM4/1/4, 3.6.1836; Owen, p. 179.

10 MS3472, 2.7.1836; MS1503/14/11, 11.6.1836; BJ3/18, 12.6.1836.

11 MM4/1/4, 3.6.1836.

12 Owen, p. 179.

13 H6/24, 27.8.1836, 2.9.1836, 28.9.1836; MS248/84, 25.9.1836, 16.10.1836, 23.10.1836.

14 MS248/84, 16.9.1836, 21.9.1836, 29.9.1836, 4.10.1836, 29.10.1836, 1.11.1836, 3.11.1836, 7.12.1836.
15 MS248/84, 8.9.1836, 10.10.1836.
16 MS248/84, 19.11.1836.
17 MS248/84, 16.11.1836.
18 MS248/84, p. 369ff; D3287/26/21/13.
19 West, *History of Tasmania*, p. 81.
20 Alexander, *Governors' ladies*, Chapters 1–7.
21 Alexander, *Governors' ladies,* Chapter 8.
22 Information from Frances Underwood.
23 *HTC,* 19.8.1836, 26.8.1836; *CT,* 23.8.1836, 11.10.1836.

Chapter 5 The governor's lady

1 MS248/170, 6.1.1839.
2 *CT,* 10.1.1837; *HTC, TC,* 13.1.1837.
3 *Sydney Gazette*, 26.1.1837; *CT,* 6.2.1838.
4 MM4/1/3, 9.1.1837; *CT,* 10.1.1837.
5 *HTC,* 13.1.1837; *CT,* 17.1.1837.
6 *CT,* 31.1.1837.
7 Heard, p. 206.
8 *CT,* 7.2.1837.
9 *CC,* 25.2.1837.
10 *HTC,* 24.2.1837.
11 Brown, pp. 62–8.
12 *CT,* 4.7.1837, 11.7.1837.
13 *CT,* 18.7.1837.
14 *CT,* 11.7.1837, 18.7.1837, 8.8.1837, 29.8.1837, 27.11.1838; *TAAR,* 14.7.1837; *CC,* 15.7.1837; *TC,* 28.7.1837, 4.8.1837; RS25/2(5), 6.7.1837.
15 *CT,* 1.8.1837; Meredith, p. 30.
16 Calder, pp. 8–9.
17 RS16/2(1) 22.1.1838; *CC,* 3.2.1838.
18 RS16/8(1).
19 RS16/8(1); RS25/2/(5), 24.5.1838; *CT,* 29.5.1838.
20 RS16/8(1).
21 *CT,* 29.5.1838; *CC,* 14.9.1839, 6.6.1840; *HTA,* 27.9.1839, 29.5.1840, 25.5.1841, 10.6.1842, 26.5.1843; MS248/88, 17.5.1840; RS25/2/(6), 21.9.1839; Chisholm, p. 54.
22 MS248/88, 27.5.1840.
23 MS248/174/5; MS248/157, 24.8.1839, 12–13.9.1839, 2–7.11.1839.
24 MS248/88, 15.5.1840.
25 *CT,* 1.2.1842; MS248/157, 3.9.1839.
26 MS248/88, 26.5.1840; Alexander, *Governors' ladies*, Chapters 8, 11.
27 RS25/2(6), 6.5.1840.

28 RS18/3, *passim.*

29 RS/25/2(6), 7.5.1839, 26.12.1839, 6.5.1840; RS25/2(7), 17.10.1842, 9.1.1843.

30 MS248/85, 14.10.1838, 2.11.1838, 9.11.1838; MS248/89, 13.9.1840, 30.7.1840; MS248/92, 24.8.1841; MS248/96, 25.3.1843; Backhouse and Tylor, p. 271.

31 Cash, p. 46.

32 *CT,* 19.6.1838; *TAAR,* 22.6.1838, 10.12.1841; MS248/85, 11.11.1838.

33 MS248/85, 14.10.1838; *CT,* 9.5.1843.

34 MS248/174/6.

35 *HTC,* 27.7.38, 8.11.1839, 15.11.1839, 31.1.1840, 22.10.1841; *CT,* 3.12.1839.

36 MS248/86, 24.8.1839; MS248/88, 8.5.1840; MS248/89, 2.10.1840.

37 *HTC,* 18.5.1841, 11.6.1841; MS248/88, 6.7.1840; *Sydney Gazette,* 16.11.1841.

38 MS248/174/4; MS248/174/14; MS114, 14.12.1840; MS248/246/5.

Chapter 6 The home front

1 RS16/8(1); *Bent's News,* 15.6.1838; Calder, pp. 9–10.

2 MM4/1/3, 10–11.1.1841; MS248/91, 30.6.1841; MS248/89, 29.9.1840.

3 MM4/1/3, 25.2.1838, 18.3.1838; MS248/175/4; MS0919, 13.3.1839.

4 MS0919, 20.10.1841; MM4/1/4, 28.3.1838.

5 MS248/295/2, 20.4.1843; MS248/174/17; RS25/2(6), 4.12.1841; MM4/1/3, 21.1.1843; MS248/295/2.

6 Information from Rose Young, Auckland Museum; Plomley, p. 530; MS248/96, 24.5.1843; MS0919, 12.2.1840; Woodward, p. 172; RS16/8(5).

7 MS248/89, 26.9.1840; D3311/122/30, 26.8.[1849]; RS1784/A73.

8 MS248/174/19; MS248/85, 8.11.1838.

9 Calder, pp. 9–12, 18, 51–2; MM4/1/4, Notes on Jane Franklin.

10 RS16/7.

11 MS248/88, 17.5.1840; MS248/174/5–6; MS248/92, 4.8.1841; MS114, 27.4.1839.

12 *Sydney Monitor,* 20.1.1837; B1566, CY/160, 14.3.1842; Gates, p. 39.

13 Traill, p. 437.

14 MS248/85, 23.9.1838; MS248/174/6; MS248/89, 29.8.1840; *CC,* 9.4.1842; FitzSymonds, p. 279.

15 *Bent's News,* 15.6.1838.

16 MS248/85, 23.9.1838.

17 MS248/174/6, 9; MS248/157, 7.12.1839.

18 MM33, 17.5.1839; RS16/1(1), 13.4.1841; MS114, 1.1.1841; MS248/85, 20.12.1838.

19 RS16/8(1).

20 MS248/92, 17.9.1841.

21 RS16/2(2); MS248/174/6; MS248/86, 24.8.1839; MS248/87, 3.9.1839.

22 Crooke, pp. 51–2.

23 RS16/2(1), 4.1.1838; MS248/85, 13.12.1838; MS248/157, 11.12.1839.

24 MS248/92, 10.9.1841; MS248/174/6; Crooke, pp. 44, 51–2.

25 RS16/8/(2).

26 MS248/89, 1.10.1840; MS248/174/11; MS248/87, 5.11.1839, 6.11.1839, 28.11.1839.

27 MS248/303/77.

28 MS248/85, 23.9.1838; MS248/157, 5.6.1839, 7.7.1839; MS248/96, 18.6.1843; RS16/8(9).

29 MS248/92, 5.10.1841.

30 CEN1/1/16-3, 8.1.1842.

31 MS248/239, p. 51; RS16/8(3).

32 RS18/4(1); MM4/1/4, June 1837; MS248/411/12.

33 Susan Adams, CON40/1/1/A83; Mary Ann Andrews, CON40/1/2/A123; Ann Balfour, CON40/1/1/B321; Elizabeth Bell, CON40/1/2/B482; Mary Bleeze, CON40/1/1/B201; Mary Braid, CON40/1/1B322; Margaret Callaghan, CON40/1/2/C438; Helen Curle CON40/1/2/C340; Ann Eccles CON40/1/4/ E60; Marianne Galey CON40/1/4/G222; Rhoda Gunn CON40/1/4/G273; Mary Harper, CON40/1/6/H307; Lydia Hart, CON40/1/5/H148; Ellen Holden, CON40/1/6/H406; Rachael Jones, CON40/1/6/J193; Elizabeth King, CON40/1/6/ K127; Judith McCoy, CON40/1/2/C335; Ellen Malen, CON40/1/8/M265; Susannah Miles CON40/1/8/M421; Margaret Murray CON40/1/8/M276; Mary Power, CON40/1/8/P221; Mary Stewart, CON40/1/10/S427; Elizabeth Such, CON40/1/10/S497; Bridget Tway, CON40/1/9/T104; Ann Williams, CON40/1/10/W524; Jane Willis, CON40/1/10 W431; Jane Wilson CON40/1/10/ W412, CON19/1/1.

34 MS248/87, 16.9.1839; MS248/92, 21.9.1841; MS248/89, 30.9.1840; *Caledonian Mercury*, 30.1.1834.

35 CON40/1/4/G222, CON15/1/9, CON19/1/13; MS248/89, 25.8.1840.

36 MS248/88, 27.5.1840; MS248/90, 20.2.1841, 28.3.1841, 8.4.1841; MS248/91, 5.5.1841, 8.5.1841, 24.5.1841.

37 Owen, p. 181; MS248/174/3; MS248/92, 3.9.1841.

38 MS248/174/6; MS248/174/22.

Chapter 7 Female convicts

1 MS0919, 14.1.1839.

2 MS248/174/4.

3 MS248/87, 4.11.1839; MS248/86, 26.8.1839.

4 RS16/1(2), 3.8.1841.

5 MS0375, 30.7.1841; RS16/1(2), 29.4.1842.

6 NS202/1, 9.2.1842; MS248/91, 23.7.1841.

7 MS248/158, 28.7.1841; RS18/4(2); MS248/171/5; D/EHX/F29, 11.10.1841.

8 MS248/158, 1.9.1841, 4.9.1841.

9 MS248/92, 16.9.1841, 18.9.1841, 21.9.1841, 28.9.1841, 2.10.1841, 4.10.1841; *TAAR*, 1.10.1841, 4.11.1841; *CT*, 5.10.1841.

10 MS0919, 4.1.1842; RS16/8(3), 5.9.1842; *CT*, 1.2.1842, 8.3.1842; NS202/1, 3.3.1842.

11 NS202/1, 22.1.1842, 26.1.1842, 6.4.1842; MS248/174/17.

12 MS248/96, 30.5.1843; MS248/174/17; MS248/174/20.

13 MS248/97.

14 West, *The hope of life eternal*, pp. 119–20, 123–4.

15 Crooke, pp. 2–4, 22–6.

16 Crooke, pp. iii–vii; MS248/92, 2.8.1841; MS248/95, 11.2.1843; *Examiner*, 6.6.1857; *Mercury*, 23.9.1857, 12.10.1857.

17 Fitzpatrick, pp. 80–1, 381.

18 Connor; Woodward, pp. 213–14, 367; Alexander, *Governor's ladies*, p. 32; Lambert, pp. 105, 364.

19 Cowley, pp. 66–70.

20 *Examiner*, 19.11.1892; CON40/1/5/L19, L43.

Chapter 8 Improving the colony

1 RS16/8(2); 28.4.1840.

2 West, *History of Tasmania*, pp. 215–6.

3 RS16/8, 7.9.1840; RS16/8(2); Woodward, p. 220.

4 MS248/89, 15.8.1840; *TC*, 13.11.1840; *TAAR*, 1.7.1842.

5 MS248/89, 17.9.1840; MS248/92, 2.9.1841, 9.9.1841; MS248/174/11; MS114/12.

6 MS248/89, 8.10.1840, 17.9.1840.

7 MS248/174/10.

8 MS248/85, 21.12.1838.

9 *HTC*, 17.11.1827, 25.6.1831, 1.6.1832, 27.2.1835.

10 *CT*, 18.12.1829, 26.3.1830; *HTC*, 23.1.1830, 29.5.1830, 19.10.1832, 25.10.1833.

11 *HTC*, 19.2.1836, 8.4.1836, 26.8.1836.

12 MM4/1/4, 28.3.1838, 5.12.1840; Fitzpatrick, p. 195; MS248/95, 1.3.1843; MS248/156, March 1837; MS248/85, 13.12.1838; Oats, p. 14.

13 *HTC*, 14.4.1837, 21.4.1837; *CT*, 24.8.1841; *TC*, 3.7.1840.

14 MS248/174/6; Huxley, p. 455; MS0919, 31.3.1839; MS248/87, 19.9.1839.

15 MS248/87, 17.9.1839, 5.11.1839; MS248/88, 18.5.1840; MS248/92, 3.9.1841; MS248/89, 24.8.1840; D3287/26/21/2; information from Rhiannon Evans.

16 *Tasmanian Journal of Natural Science*, vol. 1, p. 414; MS0919, 21.12.1841; RS16/4; MM4/1/3, 25.5.1841, [undated, around September 1840].

17 MS248/89, 24.8.1840; Burns and Skemp, p. 84.

18 MM4/1/3, 20.11.1840.

19 RS16/4; MS248/92, 21.8.1841, 27.8.1841; *Tasmanian Journal of Natural Science*, vols 1, 2; MM4/1/3, 27.10.1842.

20 MS248/87, 18.9.1839; MS248/88, 8.5.1840; MS0919, undated letter [September 1839?]; MS248/91, 5.5.1841.

21 RS25/2(6), 4.8.1841, 25.8.1841; RS25/2(7), 2.1.1843, 6.7.1843.

22 *Van Diemen's Land Chronicle*, 3.9.1841; *HTC*, 10.9.1841; *Sydney Morning Herald*, 6.4.1843.

23 Burns and Skemp, pp. 66, 71, 74, 81–4, 86, 91; RS25/2(7), 23.8.1842.

24 MS248/174/4–5, 7; RS16/8(15); MS248/88, 29.4.1840; Chisholm, pp. 29, 38, 49, 53.

25 RS16/7(12); MS248/92, 3.10.1841, 4.10.1841; RS16/8(3); MS0919, 21.12.1841.

26 MS248/89, *passim* and 27.9.1840; James Ross, p. 110; Huxley, pp. 106–07.

27 RS16/7(12), 7.9.1840; MM4/1/4, 5.12.1840, 13.4.1841.

28 MS248/89, 18.8.1840, 20.8.1840, 24.8.1840.

29 *CT*, 4.5.1841; MM4/1/3, 22.5.1841.

30 MS248/85, 17.11.1838; MS248/87, 5.11.1839; MS0919, 14.1.1839; Burns and Skemp, pp. 71, 74.

31 Burns and Skemp, pp. 74, 84.

32 MS248/89, 8.10.1840; RS16/8(9).

33 MS248/174/15; *HTA*, 3.10.1843; MS114, 27.5.1839, 3.6.1839, 7.10.1839; MS248/158, 17.3.1844.

34 MS248/85, 18.10.1838; MS248/89, 22.9.1840; Buscombe, pp. 9, 128, 132, 293–304; MS248/170/6; Owen, p. 429.

35 MS248/92, 24.8.1841; *CT*, 16.6.1840.

36 RS16/8(2); Dietrich, pp. 80–7; MS248/175/6.

37 MS248/175/6; RS16/5.

38 MM4/1/3, 16.3.1842.

39 MS248/95, 9.2.1943, 11.2.1843; MS248/96, 27.5.1843, 6.7.1843; RS25/2(7), 26.10.1843.

40 MS248/89, 1.10.1840.

41 *HTC*, 13.3.1835, 19.6.1835, 4.3.1836; *CT*, 20.9.1836, 21.3.1837; Woolley and Smith, pp. 58–63.

42 RS16/2(1), 22.1.1838; MS248/95, 23.9.1838; *Mercury*, 25.7.1885.

43 MM4/1/3, 8–12.9.1838; *CT*, 18.9.1838.

44 RS16/8(9); *Mercury*, 25.7.1885; MS248/87, 11.7.1839, 22.8.1839, 24.8.1839, 2.9.1839, 6.10.1839, 4.11.1839.

45 MM4/1/3, 27–29.10.1839, 23.11.1839; MS248/88, 26.6.1840; MS248/89, 1.8.1840, 28.9.1840.

46 MS248/89, 28.8.1840; MS248/174/20.

47 MS248/91, 28.8.1841; MS248/93, 3.1.1842; *HTA*, 8.11.1839; CB7/39, 15.10.1842, 27.10.1842, 1.11.1842, 17.2.1843, 18.2.1843.

48 RS16/2(3), 4–6.11.1843.

49 *Mercury*, 1.8.1900.

50 Calder, pp. 18–19; *CC*, 25.12.1841, 31.12.1842, 25.2.1843; MS073(417), 9.8.1838, 24.8.1838; Owen, pp. 193–4; MS114, 20.4.1839; *HTC*, 27.12.1839; *TC* 4.10.1839; MS248/174/6.

51 MS248/174/11; *HTC*, 3.12.1841; *CT*, 7.12.1841; MS0919, 21.12.1841.

52 MS248/89, 12.10.1840, 13.10.1840; MM4/1/3, 12.3.1842, 9.10.1842.

53 RS16/1(1).

54 MS0919, 13.3.1839.

Chapter 9 The Aborigines

1 *HTC*, 23.1.1830.

2 MS248/92, 10.9.1841; MS248/94, 12.2.1842; Boyce, p. 18.

3 Plomley, pp. 524–30; Burns and Skemp, p. 72.

4 D3287/26/21/1; Keynes, pp. 34–6, 45–6.

5 Plomley, pp. 605, 610, 779, 837.

6 MM4/1/3, JF to Eleanor Franklin, [March 1839]; MM4/1/3, 30.7.1839, 7.8.1839, 14.3.1842; MS248/87, 4.11.1839; Owen, p. 184; MS248/157, 21.12.1839; MS248/94, 11.3.1842; Plomley, pp. 779, 887.

7 Plomley, p. 783; MS1503/28/10.

8 MS248/92, 3.9.1841; Plomley, pp. 830, 833, 858.

9 MM4/1/3, 22.5.1841, 14.9.1841.

10 MM4/1/3, 25.4.1842; MM4/1/1, 9.2.1842.

11 MS248/94, 11.3.1842; MM4/1/1, 18.8.1842.

12 MS248/94, 14.2.1842; MS1503/28/10; MS248/174/20–21.

13 MM4/1/3, 14.2.1843; Traill, p. 431.

14 Crooke, p. 45.

15 *Mercury*, 7.6.1869.

16 MS248/95, 29.3.1843.

17 *Mercury*, 7.6.1869; MS1503/28/10.

18 Plomley, p. 144; CSO24/1/7/101, 9.6.1847, 19.6.1847, 4.10.1847; GO33/55/1205, 22.5.1846.

19 CSO24/1/32/922, p. 89, 97; CSO24/1/32/911, 4.11.1847; Davis and Petrow, pp. 74–7, 83–4.

20 CSO24/1/280/6187, 4.7.1851.

21 SC195/31/2798; Plomley, p. 173, 181; CSD1/1/51/1009; CSD1/18/703.

22 CSO89/1/1, 5.11.1857; *Mercury*, 7.6.1869, 6.12.1869.

23 *Mercury*, 5.8.1879; Bonwick, pp. 382–3.

Chapter 10 Mount Wellington, Sydney and beyond

1 MS248/156, 21.3.1837.

2 Heard, p. 208; MS248/156, 21–27.3.1837.

3 De Quincey, pp. 15, 19; *HTC*, 22.12.1837, 29.12.1837; *AAR*, 26.12.1837.

4 Information from Chris Goodacre and Jean Elder; *TC*, 29.12.1837.

5 MS248/85, 'Excursion to Port Davey', December 1838; MM4/1/3, 11–20.12.1838.

6 MM4/1/3, 31.10.1839.

7 Russell, *This errant lady*, p. 30; *HTC*, 26.4.1839; MS114, letter 2, 5.4.1839; MS114, 6.4.1839.

8 MS114, 5.4.1839, 14.4.1839, 6–30.4.1839; MS114/12; Parris, *passim*, especially 13.4.1839.

9 MS114, 10–14.4.1839; Parris, 12.4.1839, 14.4.1839.

10 MS114, 24.14.1839, 29.4.1839.

11 MM4/1/3, 6.9.1839, 21.6.1839; Parris, 10–14.4.1839.

12 MS114, 10.4.1839, 20.4.1839; Parris, 14.4.1839, 19.4.1839.

13 MS114, 21–29.4.1839; MS114, 27.4.1839.

14 MS114, 30.4.1839.

15 MS114, diary 6–27.5.1839, letter to Sir John 18.5.1839.

16 MS114, 20–27.5.1839; MS114/8, 21.5.1839.
17 MS114, undated (probably 27.5.1839, 31.5.1839, 2.6.1839).
18 MS114, undated (probably 27.5.1839), 4–29.6.1839.
19 MS114, 29.6.1839.
20 MS114, 30.6.1839–16.7.1839, especially 9 July; Russell, *This errant lady*, p. 251.
21 MS114, 12–16.7.1839, 23.9.1839.
22 Article from Sydney newspaper (*Australian*? *Australasian*?) dated 27.8.1839 copied by Jane Franklin 23.9.1839; *Sydney Colonist*, 15.5.1839, 24.4.1839, 1.6.1839.
23 *CT*, 30.4.1839, 14.5.1839, 28.5.1839, 4.6.1839; *TC*, 4.10.1839; MS248/174/8.
24 MS114, 16.7.1839–19.8.1839; *CT*, 20.8.1839.
25 MS114, 'Visit to South Australia in Dec^br 1840'; MM4/1/3, 25.12.1840; Owen, p. 200.
26 MS114, 'Visit to South Australia'; MM4/1/3, 1.1.1841, 2.1.1841, 5.1.1851.
27 MS114, 'Visit to South Australia'; MM4/1/3, 6.1.1841–14.1.1841.
28 RS16/8(2).
29 MS248/90, Captain Hobson to Mr Davis, 23.4.1839.
30 RS16/6(1).
31 MS248/90, 12.3.1841–21.4.1841; RS16/6(1).
32 MS248/90, 21.4.1841–1.5.1841; MS248/91, 2.5.1841–30.6.1841.
33 Burn, p. 8, 12–13; Calder, pp. 51–2, 55–6.
34 Calder, pp. 51–4.
35 Burn, pp. 8, 13–31; RS16/8(3).
36 Calder, pp. 50, 69–76; *Examiner*, 16.7.1887; Burn, pp. 15–26; Pasco, p. 153; A316, Milligan to Gunn, 16.5.1842; MS248/174/15.
37 MM4/1/3, Franklin to Boyes, May 1842; RS16/7, 23.7.1842; MM4/1/4, 16.5.1842; RS25/2(7), 12.4.1842–20.5.1842.
38 *CT*, 28.6.1842; *CC*, 30.4.1842; *HTA*, 24.5.1842.
39 MS248/246/5–6.
40 RS16/8(1), 21.6.1838.

Chapter 11 Three women's lives

1 MM4/1/3, 29.1.1837; MS248/170/5.
2 Barry, pp. 1–9; *HTC*, 14.7.1837; MM4/1/3, 21.12.1837, 25.2.1838.
3 RS16/8(1); MM4/1/3, 18.3.1838.
4 Barry, pp. 11–13; MS248/174/7.
5 MS248/87, 3.10.1839; MM4/1/3, 3.10.1839, 18.6.1840; Barry, p. 13.
6 MS248/89, 28.9.1840; MS248/95, 1.3.1843; MS248/158, 4.11.1843; *CC*, 11.12.1841; Barry, pp. 14–16.
7 Barry, pp. 24–153; 'Rogers, Thomas George', *Australian Dictionary of Biography*, vol. 2.
8 MM4/1/3, 21.12.1837.
9 MS248/157, 23.5.1839, 1.6.1839, 19.6.1839; MS248/87, 6.10.1839.

10 MS248/96, 24.6.1843; NS202/1, 3.3.1842; Nixon, p. 8.

11 NS202/1, 17.1.1842; MM4/1/3, 13.3.1841, 18.3.1841, August 1841, 14.2.1843.

12 MS248/239, pp. 59, 119, 13.5.1844, 20.5.1844.

13 Owen, p. 208; MS248/87, 11.9.1839; MS248/92, 28.9.1841; MS248/174/15.

14 Michael Smith, p. 89; Lubbock, pp. 136–7.

15 MS248/228, 20.6.1844, 9.7.1845; MS248/174/15.

16 CC, 17.9.1840; MS248/228, 9.7.1845.

17 Owen, p. 208; MS114/12, 14.4.1839; MS248/246/5; MM4/1/3, 23.11.1839; D3287/26/21/9.

18 MS248/246/3; MM4/1/3, 31.2.1837, 31.3.1838.

19 MM4/1/3, 31.2.1837; MS248/170/6, 12.10.1841; D3311/123/242; MM4/1/4, Notes on Jane Franklin.

20 MM4/1/3, [March 1839]; MS248/96, 24.5.1843.

21 MM4/1/3, 26.5.1842, 18.6.1840; MS248/239, 18.4.1844; MS248/246/2, 5.

22 MM4/1/3, 18.6.1840; MS248/174/15.

23 RS16/1(3), 6.11.1843; MS248/95, 1.3.1843.

24 MS248/174/15.

Chapter 12 The political question

1 Fleming, p. 339.

2 NS279/1/1, 18.4.1841; Laidlaw, Chapter 4.

3 MS248/174/18; RS16/8(3); *The Times*, 2.8.1839.

4 RS16/1(1) letter 3; MS248/87, 9.10.1839; MS248/174/6.

5 MS248/85, 2.11.1838.

6 RS16/1(1).

7 MS248/174/9; A2187, 7.10.1838, 9.3.1840; Crooke, p. 42–4.

8 *Sydney Monitor*, 23.10.1837.

9 West, *History of Tasmania*, pp. 227–8.

10 MM4/1/4, 18.9.1837.

11 MS248/174/1.

12 RS16/8(3), 12.10.1841.

13 MS395/54/2; MS248/411/9; Owen, p. 187.

14 MS248/84, 29.9.1836, 18.10.1836, 7.11.1836, 18.11.1836.

15 A2176, 22.2.1837; MS395/53/1; MM4/1/4, 18.9.1837; MS248/87, 24.10.1839; MS395/54/2.

16 MS395/54/2.

17 NS473/1/6, pp. 3, 17; Franklin, *Narrative of some passages in the history of Van Diemen's Land*, p. 9; MM4/1/4, 18.9.1837; CC, 15.4.1837.

18 HTC, 8.6.1838; CT, 2.1.1838, 6.2.1838; A2176, 9.12.1837.

19 West, *History of Tasmania*, p. 228; RS25/2/(5), 14.12.1837; MS1503/18/1, 20.

20 MS248/156, 25.3.1837; MS48/174/18; *Town and Country Journal*, 25.6.1870; *Mercury*, 11.11.1870; A2176, 15.3.1838; MS248/85, 2.11.1838.

21 MS248/174/5; MS248/303/75; Owen, p. 199 (illustration).

22   MS248/85, 20.12.1838, 26.8.1838, 14.10.1838.
23   A2176, 15.3.1838.
24   MS248/316/11.
25   MS248/174/4, 7; MS248/157, 26.12.1839; MS395/53/1; MS395/54/1.
26   MS248/174/5.
27   A2187, 16.2.1840, 29.7.1840.
28   MS248/174/9; RS16/1(1).
29   MS248/174/5.
30   RS16/1(1); RS16/6(1).
31   MS248/87, 7.10.1839; MS248/89, 15.8.1840.
32   MS248/174/9.
33   NS473/1/6, pp. 116–17; MS248/157, 6.12.1839.
34   RS16/8(10); MS248/174/11–12; MS248/86, 28.8.1839.
35   MS248/174/6.
36   MS248/174/6; MS248/174/9.
37   RS16/8(10); MS248/174/5, 11.
38   *CT*, 14.11.1837; *Bent's News*, 29.6.1838; *CC*, 13.4.1839; *AAR*, 10.12.1839.
39   *TC*, 4.10.1839.
40   *Mercury*, 21.6.1887; *Tasmanian*, 1.3.1839; MS248/174/6.
41   *HTA*, 26.1.1841, 18.5.1841; MS248/92, 7.9.1841.
42   Crooke, pp. 44–5; MS248/174/10.
43   Truman, pp. 89–94, 96–101; Adler, p. 49.

Chapter 13 Jane Franklin v. John Montagu

 1   NS473/1/6 p. 3; NS279 *passim*, especially 30.4.1841.
 2   RS16/6(1), 21.4.1841.
 3   MS248/174/11, 15; A2176, 12.12.1841.
 4   A2176, 12.12.1841.
 5   MS248/174/15.
 6   NS473/1/6, pp. 3, 15–16; MS248/174/11.
 7   MS248/316/8; A2176, 12.12.1841; RS25/2(7), 21.1.1842.
 8   *VDLC*, 24.12.1841; *CC*, 29.1.1842, 5.2.1842, 12.3.1842; MS248/174/13.
 9   RS25/2(7), 15.1.1842, 19.1.1842.
10   MS248/174/12.
11   NS473/1/6 p. 11; MS248/93, 27.12 (mistake for January) 1842, 14.2.1842;
     MS248/174/12.
12   MS248/316/11.
13   NS1250/1/1, p. 3; RS25/2(7), January 1842 *passim*; West, *History of Tasmania*,
     p. 227.
14   RS25/2(7), 23.1.1842, 1.2.1842, 21.6.1842, 22.10.1842, 30.6.1842, 1.7.1842.
15   MS248/93, 10.2.1842, 12.2.1842; MS248/93, undated letter [10.2.1842].
16   *Australasian Chronicle*, 25.1.1842; *TAAR*, 12.5.1843; MS248/174/17.
17   *TC*, 14.10.1842, 21.10.1842, 4.11.1842; *CT*, 9.5.1843; RS25/2(7), 23.8.1842.

18 MS248/225/3.
19 *TC*, 21.10.1842, 28.10.1842.
20 Meredith, p. 29; West, *History of Tasmania*, p. 227; *HTA,* 26.5.1843.
21 MM4/1/3, 17.12.1842; RS25/2(7), 20.12.1842.
22 CO280/93, f.41 6.1.1838, f.179 13.2.1838; CO280/94, f.253 30.4.1838; CO280/97, f.342 8.10.1838; CO280/111, f.17 13.11.1839; CO280/120, f.43 June 1840; CO280/123, ff.209, 214 10.10.1840; CO280/129, f.13 2.1.1841, f.184 18.1.1841; CO280/134, f.554–5 16.12.1841; CO280/135, f.231 16.12.1841; CO280/136, f.270 22.7.1841; Shaw, pp. 141–53.
23 Shaw, pp. 145–6; CO280/148, ff.36–9.
24 CO280/158, f.291, 26.7.1843.
25 RS25/2(7), 2.12.1842; NS473/1/6, despatch from Stanley; CO280/148, ff.38, 41.
26 MM4/1/4, 19.4.1843; RS25/2(7), 18.1.1843, 3.3.1843; MS248/96, 20.6.1843.
27 MS248/174/22; MS248/96, 6.7.1843.
28 NS473/1/6, pp. 113–22, 132–6.
29 Nixon, pp. 10, 14.
30 MS248/316/11.
31 *CC*, 15.7.1843; *TAAR*, 12.5.1843, 25.8.1843; MS248/96, 7.7.1843.
32 Nixon, pp. 10–11; MS248/316/11.
33 *HTC*, 1.9.1843; Nixon, p. 14; MS248/316/11; *HTA*, 22.8.1843, 25.8.1843.
34 RS16/1(3), 9.9.1843.
35 *HTA*, 3.11.1843; RS25/2(7), 3.11.1843.
36 MS248/158, 6.11.1843.
37 RS16/1(3), 6.11.1843.
38 West, *History of Tasmania*, p. 228.

Chapter 14 John Franklin disappears
1 MS248/316/12–13, 15; MS248/175/7, 9–10; Traill, p. 328; Woodward, p. 249.
2 MS248/316/16–19; MS248/303/80–1; MS248/175/13; MS248/364/21–2; LA447/1, pp. 10–16, 1.6.1845; Cyriax, pp. 26–7.
3 Traill, pp. 334–5; MS248/316/17, 21; MS248/303/85; LA447/1, pp. 13, 26, 28.
4 MS248/316/13; MS248/175/9, 10; MS248/228, 29.3.1845; Traill, p. 436.
5 MM4/1/4, Sophy Cracroft to JF, [mid-1844]; MS248/175/12; MS248/228, 9.7.1845; Lubbock, p. 155; MM4/1/3, JF to Eleanor Franklin, three letters [1844–45].
6 MS1503/30/23; LA447/1, pp. 7–8; Owen, p. 243.
7 MS248/175/14, 16; *The Times*, 14.6.1847, 27.11.1847.
8 W. Gillies Ross, 'The Admiralty and the Franklin Search', p. 289; Potter, p. 4; *Taranaki Herald*, 9.5.1857; Owen, p. 281.
9 W. Gillies Ross, 'False Leads in the Franklin Search', pp. 131–60; W. Gillies Ross, 'Admiralty', p. 289; Owen, pp. 264–4; Rich, *John Rae's correspondence*, p. 233.
10 MS1503/58/25; Elce, p. 170.

11   LA447/1, pp. 82–5, 90–1, 123; MS248/175/18–19; MS248/103, 26.2.1848, 9.3.1848; Owen, p. 267.

12   MS248/266/1.

13   *The Times*, 28.3.1848; MS248/103, 11.1.1848, 26.2.1848, 8.4.1848; MS248/228, 8.11.1848; [Anon], p. 55.

14   MS395/40, 1.1.1849; MS1100/2/1; *The Times*, 24.3.1849; MS248/212/1; MS248/104, 29.12.1849.

15   D3311/118/(i), 6.5.1849; *Standard*, 14.2.1849; *Daily News*, 16.2.1849; *The Times*, 13.6.1849, 3.7.1849; *Bristol Mercury*, 16.6.1849; Cyriax, p. 76.

16   MS1100/2/2; MS248/212/1; *Hull Packet*, 8.6.1849; *Bradford Observer*, 14.6.1849; *Morning Post*, 30.6.1849; *Standard*, 27.7.1849; NS1004/1/10–11; D3311/122/30, 26.8.1849; D3311/116/1, 11.5.1849.

17   Skewes, p. 98.

18   MS248/247/33, 19.11.1852.

19   Skewes, p. 107–08; MS72063, 30.3.1853; Woodward, p. 269; MS248/112, 16.7.1856.

20   Stone, 'An episode in the Franklin Search', Part 2, pp. 200–03; MS248/108, 13.1.1851; LA447/1, 12.4.1850; Barr, '"The cold of Valparaiso"', p. 209–10; thanks to Graeme Broxam.

21   MS248/247/1.

22   MS248/247/22; MS248/104, 28.11.1849; *Standard*, 27.6.1851; *The Times* 1.12.1849, 7.12.1849; NS1004/1/11; LA447/1, pp. 101, 104.

Chapter 15 Jane Franklin's Search

1   MS248/175/20.

2   Jacobs, '"Excited hopes and weary silence:"', *passim*.

3   MS248/104, 29.12.1849; MS248/175/20; MS248/179; LA447/1, pp. 110, 114, 119, 143, 147, 157–8, 169; Woodward, p. 271; *The Times*, 1.1.1850, 9.1.1850.

4   MS248/105; LA447/1, pp. 165, 167; MS248/179; Woodward, p. 272–5; *The Times*, 31.1.1850, 16.2.1850, 13.3.1850, 4.4.1850, 16.4.1850; Elce, p. 187.

5   W. Gillies Ross, 'Clairvoyants and mediums search for Franklin', pp. 1–18.

6   MS248/267/1–4; MS248/184, 23.9.1850; Owen, pp. 284–6.

7   Owen, pp. 286–9; Skewes, *passim* and pp. 80, 264–5, 283–4, 296; Lloyd-Jones, pp. 27–34; Stone, 'An episode in the Franklin Search', Part 1, pp. 130–2; Ross, 'Clairvoyants', p. 5; D3311/28/14, 6.5.1849.

8   *Standard*, 28.2.1850, 16.4.1850.

9   Stone, 'An episode', parts 1 and 2.

10   LA447/1, p. 202; MS248/108, 14.1.1851; MS248/106, 18.1.1851; MS248/107, *passim*; [Bellot], p. 46.

11   MS248/106–108 *passim*; MS248/247/23, 28; MS248/228, 21.7.1851, 21.8.1851.

12   W. Gillies Ross, 'False Leads in the Franklin Search', p. 134; MS248/162; MS248/241, 20.12.1851.

13   Jacobs, 'Lady Jane's lament', *passim*.

14 Inglefield, *passim*; Stone, 'An episode', Part 2, p. 204; MS72063, 30.3.1853; Woodward, pp. 279–80; MS248/247/40.

15 MS248/228, 23.11.1852; *The Times*, 8.10.1851, 21.10.1851.

16 MS248/212/5; MS248/110 *passim*; Barr, '"The cold of Valparaiso"', pp. 203–18; *HTC*, 31.3.1853.

17 *HTC*, 31.3.1853, 23.4.1853, 4.6.1853, 20.8.1853; Barr, 'Searching for Franklin from Australia'.

18 MS248/212/6–7; LA447/1, p. 287.

19 Rich, *John Rae's correspondence*, p. 342; *The Times*, 8.12.1853, 5.4.1854; Owen, p. 346.

20 NS1004/1/15; Rich, *John Rae's correspondence*, pp. 265–77, 288.

21 NS1004/1/15; LA447/1, p. 321.

22 MS248/178, 31.5.1855; *The Times*, 23.10.1855, 30.10.1855; Stone, ' "The contents of the kettles" ', pp. 6–16.

23 McGoogan, p. 358 and *passim*.

24 MS72063, 30.3.1853.

25 Owen, p. 282.

26 MS248/266/1, 2; Woodward, p. 291.

27 LA447/1, p. 252; Elce p. 77; Spufford, p. 122; Russell, 'Wife stories', *passim*.

28 MS248/228, 8.12.1849; MS248/104, 29.12.1849; MS248/241, 6.1.1852; MS248/110, 2.4.1853; Woodward, p. 295.

29 MS248/256/1; MS248/342/2–4.

30 MS248/106, p. 123; MS248/175/7; Elce, pp. 77, 84–5, 115–18, 158–9, 195–7, 204; Stone, 'The Franklin Search in Parliament', pp. 209–16.

31 MS248/247/39.

32 MS248/241, 11.11.1851; LA447/1, p. 238; MS248/114, 4.12.1856; McClintock, Preface by Murchison, pp. vii–xxii; Herbert, p. 174.

33 Elce, pp. 84, 104; Stone, 'An episode', Part 1, p. 129.

34 Spufford, p. 121.

35 *Standard*, 4.10.1850, 16.4.1850, 21.5.1850, 8.6.1850; *Morning Chronicle*, 11.2.1850, 8.4.1851, 29.9.1851, 28.7.1852; MS248/181; MS248/247/38.

36 LA447/1, pp. 348–9; Elce, p. 78.

37 Simmonds, pp. vii–ix.

38 MS248/212/1; Fleming, p. 382; Skewes, pp. 86, 92, 266; Elce, p. 150; MS248/107, 25.4.1851.

39 Elce, p. 202; MS248/111, 22.11.1855.

40 Stone, 'An episode', Part 2, p. 204; MS248/105; MS248/107, 24.4.1851.

Chapter 16 Family upsets

1 MM4/1/3, 23.5.1845.

2 MS1503/33/1; MM4/1/3, 21.11.1846; D3287/31/1(xxxix), 11.1.1846.

3 Owen, p. 329–30; D3311/122/3, [July 1849?]; D3311/116/1, 11.5.1849; D3287/32/2/6, undated; D3311/122/27(i), [summer 1849]; D3311/122/12, pp. 63–4.

4   D3311/28/14, 6.5.1849.

5   D3311/116/3, 11.6.1849; MS248/228, 4.1.1849; D3287/7/3/3/13, 15.6.1849.

6   D3311/122/4, 4.7.1849; MS248/247/38.

7   MS248/247/6–17.

8   D3287/7/3/1/2–3.

9   Owen, pp. 291–2, 348, 402; NS1004/1/12; MS248/228, 25.9.1850; MS248/111, 29.3.1855, 5.5.1855, 6.8.1855.

10 D3311/122/123, 11.11.1849; D3287/31/7(iv), 22.9.1851; D3311/122/34, 29.8., no year.

11 MS248/228, 4.8.1854; NS1004/1/12; MS248/249/1, [1851]; MS248/162, 27.9.1851.

12 MS248/162, 3–13.11.1851, 25.12.1851; *The Times*, 9.11.1853; D3287/122/22, 21.10.[1852]; MS248/228, July 1854; MS248/247/38.

13 *The Times*, 29.10.1853, 5.11.1853, 7.11.1853, 8.11.1853; Owen, p. 347.

14 *The Times*, 9.11.1853.

15 Owen, pp. 347–8; D3287/31/9/VI, 3.11.[1854]; D3311/122/35, 6.11.1853; D3311/122/37, 26.11.1853; D3311/57/2(i), 25.11.1853.

16 D3287/31/13, 28.1.1854; Owen, pp. 346, 348, 360–2; NS1004/1/15.

17 MS248/111, 1–22.2.1855, 1.8.1855, 20.10.1855, 5.12.1855, 12.12.1855; D3311/122/18, 11.8.[1855]; MM4/1/4, Notes on Jane Franklin.

18 MM4/1/2, 15.9.1844; D3311/122/33, 4.1.1853; D3311/122/21, [late 1849]; D3287/31/1(xx), 6.11.1853; D3311/122/8, 7.11.1850.

19 D3311/122/21, [late 1849].

20 MS248/162, 2.11.1851, 3.11.1851, 7–8.11.1851, 13–24.11.1851.

21 NS1004/1/14–15; MS248/228, 20.7.1853; LA447/1, p. 244; MS248/247/39; MS248/247/44.

22 D3287/31/13, 8 November [year unknown]; D3287/31/1(xx), 6.11.1853; D3311/122/22, 21.10.[1852]; MS248/247/42; MS248/111, 1–24.1.1855, 13.3.1855, 17.11.1855.

Chapter 17 Victory

1   MS248/113, 1.7.1855; Owen, p. 366.

2   MS1100/8; MS1503/50/19; MS1503/49/22, 20.12.1855; MS248/112, 28.1.1856; MS248/103, 25.1.1848.

3   MS248/112, 13–25.12.1856; Woodward, p. 293.

4   Corner, pp. 104, 241–7; LA447/1, p. 333, 343–9.

5   [Anon], p. 59; McClintock, pp. viii–ix, 1–9, 13–14, list of subscribers; LA447/2, pp. 394, 403.

6   McClintock, *passim*; Eber, p. 80.

7   Information from Dr Ian Stone.

8   MS248/247/54–72, quotations from letters 55, 60, 63, 64, 70.

9   McClintock, pp. xv, 11–14; Potter, p. 154.

10 Armstrong, p. xviii; Osborn, pp. 71–2, 111.

11 MS248/378; Clayton, pp. 5–44.

12 'Presentation of the Gold Medals', *Proceedings of the Royal Geographical Society*, 1859–60, p. 111.

13 [Anon], Appendix p. iv–v.

14 Rawnsley, p. 177; MS248/256/3.

15 DeArmond, pp. 17–29, 42; Dorothy Blakey Smith, pp. 35–59; MS248/266/1; Woodward, p. 315.

16 MS248/131–3, especially 21.7.1864; MM4/1/4, 'Notes on Jane Franklin'; MS1305/1.

17 MM4/1/4, 'Notes on Jane Franklin'; LA447/2, p. 230; MS248/139, 13.10.1866.

18 Korn, pp. 203–78; MS248/135–6; Rawnsley, p. 176; MM4/1/4, 'Notes on Jane Franklin'.

19 Traill, p. 424; MS248/266/1; [Anon], p. 43; MM4/1/2, 1.10.1869; LA447/2, p. 225; Woodward, p. 358.

20 *Lincoln, Rutland and Stamford Mercury*, 29.11.1861; Woodward, p. 349; *Mercury*, 12.1859, 21.9.1860, 23.2.1861, 18.9.1863, 23.2.1865.

21 MS248/266/1; Owen, pp. 426–7; *Mercury*, 16.3.1881, 23.6.1917.

22 Owen, pp. 427–8; MS248/266/1; Young, pp. v, lii, 80.

23 Woodward, pp. 363–4.

24 *York Herald*, 20.7.1875; *The Times*, 19.7.1875; *Essex Standard*, 23.7.1875; *Glasgow Herald*, 20.7.1875.

25 *Morning Post*, 24.7.1875; Inscriptions, Kensal Green Cemetery, Westminster Abbey.

26 Owen, pp. 430–1.

27 Stone, 'An episode' Part 1, pp. 129, 142; Woodward, p. 7.

28 *Examiner*, 22.12.1906; *HTC*, 26.10.1857, 25.6.1853, 1.7.1853.

29 *Mercury*, 2.12.1891, 21.11.1894, 27.7.1895, 29.8.1931, 22.7.1875, 23.7.1875.

30 *Mercury*, 25.7.1885, 17.8.1907, 4.8.1909.

31 *Mercury*, 4.4.1923, 28.10.1926, 23.1.1940.

32 *Mercury*, 14.10.1895, 17.1.1902.

33 *Mercury*, 27.7.1897, 2.4.1937, 12.3.1927, 8.10.1937, 11.2.1943, 24.3.1953, 22.1.1954.

34 [Anon]. p. 51.

35 Butler, *passim*.

36 West, *History of Tasmania*, p. 228; Fenton, p. 155; Robson, pp. 322, 375–6; Reynolds, *passim*.

37 Fitzpatrick, *passim*; Bethell, p. 116.

38 Alexander, *Jane Franklin Hall*, p. 5.

39 Russell, *For richer, for poorer*, Chapter 3, especially pp. 52, 63.

40 Information from Richard Geeves, Naomie Clark-Hansen.

41 Author present at meeting, Lenah Valley hall, 10 October 2011.

BIBLIOGRAPHY

Books and articles

Adler, Bill, *America's First Ladies*, Taylor Trade Publishing, Maryland, 2003

Alexander, Alison, *Governors' ladies*, Tasmanian Historical Research Association, Hobart, 1986

——*Jane Franklin Hall 1950–2010*, Jane Franklin Hall, Hobart, 2010

[Anon], *A brave man and his belongings: being some passages in the life of Sir John Franklin*, S. Taylor, London, 1874

Armstrong, Alex, *A personal narrative of the discovery of the North-West Passage*, Hurst & Blackett, London, 1857

Australian Dictionary of Biography

Backhouse, James and Tylor, Charles, *The life and labours of George Washington Walker*, A.W. Bennett, London, 1862

Barr, William, 'Searching for Franklin from Australia; William Parker Snow's initiative of 1853, *Polar Record* 33/185, 1997

——'"The cold of Valparaiso": the disintegration of William Kennedy's second Franklin search expedition, 1853–54', *Polar Record* 34/190, 1998

Barry, John Vincent, *The life and death of John Price*, Melbourne University Press, Melbourne, 1964

[Bellot, J.R.], *Memoirs of Lieutenant Joseph René Bellot*, vol. 1, Hurst and Blackett, London, 1855

Bethell, L.S., *The valley of the Derwent*, Education Department, Hobart, [1956]

Bonwick, James, *The last Tasmanians*, J. Walch, Hobart, 1870

Boyce, James, *1835: The founding of Melbourne & the conquest of Australia*, Black Inc, Melbourne, 2011

Brown, P.L. (ed.), *Clyde Company Papers*, vol II, Oxford University Press, London, 1952

Burn, David, *Narrative of the overland journey of Sir John and Lady Franklin ...*, D.S. Ford, Sydney, 1955

Burns, T.E. and Skemp, J.R., *Van Diemen's Land correspondents*, Queen Victoria Museum, Launceston, 1961

Buscombe, Eve, *Artists in early Australia and their portraits*, Eureka Research, Sydney, 1978

Butler, Ethel Nairn, *V.D.L. a hundred years ago,* J. Walch, Hobart, [1936]

Calder, James, *Recollections of Sir John and Lady Franklin in Tasmania*, Sullivan's Cove, Adelaide, 1984

Cash, Martin, *Martin Cash; the bushranger of Van Diemen's Land*, J. Walch, Hobart, 1929

Chisholm, Alec, *The story of Elizabeth Gould*, Hawthorn Press, Melbourne, 1944

Clayton, Ellen C., *Celebrated women: Stories of their lives and example*, Dean & Son, London, [1860]

Connor, Michael, 'Fabricated feminist flashers', *Quadrant*, LIV/5, May 2010

Corner, George W., *Doctor Kane of the Arctic seas*, Temple University Press, Philadelphia, 1972

Courtney, Nicholas, *Gale Force 10: The life and legacy of Admiral Beaufort*, Review, London, 2002

Cowley, Trudy, 'Ellen Scott of the Flash Mob', *Convict lives*, Female Factory Research Group, Hobart, 2009

Crooke, Robert, *The convict: A fragment of history,* University of Tasmania Library, Hobart, 1958

Cyriax, R.J., *Sir John Franklin's last Arctic expedition*, Methuen, London, 1939

Davis, Richard and Petrow, Stefan (eds), *Varieties of vice-regal life*, Tasmanian Historical Research Association, Hobart, 2004

Davis, Richard C. (ed.), *Sir John Franklin's journals and correspondence: The first Arctic land expedition*, Champlain Society, Toronto, 1995

——'Fact and fancy in history and biography: The case of Greenstockings', *Polar Record* 37/200, 2001

DeArmond, R.N. (ed.), *Lady Franklin visits Sitka, Alaska 1870*, Alaska Historical Society, Anchorage, 1981

De Quincey, Elizabeth, *The history of Mount Wellington*, E. De Quincy, Hobart, 1987

Dietrich, Jessica, 'Lady Jane Franklin Empress of Tasmania?', *Tasmanian Historical Studies* 14, 2009, pp. 79–91

Eber, Dorothy Harley, *Encounters on the Passage: Inuit meet the explorers*, University of Toronto Press, Toronto, 2008

Elce, Erika Behrisch (ed.), *As affecting the fate of my absent husband*, McGill–Queen's University Press, Montreal, 2009

Fenton, James, *History of Tasmania*, J. Walch, Hobart, 1884

Fitzpatrick, Kathleen, *Sir John Franklin in Tasmania*, Melbourne University Press, Melbourne, 1949

FitzSymonds, E., *A looking-glass for Tasmania*, Sullivan's Cove, Adelaide, 1980

Fleming, Fergus, *Barrow's boys*, Granta Books, London, 1999

Franklin, John, *Narrative of a journey to the shores of the Polar Sea, in the years 1819–20–21–22*, John Murray, London, 1824

[Franklin, John], *Narrative of some passages in the history of Van Diemen's Land*, Platypus Publications, Hobart, 1967

Gates, William, *Recollections of life in Van Dieman's Land*, Part 1, D.S. Ford, Sydney, 1961

Gell, Mrs, *John Franklin's bride: Eleanor Anne Porden*, John Murray, London, 1930

Heard, Dora, (ed.), *The journal of Charles O'Hara Booth*, Tasmanian Historical Research Association, Hobart, 1981

Herbert, Kari, *Polar wives*, Greystone Books, Vancouver, 2012

Huxley, Leonard, *Life and letters of Sir Joseph Dalton Hooker*, vol. 2, John Murray, London, 1918

Inglefield, E.A., R.N., *A summer search for Sir John Franklin*, Thomas Harrison, London, 1853

Jacobs, Annaliese, ' "Excited hopes & weary silence": Explorers' families, Inuit maps, and British information anxiety, autumn 1849', unpublished paper

——'Lady Jane's lament: British maritime communities, Arctic exploration, and the making of a national heroine, 1851', unpublished paper

Keynes, Randal, *Annie's box: Charles Darwin, his daughter and human evolution*, Fourth Estate, London, 2001

Korn, Alfons L., *The Victorian visitors: An account of the Hawaiian Kingdom, 1861–1866*, University of Hawaii Press, Honolulu, 1958

Laidlaw, Zoe, *Colonial connections: Patronage, the information revolution and colonial government*, Manchester University Press, Manchester, 2005

Lamb, G.F., *Franklin—Happy voyager*, Ernest Benn, London, 1956

Lambert, Andrew, *Franklin: tragic hero of polar navigation*, Faber and Faber, London, 2010

Lloyd-Jones, Ralph, 'The paranormal Arctic: Lady Franklin, Sophia Cracroft, and Captain and "Little Weesy" Coppin', *Polar Record* 37/200, 2001

Lubbock, Adelaide, *Owen Stanley R.N.*, Heinemann, Melbourne, 1967

McClintock, Captain, *A narrative of the discovery of the fate of Sir John Franklin and his companions*, John Murray, London, 1859

McGoogan, Ken, *Lady Franklin's revenge*, Bantam Books, London, 2006

McIlraith, John *Life of Sir John Richardson*, Longman's Green, London, 1868

Markham, Albert Hastings, *Life of Sir John Franklin and the North-West Passage*, George Philip, London, no date

Meredith, Louisa Anne, *Nine years in Tasmania*, John Murray, London, 1852

Nixon, Norah, (ed.), *The pioneer bishop in Van Diemen's Land*, N. Nixon, Hobart, 1953

Oats, W.N., *Backhouse and Walker*, Blubberhead Press, Hobart, 1981

Osborn, Sherard, C.B., *The career, last voyage and fate of Captain Sir John Franklin*, Bradbury and Evans, London, 1860

Owen, Roderic, *The fate of Franklin*, Hutchinson, Melbourne, 1978

Parris, H.S., 'From Melbourne to the Murray in 1839' Parts 1 and 2, *Victorian Naturalist,* vol. 66, February 1950, March 1950

Parry, Edward, *Memoirs of Rear-Admiral Sir W. Edward Parry,* Longman Brown, London, 1857

Pasco, Commander Crawford, *A roving commission,* George Robertson, Melbourne, 1897

Plomley, N.J.B., (ed.), *Weep in silence: A history of the Flinders Island Aboriginal Settlement,* Tasmanian Historical Research Association, Hobart, 1987

Potter, Russell, *Arctic spectacles: The frozen north in visual culture, 1818–1875,* University of Washington Press, Seattle, 2007

Proceedings of the Royal Geographical Society, 1859–60

Rawnsley, Willingham, *The life, diaries and correspondence of Jane Lady Franklin,* Erskine Macdonald, London, 1923

Reynolds, Henry, *A History of Tasmania,* Cambridge University Press, Cambridge, 2012

Rich, E.E., (ed.), *Journal of Occurrences in the Athabasca Department by George Simpson, 1820 and 1821, and report,* Hudson's Bay Record Society, London, 1938

——(ed.), *John Rae's correspondence with the Hudson's Bay Company,* Hudson's Bay Record Society, London, 1953

Robson, Lloyd, *History of Tasmania,* vol. 1, Oxford University Press, Melbourne, 1983

Ross, James Clark, R.N., *A voyage of discovery and research in the southern and Antarctic regions,* vol. 1, John Murray, London, 1847

Ross, W. Gillies, 'Clairvoyants and mediums search for Franklin', *Polar Record* 39/1, 2003, pp. 1–18

——'False Leads in the Franklin Search', *Polar Record* 39/2, 2003, pp. 131–60

——'The Admiralty and the Franklin Search', *Polar Record* 40/4, 2004

Russell, Penny, (ed.), *For richer, for poorer: Early colonial marriages,* Melbourne University Press, Melbourne, 1994

——'The allure of the Nile: Jane Franklin's voyage to the Second Cataract, 1834', *Gender & History* 9(2), 1997

——*This errant lady: Jane Franklin's overland journey to Port Phillip and Sydney,* National Library of Australia, Canberra, 2002

——'Antipodean Queen of Sheba', *Meanjin* 62(4), December 2003

——'Wife Stories: Narrating marriage and self in the life of Jane Franklin', *Victorian Studies* 48(1), Fall 2005

Shaw, A.G.L., 'Three Knights: Sir James Stephen, Sir John Franklin and Sir John Eardley Wilmot', Tasmanian Historical Research Association 36/4, 1989

Simmonds, P.L., *Sir John Franklin and the Arctic regions,* Geo. Derby, Buffalo, 1852

Skewes, J. Henry, *Sir John Franklin. The true secret of the discovery of his fate,* Bemrose & Sons, London, 1890

Smith, Dorothy Blakey, (ed.), *Lady Franklin visits the Pacific Northwest,* Archives of British Columbia, Victoria, 1974

Smith, Michael, *Captain Francis Crozier*, The Collins Press, Cork, 2006

Spufford, Francis, *I may be some time: Ice and the English imagination*, Faber and Faber, London, 1996

Stock, Eugene, *The short history of the Church Missionary Society*, Church Missionary Society, London, 1899

Stone, Ian R., ' "The contents of the kettles": Charles Dickens, John Rae and cannibalism on the 1845 Franklin Expedition', *The Dickensian*, 83/1, 1987

——'An episode in the Franklin search: the *Prince Albert* expedition, 1850', Part 1, *Polar Record* 29/169, 1993, pp. 127–42; Part 2, *Polar Record* 29/170, 1993, pp. 197–208

——'The Franklin Search in Parliament', *Polar Record* 32/182, 1996, pp. 206–19

Tasmanian Journal of Natural Science, Agriculture, Statistics, &c vol. 1, Tasmanian Government Printer, Hobart, 1842; vol. 2, Henry Dowling, Launceston, 1846

Traill, H.D., *The life of Sir John Franklin, R.N.*, John Murray, London, 1896

Truman, Margaret, *First Ladies*, Random House, New York, 1995

West, John, *The hope of life eternal*, J.S. Waddell, Launceston, 1850

——*History of Tasmania*, vol. 1, Henry Dowling, Launceston, 1852

Woodward, Frances, *Portrait of Jane: A life of Lady Franklin*, Hodder and Stoughton, London, 1951

Woolley, Richie and Smith, Wayne, *A history of the Huon and far south*, Huon Valley Council, Huonville, 2004

Young, Allen, *The cruise of the 'Pandora'*, William Clowes, London, 1876

Roderic Owen, a Franklin descendant, wrote a biography of John Franklin using family papers unobtainable publicly (as did Frances Woodward, on a smaller scale). Owen did not include footnotes or a bibliography, but I have quoted his quotations as he seems accurate (with no particular axe to grind) and they provide information unobtainable elsewhere.

Newspapers
Australia

Austral-Asiatic Review (AAR), Australasian, Australian Chronicle, Bent's News, Colonial Times (CT), Cornwall Chronicle (CC), Examiner, Hobart Town Advertiser (HTA), Hobart Town Courier, Mercury, Sydney Colonist, Sydney Gazette, Sydney Monitor, Sydney Morning Herald, Tasmanian and Austral-Asiatic Review (TAAR), Town and Country Journal, True Colonist (TC), Van Diemen's Land Chronicle

United Kingdom

Britannia, Bradford Observer, Bristol Mercury, Caledonian Mercury, Daily News, Era, Essex Standard, Glasgow Herald, Hull Packet, Lincoln Rutland and Stamford Mercury, Morning Chronicle, Morning Post, Standard, The Times, York Herald

New Zealand
Taranaki Herald

Archival collections

Derbyshire County Archives

D3287/7/3/3/13, letter, Isabella Cracroft to Eleanor Gell

D3287/7/3/1/2, letter, Philip Gell to Eleanor Gell

D3287/26/21, Gell family personal correspondence 1837–97

D3287/31/1, letters, Emma Simpkinson to Eleanor Gell

D3287/31/7, 22, letters to Eleanor Gell

D3287/31/9, letters to Eleanor Isabella Franklin

D3287/31/13, letters, Mrs Wright to Eleanor Gell

D3287/32/2, letters, A.M. Dixon to Eleanor Gell

D3311/28 letters, John Franklin to Eleanor Franklin

D3311/57/2, letters, John Richardson to Eleanor Gell

D3311/109/2, letter, JF to Mrs Kay

D3311/116, letters, Edward Parry to Eleanor Franklin.

D3311/118 letters, Eleanor Franklin to John Franklin

D3311/122/3, letter, Fanny Majendie to Eleanor Franklin

D3311/122/4, letter, JF to Eleanor Gell

D3311/122/8, letter, Marianne Simpkinson to Eleanor Gell

D3311/122/18, letter, Louisa Dixon to Eleanor Gell

D3311/122/21, 22, 27 letters, Marianne Simpkinson to Eleanor Gell

D3311/122/30, letter, Isabella Cracroft to Eleanor Gell

D3311/122/32, 33 letter, Emma Simpkinson to Eleanor Gell

D3311/122/34, letter, Henrietta Wright to Eleanor Gell

D3311/122/35, 37 letters, Aunt Booth to Eleanor Gell

D3311/122/123, letter, Mary Anne Kendall to Eleanor Gell

D3311/123, notes about Eleanor Franklin's life by Philip Gell

The Goldsmiths' Company, London

Apprentice Books 7, 8; Freedom Book 2; Court Book 23; Griffin windowpane in Great Hall

Hertfordshire Record Office

D/EHX/F29, Kezia Hayter to Mary Ann Stoddart

Lincolnshire County Archives

MISC DON LA447/1, LA477/2, two books of typed Franklin documents

Mitchell Library, Sydney

A316, Gunn Papers

B1566, CY/160, journal of William Cleveland, April 1842

National Archives, Kew, England

BJ3/18, letters, Edward Sabine–John and Jane Franklin

National Library of Australia
MS114, diaries and letters of JF
MS3472, John Franklin to Thomas Ainger

National Maritime Museum, Greenwich
MS74/101, JF to Mr Crowe
MS72063, JF to John Franklin

Scott Polar Research Institute, Cambridge
MS248/2, JF journal 1809
MS248/11, JF books read, 1814–24
MS248/12, JF journal 1813–25
MS248/28, JF journal 1817
MS248/35, JF journal 1819
MS248/39, JF journal 1819–20
MS248/43, JF journal 1820–21
MS248/44, JF journal 1821
MS248/45, JF journal 1821–22
MS248/50, JF journal 1823–25
MS248/56, JF journal 1825–26
MS248/66, JF journal 1828
MS248/72–75, JF journal 1832
MS248/76–78, JF journal 1833
MS248/79, JF journal 1833–34
MS248/80–81, JF journal 1835
MS248/84, JF journal 24.8.1836–5.1.1837
MS248/85, JF journal 26.8.1838–20.12.1838
MS248/86, JF journal 22.8.1839–9.9.1839
MS248/87, JF journal 11.9.1839–30.11.1839
MS248/88, JF journal 29.4.1840–7.7.1840
MS248/89, JF journal 12.7.1840–13.10.1840
MS248/90, JF journal 20.2.1841–1.5.1841
MS248/91, JF journal 4.5.1841–10.7.1841
MS248/92, JF journal 1.8.1841–5.10.1841
MS248/93, JF journal 1.1.1842–29.1.1842
MS248/94, JF journal 10.2.1842–12.3.1842
MS248/95, JF journal 1.1.1842–29.3.1842, January–March 1843
MS248/96, JF journal 8.5.1843–26.7.1843
MS248/97, 'Notes on the treatment of convicts in V.D.L'
MS248/103, JF journal 1848
MS248/104, JF letterbook 1849–50
MS248/105, list of stores for *Prince Albert*
MS248/106, 107, JF letterbooks 1851

MS248/108, JF journal 1851
MS248/110, JF letterbook 1853
MS248/111, JF journal 1855
MS248/112, JF journal 1856
MS248/113, JF letterbook 1855–58
MS248/114, JF letterbook 1856–57
MS248/131, JF journal 1864
MS248/135–6, JF journals 1865
MS248/139, JF journal 1866
MS248/150, JF journal 1827
MS248/151, JF journal 1828
MS248/152, JF journal 1831
MS248/154, JF journal 1834
MS248/156, JF journal March 1837
MS248/157, JF journal 1839
MS248/158, JF journal 1843–44
MS248/162, JF journal 1851
MS248/167, Career of Sir John Franklin
MS248/168, JF 'Plan for the employment of time ...'
MS248/169, JF school report 1803–04
MS248/170, letters, JF to John Griffin
MS248/171, letters, JF to Mrs Leeves
MS248/172, letters, JF to John Franklin
MS248/173–4, letters, JF to Mary Simpkinson
MS248/175, letters, JF to James Ross
MS248/178, letter, JF to Turner (solicitor)
MS248/179, letter, JF to Charles Phillips
MS248/181, letter, JF to Joseph Bellot
MS248/184, letters, JF to Hogarth
MS248/190, letters, Sophia Cracroft to Isabella Cracroft
MS248/212, letters, JF to Admiralty
MS248/225, letters, John Franklin to Roderick Murchison
MS248/228, Sophia Cracroft, notes on letters sent 1844–56
MS248/229, JF journal 1817–18
MS248/239, Sophia Cracroft journal, 1843–44
MS248/241, JF journal 1851–52
MS248/246, letters, Sophia Cracroft to Thomas Cracroft
MS248/247, letters, Sophia Cracroft to Isabella Cracroft
MS248/249, letters, Sophia Cracroft to Henry Elliot
MS248/256, letters, Sophia Cracroft to Leopold McClintock
MS 248/266/1, obituary of JF by Sophia Cracroft
MS248/266/2, notes for memoir of JF
MS248/267, statements about the Franklin Search

MS248/295, letters, John Franklin to Francis Beaufort
MS248/296, letters, John Franklin to Robert Brown
MS248/298, letters, JF to Isabella Cracroft
MS248/303, letters, John Franklin to JF
MS248/311, letter, JF to Rev. Leeves
MS248/316, letters, John Franklin to James Ross
MS248/342, letters, Francis Beaufort to Sophia Cracroft
MS248/343, letters, Francis Beaufort to LF
MS248/364, letters, F Crozier to James Ross
MS248/378, letter, John Ferard to JF
MS248/388, letters, John Franklin to Isabella Cracroft
MS248/410/3, letter, Fanny Griffin to JF
MS248/411, letters, John Griffin to JF
MS248/472, letters, Mary Simpkinson to JF
MS395/40, letter, JF to Lady Back
MS395/53–54, letters, Alexander and Mary Maconochie to George Back
MS580/1, reminiscences of Franklin by Frank Simpkinson
MS580/2, letter, Frank Simpkinson to [F.H.H. Guillemard]
MS1100/2, letters, Eleanor Franklin to William Scoresby
MS1100/8, letter, JF to Lord Palmerston
MS1305/1, letter, Edith Hansard to Alan Frant
MS1503/11/5, letter, John Franklin to JF
MS1503/14/1,11,12, letters, JF to John Richardson
MS1503/18/1, 20 letters, John Richardson to Mary Richardson
MS1503/28/10, letter, JF to Josephine Richardson

State Library of Victoria
MS073(417), letters, JF to Captain Moriarty

Tasmanian Archive and Heritage Office
CB7/39, daily journal of proceedings in the Immigration Quarters
CEN1/1/16–3, census 1842
CEN1/1/90-397/1848, census 1848
CON40, CON15, CON19, female convict records
CSD1/1/51/1009, CSD1/18/703, CSO24/1/7/101, CSO24/1/32/911, CSO24/1/32/922,
    CSO24/1/280/6187, GO33/55/1205, records of Aboriginal community
CSO89/1/1, Oyster Cove visitors' book
MM4/1/1–4 Gell and Franklin Papers (MM4/1/3 includes Eleanor Franklin's diary;
    MM4/1/4 includes Franklin–Richardson correspondence)
NS52/1/16, deed to Ancanthe, 1842
NS202/1, diary, Kezia Hayter
NS279/1/1, diary, John Franklin, 1841
NS473/1/6, Montagu's 'Book'

NS1004, letters to Mary Price
NS1250/1/1, journal of Dr Haslett
SC195/31/2798, inquest of Arminia
Turnbull Library, New Zealand
MS0919, letters, JF to Ronald Gunn
MS0375, letter, JF to Mary Simpkinson

University of Tasmania Archives
A2176, A2186, A2187, Arthur Papers
H6/24, diary of William Henty
RS16/1(1) letters, John Franklin to JF
RS16/1(2), letter, JF to Elizabeth Fry, Fry's reply
RS16/1(3), letter, JF to Turnbull
RS16/2(1), visit to Port Arthur 1838
RS16/2(2), excursion to Port Davey 1838
RS16/2(3) departure 1843
RS16/4, list of recipients, *Tasmanian Journal of Science*
RS16/5, admission card to opening of Ancanthe
RS16/6, letters, JF to John Franklin
RS16/7, letters, JF to John Griffin
RS16/8, letters, JF to Mary Simpkinson
RS18/3, dinner engagement book
RS18/4/(1), letter, JF to Archdeacon Davis
RS18/4(2), letter, JF to Kezia Hayter
RS25/2, diary, George Boyes
RS1784/A73, letter, JF to Turnbull
W9/A1/11, letter, JF to G.W. Walker

Websites
http://en.wikipedia.org/wiki/Native_American_name_controversy [31 October 2012]
http://search.ancestry.com/iexec?htx=view&r=an&dbid=8978&iid=MDX-HO107_671_672-0468&fn=John&ln=Griffin&st=r&ssrc=&pid=7159363 [29 October 2012]
http://search.ancestry.com/iexec?htx=view&r=an&dbid=8860&iid=MDX-HO107_1507_1507-0526&fn=Janes&ln=Franklin&st=r&ssrc=&pid=2620611 [29 October 2012]

Information from the following people: Naomie Clark-Hansen, Rhiannon Evans, Craig Joel, Robert Nash, Richard Geeves, Marion Sargent, Edward Simpkinson, Claire Smith, Ian Stone, Alan and Hilary Wallace, Frances Underwood and Rose Young

INDEX